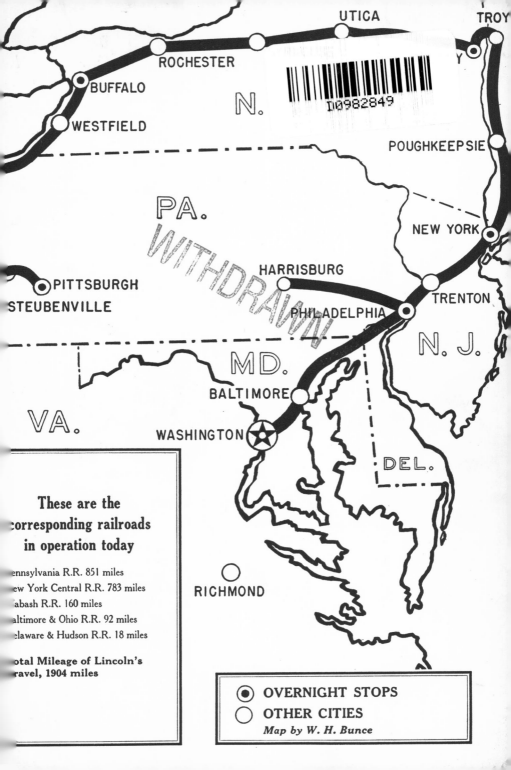

UTICA

TROY

ROCHESTER

Y

N.

D0982849

BUFFALO

WESTFIELD

POUGHKEEPSIE

PA.

WITHDRAWN

NEW YORK

HARRISBURG

PITTSBURGH

STEUBENVILLE

PHILADELPHIA

TRENTON

N. J.

MD.

BALTIMORE

VA.

WASHINGTON

DEL.

RICHMOND

⊙ OVERNIGHT STOPS
○ OTHER CITIES
Map by W. H. Bunce

LINCOLN'S JOURNEY TO GREATNESS

The marble statue that Thomas D. Jones chiseled from a clay model which he made while Lincoln was reading his mail and composing his journey speeches. The bust now stands at the head of the north stairs, just outside the Senate chamber, in the Ohio State Capitol at Columbus. It is claimed to be the only sculpture for which Lincoln actually posed until it was complete.

LINCOLN'S JOURNEY
TO GREATNESS

A FACTUAL ACCOUNT OF THE TWELVE-DAY
INAUGURAL TRIP

By VICTOR SEARCHER

THE JOHN C. WINSTON COMPANY
PHILADELPHIA · TORONTO

For Madeleine

Author's Note

In view of the voluminous Lincoln literature produced in the preceding one hundred years, it is incredible that this is the first work to cover comprehensively the inaugural trip from Springfield to Washington. Moreover, it is the only such book, with the single exception of a slim volume of news clips assembled from the *Ohio State Journal* by its editor, William T. Coggeshall, and published in 1865.

It is to be noted also that the narrative presented in the following pages is a true story. No incidents are invented. No words are put into Lincoln's mouth. The subject-matter is not fictionized or novelized. It is all solid fact and based on firsthand sources.

To make sure this work is authentic required over two years of full-time research and writing, plus the resources of the Library of Congress, National Archives, Association of American Railroads, the railroads involved, state, local and university libraries, historical societies, newspapers, and other special sources, to all of whom grateful appreciation is hereby extended for information generously supplied.

The chapters were developed under the scrutiny of Lincoln experts David C. Mearns, Chief, Manuscript Division, Library of Congress, and Dr. C. P. Powell, Research Director, Lincoln Sesquicentennial Commission. The manuscript was checked by Carlton Corliss, practical railroader, author of *Mainline of Mid-America,* and by Dr. T. J. Sinclair, head of the School and College Service of the Association of American Railroads. The historical background material was evaluated by Dr. George H. Mayer, professor of History and Government at Purdue University, author of *The United States and the Twentieth Century* and other college texts. The Southern viewpoint was represented by Robert S. Henry, author of such historical works as *The Story of the Confederacy*.

To make certain the facts stood out clearly, the script was read by Georgia Cowan, History Department, District of Columbia Library; Lucy Kelley, Special Studies Division, Association of American Railroads; and George M. Hall, Newspaper and Periodical Department, Library of Congress.

Everything said herein, however, is the responsibility of the author. No political, financial or institutional aid entered into the making of this book or influenced its writing. It stands as evidence of the Lincolnian way of life in freedom of expression and freedom of enterprise.

V. S.

Washington, D.C.

CHAPTER 1

Chuffing and panting through its huge balloon stack, steam dome hissing and brasswork gleaming, cordwood piled high on the tender, the locomotive *L. M. Wiley* waited impatiently at the Great Western railroad depot. The powerful Hinkley engine proudly headed a Presidential Special that consisted of two cars, a baggage car and an ordinary passenger coach, both painted bright yellow.

The time was 7:55 A.M. The date was February 11, 1861. The day was Monday and it was drizzling.

Cold mist and overcast sky were typical of central Illinois winter weather. The occasion, however, was most untypical for Springfield's 9,320 inhabitants. They were seething with the excitment of sending Old Abe to the White House as Sixteenth President of the United States.

Seething also were thirty-four states and seven territories. The Union was being dismembered. Seven slaveholding states had broken away from the Republic fathered by George Washington. Two days before, in Alabama's capital city, the Confederate States of America had adopted a constitution and appointed a president and vice-president. The American people would soon be ruled by two separate national governments.

[1]

Was the United States of America an association of sovereign states from which any could withdraw at will? Or were federal and state governments to cooperate within the framework of a union so as to better assure the body politic of life, liberty and the opportunity to pursue happiness? The point was this: was the United States a government proper, or was it merely a confederacy subject to unrestricted secession? The question of state sovereignty had wracked the Republic since its formation.

The Constitution was not clear. Nor is it clear today, never having been altered or amended in this regard. The sentiment of the American people, however, was crystallized by the subsequent passage-at-arms, a conflict commonly called the Civil War although it was not a war to overthrow existing government, but to withdraw and establish another on the basis of a state's sovereign rights.

Already a succession of hostile acts threatened the peace of the land. The supply ship, *Star of the West,* had been fired on at the turn of the year when attempting to provision the federal garrison stationed on Fort Sumter in Charleston harbor. The new Republic of Louisiana had seized the United States Mint and Customhouse in New Orleans. Mississippi had posted artillery at Vicksburg, dominating river traffic. Florida had grabbed the Pensacola navy yard. Georgia had taken Fort Pulaski. Arkansas troops had occupied the Little Rock arsenal. Texas had confiscated southwestern forts including arms, ammunition and equipment.

The intense political ferment had raised personal emotions and caused threats of violence to be made against Lincoln. Black-bordered letters arrived warning him that he would be killed before he could take office. Funeral wreaths, pictures of coffins, skulls and crossbones, vituperative messages, "you damned old nigger thief," and other obscene expressions, cluttered the daily mails.

Senator William H. Seward of New York, who would be Lincoln's Secretary of State, wrote imploring him to call off the extended inaugural journey that he had announced, or at least to advance the date in order to foil assassination plotters.

Official necessity did not require that Lincoln make a long cross-country excursion. He could have taken the oath of office in his own home, or at the nearest justice of the peace office. And the manner in which a President-elect traveled to the federal capital was a purely personal choice. Lincoln's roundabout itinerary was unique. Scheduled to extend from the eleventh of February to the twenty-sixth, stopping overnight at Indianapolis, Cincinnati, Columbus, Pittsburgh, Cleveland, Buffalo, Albany, New York City, Philadelphia and Harrisburg, it would be punctuated with many stops and hesitations each day. From Harrisburg the route to Washington was by way of Baltimore.

What were Lincoln's purposes in making the prolonged trip? Why did he persist despite strong advice to the contrary? Why should he speak out now, when ever since the nomination he had stayed in Springfield and said nothing? Why jeopardize his life on the way to take office?

He never commented on the reasons behind his tour nor discussed the subject with those who might have left revealing reminiscences. He was, as law-partner William H. Herndon wrote in a later year, a most "shut-mouthed man" on political plans and purposes. His secretaries or traveling companions did not disclose anything of importance in subsequent writings. The records are silent.

[3]

Only by following him stop by stop and speech by speech can his objectives be understood and his achievements realized. That the pages of this book are the first to pursue Lincoln in detail throughout the journey may be because the next four years of bloody fratricide totally eclipsed this twelve-day expedition.

Yet it was during the travel to Washington that Lincoln first spoke out to his countrymen. Here he first came face to face with millions of his constituents and shook their hands by the thousands. Here he first met and talked with hundreds of politicians, legislators and public officials. The journey was the curtain-raiser to all that followed—an unveiling of the man and his methods. And at the end of the trip he came near to his own death when the first assassination attempt was made.

Sunday evening Lincoln went to the office to wind up partnership affairs. "Leave the sign undisturbed, Billy," he said to partner Herndon. "When I come back we'll go on practicing law as before."

Now the time for departure was at hand.

Despite the early hour, the chill rain, and an express wish that no demonstration be made, a goodly throng turned out to see him off. Willing helpers unloaded the luggage from the hotel omnibus. The crowd parted courteously as he and his family entered the one-story brick depot. A hush of respectful solemnity hung over the assembly. As hands were extended, Lincoln grasped them. He said nothing.

At five minutes to the hour, he said good-by to Mrs. Lincoln and the two younger boys who would take a later train and join him in Indianapolis. He was escorted out the door and up the steps of the passenger car. The crowd followed. Reaching the car platform, he turned to these friends and neighbors who had come to bid him farewell. The parting touched him deeply. He removed his tall hat, raised his arm as if in benediction, then let it rest on the railing. Obviously under the stress of emotion, he said slowly:

"My friends— No one, not in my situation, can appreciate my feeling of sadness at this parting.

"To this place, and to the kindness of these people, I owe everything. Here I have lived a quarter of a century, and have passed from a young to an old man. Here my children have been born, and one is buried.

"I now leave, not knowing when, or whether ever, I may return, with a task before me greater than that which rested upon Washington.

"Without the assistance of that Divine Being, who ever attended him, I cannot succeed. With that assistance I cannot fail.

"Trusting in Him, who can go with me and remain with you and be everywhere for good, let us confidently hope that all will yet be well.

"To His care commending you, as I hope in your prayers you will commend me, I bid you an affectionate farewell."

Hardly had he spoken the final words than the train started. The leave-taking throng, heedless of falling rain, stood with heads uncovered and watched their distinguished neighbor enter the moving car as it sped out of sight to the east.

The wheels of destiny were rolling for Abraham Lincoln, powered by an engine named for a Southern plantation owner and secessionist. The immortal journey had begun.

CHAPTER 2

STILL clutching the tall bea-
ver hat in his hand, Lincoln strode into the moving car.

At once he was besieged by newspaper correspondents
Henry Villard of the *New York Herald*,* Henry M.
Smith of the *Chicago Tribune,* and Edward L. Baker,
editor and co-owner of the *Illinois State Journal.* They
wanted to know about the speech. The press had been
informed that Lincoln would make no announcements
before departing. His last-minute remarks had come as
a complete surprise for which they had been unprepared.

To comply with their request, Lincoln sat down in a
coach seat that swayed and bounced as the train gathered
speed. On a pad handed him by private secretary John
G. Nicolay he put down the words he had just spoken.
At the fourth sentence he handed back pad and pencil
to Nicolay and dictated several lines. Nicolay having
trouble writing, he took over again and completed what
has become an American classic.

Lincoln's Farewell to Springfield is considered by many
to be his finest composition, since it was a spontaneous
outpouring of profound feeling.

---

*Villard's dispatches to the *Herald* were used, by arrangement, by the Associated Press; thus his same copy appeared in newspapers all over the country.

Riding with Lincoln in the flat-roofed, wooden passenger coach was, first of all, his personal suite comprising son Robert; Dr. W. S. Wallace, Lincoln's personal physician and brother-in-law; Robert Irwin, in whose care he entrusted his Springfield financial affairs; George C. Latham, Robert's chum, a Springfield boy; John Hay, assistant private secretary; and Nicolay.

What would be called his military escort, but which was not official, included Elmer E. Ellsworth, former Lincoln law student now arrayed as Colonel of a Zouave militia regiment, who would be the first officer casualty after war was declared; and Colonel Ward H. Lamon, resplendent in a personally-designed uniform as aide to the Illinois Governor, whom Lincoln so trusted he would have him serve as Marshal of the District of Columbia throughout the war, and who would be the only person to ride with him all the way to Washington.

Lamon must also be included in the Illinois delegation, having been a Lincoln law associate. Also in the Illinois group were two who had functioned as presidential campaign managers, Norman B. Judd, influential Chicago attorney who would become Lincoln's Minister to Prussia; and Judge David Davis, in whose Eighth Circuit Court Lincoln had appeared many times. Davis would have his dearest wish fulfilled when Lincoln appointed him to the United States Supreme Court.

Others in the Illinois delegation were Ebenezer Peck, another prominent Chicago attorney and political worker who would be rewarded with appointment to the Federal Court of Claims; O. H. Browning, former state senator from Quincy whom Lincoln would recommend be appointed to fill Stephen A. Douglas's unexpired term when Douglas died a few months later; O. M. Hatch, Secretary of State; Jesse K. Dubois, State Auditor; ex-

Governor "Honest John" Moore; and incumbent Governor Richard Yates, who would become noteworthy for his wise administration in the troubled times ahead.

From Wisconsin there was James M. Burgess of Janesville. Burgess had been appointed colonel and charged by his state with guarding Lincoln's person on the journey and until inaugurated. It was a thoughtful move on the part of Wisconsin Governor Alex W. Randall and state officials.

Heading the operating personnel was Lincoln's good friend, Lucian Tilton, president of the Great Western Railway, to whom he had leased his house and sold much of the furniture. Assisting were F. M. Bowen, superintendent of the road; conductor Walter Whitney; engineer Edward H. Fralick; fireman Benjamin A. Gordon; brakeman Thomas Ross; and baggagemaster Platt Williamson.

The superintendent of the Illinois-Mississippi (Caton) telegraph lines, J. J. S. Wilson, was aboard with an assistant carrying a portable instrument that could be attached to the wires at any point in case of emergency.

Over all ruled William S. Wood, former eastern railroad official said to have been recommended by Thurlow Weed, Republican leader in New York State. He was styled Superintendent of Arrangements and was assisted by Burnett Forbes of New York who stayed behind to escort Mrs. Lincoln on her later trip.

Wood had made an inspection tour of the entire route, consulting with railroad officials, perfecting arrangements, returning to Springfield the week before. He issued a timetable and operating instructions to participating lines. He had handbills printed that set forth the carriage protocol for the guidance of local committees, as well as a list naming those authorized to travel from Springfield to Washington.

Both handbill and party list named Colonel E. V. Sumner, First United States Cavalry; Major David Hunter, paymaster at Fort Leavenworth; Captain John Pope, Topographical Engineer; and Captain George W. Hazzard, Fourth Artillery. Not one of these officers was aboard the Special when it departed. Sumner and Hunter would come aboard at State Line. Pope and Hazzard would join the party at Indianapolis. Every Lincoln biography to date has carried this information improperly, misled no doubt by Wood's printed lists. And Army Chief General Winfield Scott did not detail the four regular Army officers as a military escort. These two misstatements have been widely disseminated over the years. Colonel Sumner categorically denied being so detailed in a newspaper interview.

Army records support his contention. He and Hunter were on leaves of absence each had obtained for the occasion; Hazzard was on sick leave which he had had extended. Pope was on detached service with the Lighthouse Board that permitted freedom of movement. (But no sooner did the trip end than he was cited for court martial by order of President Buchanan.) Each of the four officers volunteered his services and made his arrangements with Lincoln personally. Not one had been officially detailed to accompany Lincoln.

Lincoln traveled to Washington as a civilian—as was proper. The likelihood is that he arranged it that way. Despite importunings of associates, he would not affront his neighbors or the nation by being guarded like a prisoner of war as he moved across the country. A prime object of his tour was to allay the people's fears of war, and promote the peaceful intentions of the incoming administration. Army officers could accompany him— but only as personal friends. It appears that the "military escort" was missing when the train left Springfield, by Lincoln's own arrangement.*

Wood's printed instructions and lists were also sent to newspapers and magazines the country over as well as to local committees and public officials. In this manner the schedule of the train was made known as well as the names of the presidential party. The inaugural journey would be conducted in a blaze of publicity. But there were serious misgivings.

At length Lincoln took notice of the political ferment that was raising up personal feuds and animosities. His concern, rather than with himself, was with the situation in Washington. He wanted to know what would happen when he and his administration arrived to take over the government. Where did the Army stand? And, in particular, what about Army Commander Scott, a Virginian?

"Look him square in the eye. Note carefully what he says," Lincoln instructed Thomas B. Mather, Illinois adjutant-general, whom he asked to go to Washington as his personal representative, to ascertain the general's loyalty.

Scott, doughty old hero of Lundy's Lane, and once one of the handsomest men in the military forces of the world

---

*Lincoln had invited to ride with him not only Republicans, but also Breckinridge and Buchanan Democrats, and Bell-Everett men. So that in addition to the "through" members of the presidential party described above, the following persons accepted the invitation and were also on the train leaving Springfield. Some went no further than State Line, others to Indianapolis: William Butler, W. H. Carlin, M. H. Cassell, D. H. Gilmer, J. Grimshaw, J. A. Hough, W. Jameson, E. F. Leonard, W. R. Morrison, L. W. Ross, William S. Underwood and Hall Wilson.

It is to be noted that Villard's dispatch from Tolono, Illinois, mentioned Major Hunter as being in the party, but does not include the other three Army officers. His was the only dispatch stating this.

—six-feet-five and three hundred pounds—was sick in bed, propped up on pillows, when Mather came into the bedchamber.

"Tell Mr. Lincoln I shall expect him to come to Washington when he is ready," wheezed the conqueror of Vera Cruz, voluminous flesh lying in rolls across his warty face and neck. "Tell him I consider myself responsible for his safety. If necessary, I'll plant cannon at both ends of Pennsylvania Avenue, and if any should raise a finger I'll blow them to hell!"

Lincoln believed him. Believed him, remembering that Scott, as Secretary of War, had tangled with Jefferson Davis a few years back. Davis had questioned Old Fuss and Feathers' expense accounts. Of Davis, the general now thundered, "He is no cheap Judas! I do not think he would have sold the Savior for thirty shillings; but for the successorship to Pontius Pilate he would have betrayed Christ and the Apostles and the whole Christian church." Yes, Lincoln could well believe Scott would not team up with the confederate president.

Upon leaving Springfield, knots of friends and neighbors were gathered all along the way, cheering the little yellow cars as they sped by carrying their distinguished Illinoisan. Wayside villages were decorated with national flags as if on holiday. And as Lincoln bowed from the back platform in response to their greetings they shouted to him, "Save the Union, Abe!"

Decatur was the first stop of the journey. It was one required of every train by state law since it was the "seat of justice" of Macon County. Decatur had been an important stop in Lincoln's life. Here the Lincoln family had stayed overnight when migrating from Indiana. Here, a few miles from town, they first settled in Illinois. And here, twenty-nine years later, he received the accolade of the Republican state convention as presidential candidate. Here he was named the Railsplitter.

Right on time at 9:24 A.M., the two-car Special rolled in to be greeted by a roaring crowd. Many were on horseback, and there was a company of mounted militia. Lincoln attempted to speak and made a few very moving remarks. Unable to be heard above the din, he climbed down and shook hands right and left as fast as he could. The stop was for a few minutes only, and he had to clamber aboard as the train made for the open prairie.

A few miles out of town came a sudden unscheduled halt. Barring the right-of-way stood a stake-and-rider fence. The crew jumped to remove the obstruction and the crowd shouted lustily. They accomplished their purpose. Lincoln appeared on the back platform and exchanged greetings with old friends. There is no evidence that a pilot engine preceded the Special. Lincoln was among his own people.

The next town was Bement, where he and Senator Douglas met in 1858 at the home of Francis E. Bryant to plan their famous debates. The train slowed and Lincoln saluted the flag-waving crowd. Then the cars sped out to the wide-open prairie and a brightening sky. Soon Tom Ross was twisting the brakes again, easing the Special to a halt at Tolono where the Great Western crossed the Chicago branch of the Illinois Central Railroad. This stop was also required by state law.

The time was 10:50 A.M. Over the brown sea of long grass the sun was shining and the great oval sky showed patches of blue. Nearby, in a grove of trees, a larger crowd was waiting. A marker now commemorates Lincoln's speech here.

"My friends," he said, mounting a bench, "I am leaving you on an errand of national importance, attended, as you are aware, with considerable difficulties. Let us believe, as some poet has expressed it, 'Behind the cloud the sun is shining still.' I bid you an affectionate farewell."

The stop was only to take on wood and water. Eastward again, the train soon was steaming over the flat unbroken grassland, slowing down to greet roaring crowds at Philo, Sydney, Homer, Salina (now Fairmount) , Catlin, Bryant (now Tilton after Great Western's president); all pro-Lincoln towns in the election, with better than a five-to-three ratio. Then over the Vermilion River into Danville.

A compulsory train stop, Danville, the "seat of justice" of Vermilion County, was farthest east in the original Eighth Judicial Circuit. Lincoln had had a law partnership here with Ward Lamon, whose home it had been until Lamon moved to Bloomington to become circuit prosecutor. So he shared the platform with Lincoln on this occasion.

The train was four minutes behind schedule. Lincoln was allowed time to say only that Danville was one of the old familiar places in his memory and that if he had any blessings to bestow, he would dispense "the largest and roundest to my good old friends of Vermilion County." He thanked them for their expression of friendship and bade them farewell. Lamon had to be content merely to display his wonderful uniform.

Arrival at State Line at 12:38 P.M. was eight minutes late. Here the Great Western line terminated, connecting with the Toledo and Wabash Railroad, known locally as the Valley Road. While locomotives were being changed the party detrained and dined at the State Line Hotel "on indifferent food at double the regular price," a newspaper correspondent reported.

At this village of six hundred people, which was

divided in half by a public road, the roundhouse of one railroad in Indiana and the other in Illinois, over two thousand folk had gathered. They had come in wagons, buggies, on horseback, and on foot. Some wore the buckskin and 'coon caps of pioneers. Others were smartly attired in plug hats and coats in eastern style. Many had on plain work clothes, some old and patched. Most were men, but a sprinkling of print dresses showing behind dark coats, and some fashionable velvets in the manner of *Godey's Lady's Book* enlivened the scene. Altogether it was a typical western crowd that mirrored the passing of the frontier. All were eager to see the first President born west of the Appalachians, one from their own ranks.

Was this the purpose of Lincoln's long trip? To show himself to as many people as possible that they might meet the *person* they had voted for on *principle?*

It was a sound reason. Lincoln was little-known outside of Illinois. Even in his home state he was known mostly as a political symbol. The notable exception was to residents of the Eighth Judicial Circuit. Comprising one-fifth of the state across its central part, nearly fifteen thousand square miles, the circuit's original seventeen counties were reduced, as population increased, to fourteen counties in 1847, eight in 1853, five in 1857, and finally to three in 1861. To these people he was a well-known and welcome person. But to the millions of Americans who first heard of him in the presidential campaign, Lincoln stood wholly as a political symbol; and not a handsome one at that, many thought.

His lank stature and craggy countenance lent themselves to caricature. Photography was then in its infancy. Illustrations being drawn by hand, cartoonists made the most of their opportunity. Political writers screamed that

Lincoln had no public service to justify his candidacy. Who was this Railsplitter? they asked. To rectify the deficiency, several biographies were thrown together for the election campaign. Lincoln, supplying the data, wrote that there was not much to say because "there's so little of me."

He was astute enough not to campaign. He stayed in Springfield during those politically frenetic months, deliberately saying nothing. He realized his limitations and was aware that the nomination had come to him because of his "availability," meaning he had the least number of enemies and the best chance of appealing to all groups. He recognized the attainments of the brilliant Douglas who had been in public service for twenty-five years, fourteen as United States Senator. The contest could not be won between personalities.

"We have to fight this battle on principle and on principle alone," Lincoln had advised his associates when beginning the debates with Douglas. That strategy had won for him the popular vote for United States Senator from Illinois (a fact generally overlooked) although he was subsequently defeated by a politically-hostile legislature. (State legislatures then elected United States Senators.) That same strategy now had won the Presidency.

The President is a man. He is also a symbol. He is the man who personifies the political principle for all who stand for, or against, that principle. You elected that man President of the United States. There he stands!

By long experience in the courtroom, on the hustings, in the legislature, as well as among his fellow men, Lincoln had learned he had the gift of inspiring confidence. He found he could address and win an audience. And he found he could make friends through personal intercourse.

Much as it embarrassed him to appear like a circus on parade, he wanted to make himself known to the body politic. Having been elected Chief Executive of *all* the people, he evidently felt it to be his duty to appear before them. He had become public property.

C H A P T E R   3

Had a modern journalist been present at State Line that morning, the nation's newspapers would have been able to put out a banner headline: LINCOLN SPEAKS TONIGHT! It would have been a journalistic scoop.

Since his nomination May 18 and election November 6, Lincoln had so carefully refrained from public remarks that it was news of first importance when he did say something. To persistent reporters and political inquirers, he steadfastly repeated that his position was based on what people already knew and he had nothing to add. Several times it was necessary for him to repudiate statements erroneously attributed to him.

To a political rally that stopped before his home on a night early in August he replied to their demand for a speech, "It has been my purpose, since I have been placed in my present position, to make no speeches."

To answer many of the letters that were pouring in, he gave secretary Nicolay a wise form of reply. The reply stated that he was receiving requests to express his views on certain political points, but that he was receiving more letters advising him not to widen the area of political controversy.

He stood in the public square of a town that straddled the Illinois-Indiana border, speaking to an enthusiastic audience. Responding to the welcoming speech of the Indiana committee's chairman, he thanked them for the aid Indiana had rendered the cause in the election and for which he was under many obligations. Then he loosed this:

"Gentlemen," he said, as the train whistle shrilled, "I shall address you at greater length at Indianapolis, but not much greater."

A scoop would have resulted from the news that the President-elect was to give a prepared speech at his forthcoming Indianapolis appearance. He would break the long strategic silence. A modern journalist would have elicited the substance of the speech to put on the wires. As it was, everyone had to wait until the Hoosier capital was reached.

Lincoln's tip-off revealed that in the nine months he had been "shut up" in Springfield he had been accomplishing more than meeting delegations, shaking hands and answering letters. Exactly what he had been doing remained to be learned. He had been doing his share of worrying, along with fellow Americans, for he is said to have lost forty pounds. He, too, was carrying a burden of anxiety.

Again the Special took off eastward, northeastward to be exact, toward Lafayette. A pilot engine now preceded the train. Disturbing reports had been coming in. Maybe they were only talk, but the Hoosiers were taking no chances with their precious cargo. Lincoln, heedless of the dangers swirling about him, stood on the rear platform, waving to the crowd receding in the distance, watching the horizon of his Illinois homeland fade into a blur of sky and land. Reluctantly, he turned from the view that was to be his last. He re-entered the coach. There was work to do.

Down the aisle his ex-Danville law partner was strumming the banjo, chanting to rapt listeners "The Lament of the Irish Emigrant," a soulful ditty much admired by the sentimental Lamon. Ellsworth was studying a manual of military tactics. Colonel Sumner was brushing his uniform. Judge Davis was snoozing, as fat men will after a generous meal. That's the way conductor Walt Whitney told it to his grandchildren. Whitney had received permission to ride to Indianapolis as a passenger.

Lincoln strode to where the Indianians were mingling with the Illinoisans who were continuing the trip. Among them was General George K. Steele, Indiana state senator and chairman of the legislative reception committee, who had given the welcoming speech. Present also were Caleb B. Smith, whom Lincoln would appoint Secretary of the Interior; Schuyler Colfax, candidate for a cabinet post, who would be elected Vice-President with Grant; Henry S. Lane, United States Senator-elect; Thomas H. Nelson, unsuccessful candidate for Congress whom Lincoln would appoint Minister to Chile; and General John L. Mansfield, who would become head of Indiana's state militia during the war.

With these legal and political friends, Lincoln was stimulated. Here he could win new adherents to the cause and make acquaintances into firm friends. Here his personality could come into closer view, and his sincerity could be felt—a sincerity that was the taproot of his personal and political life. In this congenial atmosphere he began to shake off the solemnity of a morning of farewells. He was encouraged by the size of the crowds that

[19]

had been greeting him along the way. The self-imposed journey appeared to be working out. His judgment was being vindicated.

A major objective of the tedious trip no doubt was to meet political personages in the states that had made his nomination and election certain. New York and Pennsylvania had been the keystones. Vital had been New Jersey and Indiana as had Ohio and his home state. All had come through handsomely. Now was the time to consolidate the victory of the party with the personality of the man. This important political chore Lincoln would perform throughout the trip. He and party workers would get better acquainted. Personal contacts were more essential, now that another national government was asserting itself. To the many delegations that came aboard the train at speaking stops, Lincoln gave careful attention. This was a fatiguing task, but one into which he entered with zest.

The train was grinding to a halt. Conversation was interrupted by the crash of cannon. It was Lafayette, the bustling community on the banks of the Wabash adjacent to the famous Tippecanoe battleground.

"When I first came to the west some forty-five years ago," Lincoln told the eager crowd surrounding the train, "you had completed a journey of some thirty miles which you had commenced at sunrise, and thought you had done well.

"Now only six hours have elapsed," he continued, "since I left my home, and I find myself far from home surrounded by thousands who are strangers to me."

This was not what the crowd wanted to hear. Nevertheless, they cheered him and the cheers echoed down the valley. His remarks adhered to his policy of no political speeches. Far from being trite, however, the travel observation was appropriate to the occasion. It was highly personal. Lafayette was Lincoln's first speaking stop in the state of Indiana, his boyhood home.

As a lad of twenty-one, he had come west from Spencer County, Indiana, where his mother and older sister had died and where his father had remarried. He had walked from there to Macon County, Illinois—a walk of more than two hundred miles that had taken two weeks, what with leading the oxen, making and breaking camp, foraging for game, fording unbridged streams, crossing the Wabash River near Vincennes, toiling over unbroken prairie and locating a place to settle.

Before that, when he was a child, had been the move from his native state of Kentucky, across the broad Ohio River, into the wooded Hoosier country full of game and wild birds upon which the family had largely subsisted.

These hard, pioneering journeys were probably in his mind as he spoke. How different this was from his Indiana exodus thirty years before! How speedy and comfortable the train! Iron horses running on rails were developing the nation, bringing people closer to each other. It was a modern miracle.

And he was part of the miracle. He was part of the passing of the frontier and the advent of the railroads. For it was the coming of rail transportation that marked the beginning of American industrialization. Railroads initiated the change from America's pioneering and rural culture to the urban, mechanized state of today; a movement still underway in the United States and one just beginning in many parts of the world. Lincoln stands as a symbol of this stirring development. He witnessed and assisted in transforming plodding oxen into swift iron horses, a transformation that shaped the course of the American nation.

Of the change from an agriculture economy to an industrial one, Lincoln was keenly aware. He saw that quick and safe transportation was a basic need for the progress of the United States. As far back as 1832, when he was twenty-three years old and had been in New Salem Village only six months, his petition for public office, his very first, had appeared in the *Sangamo Journal* and stressed the advantages of the rail road (two words) for the county:

". . . No other improvement that reason will justify us in hoping for, can equal in utility the rail road. It is a never-failing source of communication," read his petition to the voters of Sangamo County. "Upon the rail road the regular progress of commercial intercourse is not interrupted by either high or low water, or freezing weather. . . ."

A quarter of a century later, when he was contending with Douglas in their debates, he had made further comments in a thoughtful lecture:

"Man is not the only animal who labors, but he is the only one who improves his workmanship. This improvement he effects by *Discoveries and Inventions*," he had begun the lecture. He said transportation was one of man's great necessities; that the advantageous use of steam power was a modern discovery; and he cited young America with cotton fabrics from Lowell, sugar from Louisiana, salt from Turk's Island, cigars from Havana, coffee and fruits from the tropics; saying, "The iron horse is panting and impatient to carry him everywhere in no time."

At the moment the iron horse was whistling impatiently to be off. The time was 2:40 P.M. On schedule after a ten-minute halt to change locomotives, the train was now headed southeast out of the Wabash Valley for the center of the state via the Lafayette and Indianapolis Railroad.

A wood-burning engine steaming at high speed consumes wood at a voracious rate. Soon a stop had to be made to take on fuel and water. The stop was Thorntown. A shouting crowd brought Lincoln out. He was met by demands for a speech. Holding up a hand for quiet, he said that if he were to make a speech at every stop he never would get to Washington to be inaugurated. But he would tell a story. Didn't know if he should even do that, he said, since folks might get the impression it was not becoming the dignity of the high office he now held.

"I will tell a story," he said, "if you promise not to let it out."

A candidate for county office, he began, owned a horse he set great store by. The horse was a slow animal and stubborn, but sure-footed and a good worker. On this horse the candidate canvassed the county. His efforts gave him a good chance to win. The morning of the convention he mounted his favorite steed to go to the county seat to enter his nomination. The horse lagged, biting at every bush and sprig—

At this point the engine let out two blasts and the cars pulled away, cutting off the story in the middle of the sentence. Spectators laughingly shouted they would never let out *that* story. Lincoln joined the laughter and waved farewell until they disappeared around a bend.

Some miles further was Lebanon, a scheduled two-minute speaking stop. The welcoming crowd closed around the train. Lincoln appeared on the back platform and a number of people were seen running down the tracks.

"Here come the folks from Thorntown to hear the rest of your story," joked one of the party standing with him.

When the panting newcomers caught up (they were locals, of course), Lincoln related the Thorntown incident. Amid general laughter he told the end of the story. The lagging horse, stubbornly biting at every juicy bush despite whip and spur, was so slow the candidate did not arrive at the county seat until too late to enter his nomination, and he lost out.

"I bid you an affectionate farewell," said Lincoln, "I cannot miss the inauguration."

There was a two-minute stop at Zionsville. Then the date with Indianapolis was kept on the dot. The Special was brought to a halt at 5:00 P.M., not in Union Station, but on West Washington Street where the Lafayette track crossed at Missouri Street (now over a viaduct). The train was stopped so accurately that the rear platform came to rest where Indiana's first native-born governor, Oliver P. Morton, was stationed. He was waiting in a barouche. Lincoln appeared at once on the car platform.

Governor Morton rose in the open carriage and delivered an address of welcome. Lincoln listened intently. He heard the governor say to him;

"You are about to enter upon your official duties under circumstances at once novel and full of difficulty, and it will be the duty of all good citizens, without distinction of party, to yield a cordial and earnest support to every measure of your administration calculated to maintain the Union, promote the national prosperity and restore peace to our unhappy and distracted country."

That people should yield to authority to maintain the Union brought immediate response from Lincoln. This

Reputed to be the last ortrait taken before Lincoln arted cultivating whiskers, his picture is dated August 3, 1860. Preston Butler of ringfield was the photographer. Despite his lanky ame and angular features, braham Lincoln was far om being an ugly person.

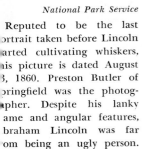

This is said to be the last picture taken of Lincoln before he left Springfield; the date is stated as February 9, 1861. The whiskers are now full grown and he appears here in the full vigor of life. The photographer is given as C. S. German.

[Feb 11 1861]

My friends.

No one, not in my situation, can appreciate my feeling of sadness at this parting. To this place, and the kindness of these people, I owe every thing. Here I have lived a quarter of a century, and have passed from a young to an old man. Here my children have been born, and one is buried. I now leave, not knowing when, or whether ever, I may return, with a task before me greater than that which rested upon Washington. Without the assistance of that Divine Being, who ever attended him, I cannot succeed. With that assistance I cannot fail. Trusting in Him, who can go with me, and remain with you and be every where for good, let us confidently hope that all will yet be well. To His care commending you, as I hope in your prayers you will commend me, I bid you an affectionate farewell.

The original farewell to Springfield speech that is now in the Library of Congress, written by the President-elect as he left Springfield. Note that his handwriting became less legible as the train picked up speed. The date of February 11, 1861, in the upper right-hand corner is that of a cataloger.

seemed a dangerous note to strike with the nation ready to explode. It was a note that needed amending. As was his wont, he addressed the people as well as the governor, thanking them for the magnificent tribute they paid to the great cause of which he considered himself a mere instrument.

"I wish you to remember now and forever, that it is your business, and not mine; that if the union of these States, and the liberties of this people, shall be lost, it is but little to one man of fifty-two years of age, but a great deal to the thirty millions of people who inhabit these United States, and to their posterity in all coming time. It is your business to rise up and preserve the Union and liberty, for yourselves, and not for me. . . . I appeal to you again to constantly bear in mind that with you, and not with politicians, not with Presidents, not with office seekers, but with you, is the question, 'Shall the Union and shall the liberties of this country be preserved to the latest generation'?"

Lincoln was making clear that "the salvation of the Union needs but one thing, the hearts of people like yours." He was making clear his implicit faith in the will of the people; that it was not government by hereditary or arbitrary rulers downward to the people, not "yielding to authority," but upward, up from the people, up from the body politic. This principle of consent of the governed underlay Lincoln's every thought and act as a politician. It made him a statesman; it set him apart from political contemporaries. Governor Morton's approach was that of imposing the Union upon the people by authority, which sharply contrasted with Lincoln's, that of the Union being wanted and supported by the people.

The difference was further sharpened by Lincoln's emphasizing that he was a "mere instrument" of a great cause; repeating the point, "An *accidental* instrument, perhaps I should say."

Newspapers paid scant heed to these extemporaneous remarks—remarks so finely phrased as to seem contrived and so sound that they stand as American political doctrine. They reveal an important political principle of the then little-known President-elect. Uttered as his first speech after the long strategic silence, his words warranted careful evaluation which they did not receive.

While the speeches were going on, a thirty-four gun salute, one for each state, boomed at intervals of a minute. Escorted by General Steele, Lincoln entered the barouche, greeting the governor and Mayor Samuel B. Maxwell. The crowd let loose a roar, surging forward for a closer look, breaking up the carriage line. With considerable difficulty, a semblance of order was restored and the march begun; a procession of brass bands, Indiana guardsmen, city firemen, Zouaves, city grays, and gaily decorated fire engines.

Through the largest winter crowd ever assembled in the capital city, the presidential parade moved down Washington Street to Pennsylvania Street, circled the business district, back to the Bates House, where the Claypool Hotel now stands. The barouche halted at the entrance. Lincoln stood up. Turning to each side, he bowed to the solid mass of people that engulfed him. Leaning over to the driver, Elijah Hedges, he complimented him on the beautifully matched team of four horses adorned with head plumes and miniature flags.

Four years later this driver would take the same white horses over the same streets through the same massing of people with the body of the tall, kind man whose life would be sacrificed that his country might remain united.

CHAPTER 4

$\mathbf{W}$HAT is coercion? What is invasion?"

Lincoln asked from the balcony of the Bates House, holding in his left hand a neatly folded paper marked For Indianapolis. This was the promised speech. And these were two questions agitating the country which he wanted to answer first.

Outgoing President James Buchanan and the Thirty-sixth Congress had been faced with the problems of what to do about states seceding from the Union. Should such states be coerced into remaining? If so, how? Should they be invaded by United States military forces to protect federal property and enforce federal laws? What could be done under the Constitution?

The subject was thoroughly confusing. Looming large in the dissension splitting the nation were the meanings of these words "coercion" and "invasion." Lincoln drove to the heart of the controversy. "Let us make sure," he said, "we do not misunderstand the meaning of *those who use them.*

"Would the marching of an army into South Carolina, for instance, without the consent of her people, and in hostility against them, be coercion or invasion? I very frankly say, I think it would be invasion; and it would be coercion too, if the people of that country were forced to submit."

Then he voiced the crux of the matter: "But if the Government, for instance, but simply insists upon holding its own forts, or retaking those forts which belong to it—or the enforcement of the laws of the United States in the collection of duties on foreign importation—or even the withdrawal of the mails from those portions of the country where the mails themselves are habitually violated; would any or all of these things be coercion?"

His question, which embodied the seceding states' political position, was so ridiculous it could only be answered by ridicule. Lincoln did not hesitate to do so. "In their view, the Union, as a family relation, would not be anything like a regular marriage at all, but only as a sort of free-love arrangement—to be maintained on what that sect calls passionate attraction. . . ."

That is to say, the seceding states were making of the federal Union no more than a convenient arrangement into which they could enter and from which they could withdraw at will, like a free-love affair. The crowd got the point and roared approval.

Lincoln balanced off the political absurdity of secession by then asking serious questions that had (and have) deep meaning for every American. The first:

"In what consists the special sacredness of the State?"

He was not speaking of a state in relation to the Constitution or to the Union, a bond well recognized. "I speak," he said, "of the assumed primary right of a State to rule all which is less than itself and to ruin all which is larger than itself."

To emphasize that deadly fact he likened a county that might be equal in size and population to a state. "Would an exchange of names be an exchange of rights?" he asked.

"Upon what rightful principle may a State, being no more than one-fiftieth part of the nation in soil and population break up the nation?

"What mysterious right to play the tyrant with its people is conferred on a district of a country by calling it a State?"

He closed by saying he was not asserting anything, merely asking questions that must be considered.

Of the huge throng that jammed the streets and filled every vantage point, how many actually heard the carefully chosen words was open to conjecture. But they applauded and hurrahed at each opportunity.

Following the speech, Lincoln made his way through crowded corridors to a dining room so overfilled that he was obliged to wait half an hour to be served, interrupted by autograph hunters and local dignitaries. After dining he moved with even greater difficulty to his suite. Here he was to hold a reception for members of the legislature, but the arrangement broke down in the face of the pressing crowd.

"Outside my door," secretary Nicolay was writing his fiancée back in Illinois, "I hear the crowd pushing and shouting in almost frantic endeavor to get to another parlor in the door of which Mr. Lincoln stands shaking hands with the multitude."

The total reached three thousand before Lincoln ended the ceremony and sought the sanctuary of his suite. He acknowledged that the task was harder than mauling rails.

Now he was pacing the floor. He was unusually agitated. Visions of the press having gotten hold of his speeches and prematurely printing them made him shudder. Impatiently, he awaited the arrival of his son Robert, into whose care he had placed the papers that morning. Robert could not be located. He was out with a group of Young Republicans who were delighted to entertain the Prince of Rails, son of the Railsplitter.

Lincoln's worry centered on the Inaugural Address, which he had prepared in Springfield and had guarded carefully from prying eyes. In the address he spelled out the policies of his administration, a program eagerly awaited by an agitated citizenry and a curious world. Lincoln's friend, William H. Bailhache, co-owner of the *Illinois State Journal,* had locked himself in with a compositor one week end and had struck off twenty copies, after which he broke up the forms.

These copies of the Inaugural Address, together with notes for his major speeches en route, Lincoln had placed in a black oilcloth handbag, and that morning he had passed the bag to Robert, not mentioning the contents, but directing the boy to keep it safely. Now when he needed them, boy and bag were missing.

He wanted to discuss the Inaugural Address with Orville Browning, for Browning had mentioned that he would return home to Quincy the next day. He also needed the speech he had prepared for Cincinnati.

The moment the panting young man entered the room, he asked him where the bag was. With the annoyance of a teen-ager pulled away from rare entertainment for a trivial thing, Robert replied to his father's anxious question that he had left the bag with the hotel clerk. He explained with an injured air that he had had to walk all the way from the train to the hotel, no carriage having been available and no room assigned when he had arrived there. Lincoln then asked what the hotel

[30]

clerk had done with the bag. Robert replied that he had put it behind the counter with other luggage.

The much-caricatured long legs of Lincoln went flying to the lobby, and in a single stride they carried him over the counter. To the horror of the clerk and the astonishment of bystanders, Lincoln unceremoniously dug through the mound of luggage. He fitted a small key to the first black bag that looked like his and opened it, and out fell a dirty shirt, some clean paper collars, a pack of cards and a half-empty whiskey pint. The unexpected collection was too much even for the distraught President-elect. He joined the general laughter.

The missing bag was found intact and carried upstairs where Lincoln extracted the documents he needed. Locking the bag, he handed it to Robert, saying, "Now, you keep it!" Robert did. Relating the incident many years later, he said his father never scolded him for what happened or alluded to it again.

So ended the first day of the journey which had brought Lincoln from the capital of Illinois to that of Indiana.

Lincoln's prepared Indianapolis speech was given banner treatment by the press all over the land. The newspapers were waiting for it. Some were hoping for fireworks on the order of Andrew Jackson's fulminations. Others looked for a blaring of bugles and beating of drums. Still others waited to pounce upon his words to twist them to their own ends.

Newspapers represented the greatest means of mass communication in that bygone era. No other medium matched their influence with the public, or remotely approached their nationwide coverage, which reached into the farthest corners of the land. Annual newspaper circulation was 927 million copies in 1860, strikingly illustrating the fact that Americans were, as the federal census superintendent remarked, "peculiarly a newspaper-reading nation."

Of the 3,242 newssheets then published, 80 per cent were classified as political. Where so large a share of the public activity was, from the nature of American civil institutions, engrossed in social and political discussions, a public press by necessity grew political. Political newspapers jumped a hundred per cent in number during the decade ending in 1860—convincing evidence that the political agitation of the time was something extraordinary.

Heading its editorial, "A President to be Trusted," the *Providence* (Rhode Island) *Journal* said that Lincoln's clear, sharp interrogations cut down secession by the roots at the very outset; that his perceptions of the difference between real coercion, and that just and firm exercise of authority which is essential to the existence of government, were "too clear to be clouded by sophistry or rhetoric." The *Journal* scored another point by noting that Lincoln had received the largest total number of votes cast for any President up to that time.

The *Boston Transcript* called him the man of the hour, noting that Lincoln's clear record, firm but modest course and high reputation for integrity had won the esteem of political opponents.

Praising the addresses as appropriate, just as the previous silence had been judicious, the *Cleveland Leader* declared that "Mr. Lincoln had acquitted himself not only creditably but nobly."

"This little speech," said the *Chicago Tribune*, "has

electrified the true Republicans and has given the fishy ones 'fever and ague!' "

Political bias so deeply colored published accounts that Lincoln was prompted to demonstrate a case to Henry J. Raymond, editor of the *New York Times*. Following the election in November, Senator Lyman Trumbull of Illinois, recognized as a Lincoln spokesman, made a speech at a rally in Springfield, part of which was written by Lincoln. Conciliatory in tone and thoughtful in text, the speech was intended to help ease the tense political feeling.

"Has a single newspaper," Lincoln wrote to Raymond, "heretofore against us, urged that speech upon its readers with a purpose to quiet public anxiety?"

Answering his own question, Lincoln wrote, "Not one, so far as I know. This is just what I expected and just what would happen with any declaration I could make. Party malice, and not public good, possesses them entirely."

To a correspondent who asked him to write something for the public and disclaim all intention to interfere with slaves or slavery in the states, Lincoln replied it would do no good, quoting Luke 16:31, "If they hear not Moses and the prophets, neither will they be persuaded though one rose from the dead."

Far away in the Nebraska Territory, yet to be reached by a railroad, the *Omaha Republican* told its readers that the policy to be pursued by the incoming administration could be understood from Mr. Lincoln's speeches. "He will feel mortally bound by his official oath to sustain the Constitution and the Union and faithfully execute the laws of the country. This is not coercion," noted the *Republican*, "it is simply defense and preservation."

The *Philadelphia Press* agreed with its Nebraska neighbor, proclaiming that Lincoln considered it the clear duty of the federal government to hold the forts and other property it possessed in the seceding states, and to retake what had been illegally captured . . . "There can be no doubt of the general correctness of these opinions."

A nearby neighbor, the *Baltimore American,* brought to light an astonishing fact: the fifth article of the South Carolina state constitution ordains that all persons holding public office shall take an oath that they will "preserve, protect, and defend, the Constitution of the State *and of the United States."* Was the oath of a South Carolinian public person worthless?

The *Lancaster* (Pennsylvania) *Express* asserted secession leaders were afraid of the word "coercion." "Hence their death yell whenever it is proposed the Government shall assert its supreme authority. . . . Any compromise to be just and honorable," observed the *Express,* "must be based upon a recognition of the right and power of the Federal government to maintain its authority."

Stating that his speeches would be subjected to misrepresentation, the *Cincinnati Commercial* did not forget Lincoln's remarks from the car platform, the first Indianapolis speech. The *Commercial* quoted Robert Dale Owen (whose father had founded the colony at New Harmony, Indiana) in a lecture he gave at Indianapolis Wednesday evening: "You were told by one who will soon be the Chief Executive of our country that the preservation of the Union was your business," declared Owen, "and that it is not the business of Presidents or politicians or office-seekers. You were bid to rise up and preserve that Union. Never was injunction more needed. Never was reminder more in place."

The *New York Times* made an effective summary of

Lincoln's prepared Indianapolis speech, saying he disclosed he had no sympathy with the theory which regards the federal government as a "voluntary league of sovereign states" from which any may secede at will.

From Washington came telegraphic dispatches saying that intense excitement had been created there. The Republicans hailed the speech as a manly and statesmanlike appeal to the sober sense of the people. The moderates were afraid it would close the door to reconciliation. "Secessionists," said one dispatch, "were glad the President-elect promised to use coercion, maintaining that is all they want."

Deep South newspapers let loose their editorial guns. That archconspirator of Secessia, the *Charleston* (South Carolina) *Mercury,* sneered that Lincoln was furnishing a dish of "fiddle-faddle," but it didn't alarm them for they knew he was a "weak compound of blockhead and blackguard." Another secessionist organ avowed that few Americans could read his speech without blushing for the country that could elect to its highest office such a "canting, ill-bred, indecent, old man." Politicians like Congressman Muscoe Garnett of Virginia trumpeted that it was the equivalent of a declaration of war. Another opposition editor declared that he had heard speeches from Monroe to Webster to Fillmore, but nothing compared to Lincoln's stuff about marriage, free love and such nonsense.

"What else did he say?" the editor asked rhetorically, then answered, "The foreshadowing of a disposition to reduce the sovereign states to the same humble basis as the counties."

Lincoln had not said or intimated such a thing. But that is the way of political propoganda; a way with men long before Esau gave up his birthright to double-talking

Jacob. Lincoln himself had experienced the twisting of words into wrong meanings. As a counselor-at-law he knew, as most attorneys and all politicians know, that the meanings of words can be distorted. Words are what hearers and readers put into them. They are symbols. To make meanings clear, words have to be guarded by aforesaids and whereases and be fortified by phrases and clauses to bar the possibility of equivocation. Legal precision was not possible in a political speech. The risks of being misquoted and of deliberate distortion had to be undertaken.

Now it was no partisan struggle for political office. With the defection of South Carolina beginning in December and six others following, political partisanship entered the realm of governmental disruption. That disruption was now pointing toward violence. False prophets had been misleading the body politic, their doctrines provoking the people into disloyalty, causing an emotional hysteria to grip the country. The time had come to speak out. Silence could only be construed as indifference or acquiescence.

Lincoln had to undergo the calculated risk of misrepresentation in the endeavor to clarify the chaotic political situation and to allay the people's apprehensions. Only three weeks remained before he would assume the Presidency. In two days he would be officially declared elected.

The moment was at hand for patriots to come forth. Lincoln would appeal directly and personally to the citizenry. His Indianapolis speeches revealed his mission: he would use the journey to Washington to rally his countrymen to the cause of freedom and the maintenance of a united nation.

CHAPTER 5

ALL night thousands of visitors, unable to secure lodging yet eager to participate in the greatest political event of their frontier lives, tramped the streets of the young Hoosier capital. Accommodations were strained to the limit. That was so even for members of the presidential party, for whom only five hotel rooms had been reserved.

"Had to sleep two in a bed, and accommodations were very poor," noted Orville Browning in his diary. "It is just about as much of that sort of thing as I want." Then he set down his daily weather observation. A beautiful springlike day, he said it was, sunny and mild.*

Outside the Bates House the crowd that had been increasing since dawn kept shouting for a speech. Lincoln finally responded by appearing on the balcony with Solomon T. Meredith, legislator from Wayne County and an active supporter. Meredith made the introduction. Excusing himself from delivering another speech, Lincoln introduced his son Robert. This was Robert's first public appearance with his father. He was unable to do more than to wave his hand. Lincoln smiled and said that his boy, Bob, "hadn't got in the way of making

---

*February 12, 1861, second day of the journey, was also the fifty-second birthday of the President-elect.

[37]

speeches." Father and son re-entered the hotel, but the audience would not be silenced by the brass band playing national airs on another balcony. The tumult mounted.

Meredith came out again, bringing with him Reverend J. W. T. McMullen, a Methodist preacher, whom he introduced, and who then delivered an inspiring address. McMullen's personal appearance was similar to Lincoln's —tall and lanky and dark. Many in the concourse failed to catch Meredith's introduction, and thought that Lincoln was making the speech.

That Lincoln delivered a speech before the Indiana Legislature has also been repeatedly recorded. He was invited to, but he did not. This was perhaps because of a conflict of invitations.

The Indiana Senate and House had passed resolutions early in the year, appointing six senators and seven representatives to act as a reception committee. They invited Lincoln to address a joint session. He accepted.

The Indianapolis City Council, not to be outdone, had appointed a welcoming committee, headed by the mayor.

A citizens' meeting, held in the old courthouse, had extended a formal invitation to Lincoln to stop over on his journey, and he formally accepted.

The conflict was solved by Lincoln's breakfasting with the governor at the gubernatorial mansion on Market Street and from there going to the Capitol and visiting the legislature informally. He then returned to the hotel, the crowd following him back and forth. Here he continued to confer with Indiana public men and greeted delegations arriving from Kentucky, Cincinnati and Columbus.

Into the room an Illinois group entered to bid him good-by. Jesse Dubois maneuvered him into a corner and held his arms while Ebenezer Peck snipped a lock of his hair. They hugged him and then rushed from the room in the manner of men who will not for the world reveal the depth of their feelings.

Orville Browning stepped over to say good-by. Lincoln drew him into the bedchamber, shutting the door. Browning, whose political opinions Lincoln valued (he had written the 1858 Illinois Republican platform), took out a printed copy of the Inaugural Address Lincoln had asked him to study. Praising the address as able, well-considered and appropriate, there was, nevertheless, one thing he did not like. That was an implied threat of war. He suggested omitting the clause wherein Lincoln declared it to be his purpose "to *reclaim* the public property and places which had fallen."

Lincoln accepted Browning's suggestion, deleting the controversial clause, thus limiting the intention to holding that which was still held. Nicolay and Hay in their authoritative biography maintain that Browning's correction changed the course of events. That may be so. Yet it is also likely that Lincoln had been pondering the subject for some time. He had a careful and deliberate mind; not, as many biographers have misinterpreted him as having, a slow-working one. He thought vigorously, but he took great care to know his ground; looking through, around and beyond the subject before he spoke or acted. He would listen to others patiently and at great length. This was a notable Lincoln characteristic. His conclusions were always his own.

Browning left the room in the company of Governor Yates and others of the Illinois group, taking with them the barrel-chested, walrus-mustachioed Ward Lamon. Unceremoniously, they bundled Lamon into another room and locked the door. They impressed upon the ex-circuit prosecutor the importance of his duties as special guardian of the President-elect on the long trip ahead.

"Now, Lamon," said Uncle Jesse, as Dubois was known to his friends, "we entrust the sacred life of Mr. Lincoln to your keeping. If you don't protect it," he warned, and the others nodded assent, "never return to Illinois, for we will murder you on sight."

With this threat, delivered in a jocular tone but with a feeling of deep alarm which everyone shared, they unlocked the door and left. Thereafter, the resplendent Lamon went about his guardianship duties with two pistols and a bowie knife stuck in his belt, commanding awesome respect. His great bulk aided in bucking crowds that filled every conceivable space to catch a glimpse of the renowned Railsplitter.

So determined was the mob that blocked the hotel entrance that Lamon had to bring all his weight to bear, like a football fullback, to get Lincoln through to the carriage in which Governor Morton was waiting. Once in the carriage, the struggle continued through the mass of people packing Meridian Street down to the depot. Here, in the nation's first Union railroad station, another jostling jam took place.

A less rugged individual than pioneering Old Abe would have been pulled apart, so overwhelming was public interest in his person. He suffered the violence good-naturedly. In private he discussed the almost savage concern being taken in the person of both himself and Bob. He posed a conundrum that became a private joke. "Which is the most savage Injuns—the hostile ones or them that goes on foot?"

To make their way through the densely-packed depot required the bulk and force of Colonel Lamon. Seven railroads centered here. Most were running half-fare excursions for the big event. Thousands of Hoosiers from all sections of the state "rode the cars" to the capital city. The legislature adjourned from 10:00 to 11:30 A.M. to join the send-off.

Preceded by Lamon, Lincoln got through to the train. Then everybody tried to get into the same car, wanting to hear the speeches of welcome of the Ohio-Kentucky delegation. This delegation included another future President of the United States, Rutherford B. Hayes, and Lincoln responded by expressing his gratitude for their respect and esteem.

To restore order required the combined efforts of manager Wood and Henry C. Lord, president of the road, and other employees, distributing the passengers in the right places, excursionists in the first two coaches, presidential party in the last two, the rear car for the President-elect.

The Indianapolis and Cincinnati Railroad management had outdone itself. The entire train was decorated with flags, and with red-white-and-blue bunting. The four attractive coaches were shiny and new-looking, redolent of fresh varnish. Across the railing of the last car stretched a rosette of national colors and draped flags, a large gilded American eagle resting in the center.

At the head of the train snorted the locomotive, *Samuel Wiggins,* named for a Cincinnati banker, a staunch Unionist and a director of the road. Thirty-four stars on a blue field encircled the balloon stack. Covering the front end completely were portraits of the fourteen Presidents and the President-elect grouped around George Washington in the center. Sides of the engine and tender were hung with flags and evergreen in unique designs.

The interior of Lincoln's car was especially attractive with a hand-carved frescoed ceiling. The walls were covered with crimson plush and blue silk studded with silver stars, and national flags were draped over the doorways.

Above the golden eagle on the rear platform stood President-elect Lincoln, soberly clad in a dark suit and long shawl. As the Special rolled out of the station at exactly 11 A.M., he bowed to the shouting spectators. The train moved through switching yards, along drab industrial sections, out to the suburbs, passing sentinels every half mile who waved American flags to signal that all was well. Finally open country was reached and Lincoln turned to enter the railway carriage.

Stepping into the car, he was greeted by the rest of his family—Mary, his wife, and sons William (Willie) and Thomas (Tad). The two boys leaped upon their famous father with joy and exuberance. He was their pal. And they were his weakness, if weakness his fondness for them can be called. As they climbed into his great arms, he stooped and kissed their blue-eyed, brown-haired* mother, and his own deep-set eyes went moist.

Some accounts said the family came along because General Scott advised that the journey would be made safer if they accompanied Lincoln. Other accounts said that Mary could not remain home, knowing her husband was traveling in constant danger. Another report asserted that she couldn't get ready in time. And there were other tangled tales. No evidence has proved the validity of one or the other. The *Chicago Tribune* reported that it became known on Saturday that Mary and the two younger boys would join the Special in Indianapolis.

---

* "When I first saw her," said law-partner Billy Herndon, "she was rather compactly built, had a well-rounded face, with dark-brown hair and bluish-gray eyes." Mary's elder sister, Elizabeth, said that even as a schoolgirl in gingham dresses Mary was very pretty. "She had clear, blue eyes, long lashes, light-brown hair with a glint of bronze and a lovely complexion. Her figure was beautiful, and no Old Master ever painted a more perfect arm and hand."

To accomplish this, Mary had to leave Springfield at 6:10 P.M. and take a sleeping car that arrived in Lafayette at 5:45 A.M. Changing railroads, she took the 7:20 A.M. train out of Lafayette, scheduled to reach the Hoosier capital at the time the Special would be leaving. Mary was so worried during her all-night trip she had conductors wire ahead to make sure she would not be left behind.

She was accompanied from Springfield by Burnett Forbes, assistant trip manager; Lockwood Todd, her cousin, of whom the boys were fond; and William Johnson, a Negro attendant. All would continue the journey to Washington.

Flushed with the exertion of the quick transfer with only minutes to spare, and happy to be reunited with her family, Mary looked radiant. Her husband did not fail to compliment her with admiring approval. Setting down the two boys, who scampered away in search of high adventure, Lincoln went about introducing his wife to the assembled company.

"Mrs. Lincoln kept up a spirited conversation during the entire journey, although much fatigued by night travel," said one correspondent. Another reported that the President-elect and "his amiable and vivacious lady" held their levee in the last car. "Merriest among the merry," telegraphed another, "the President-elect kept those around him in a continual roar of laughter." The two boys, exploring through the crowded cars, attracted attention by their sprightliness and good nature. Tad, the irrepressible one, amused everyone by suddenly asking, "Do you want to see Old Abe?" and in response to the never-failing affirmative answer would point to a nearby person and shrill in boyish treble, "That's Old Abe!" Willie, the thoughtful one, joined his younger brother in the fun, for the two were inseparable.

[43]

Robert, the shy one, was acting very seventeenish on the trip and disliked the nickname Prince of Rails although he hugely enjoyed the entertainment and attention given him all along the line.

The Lincolns loved their children and indulged them shamelessly, but Willie was the special object of their affections. Fair-haired, blue-eyed, handsome, he was like his father in disposition—sweet-tempered, sensible, gentle-mannered, "the most lovable boy I ever knew," a playmate said of him. His mother saw in him a replica of the man she had fallen in love with and married. To Lincoln, his son William Wallace represented the special joy a parent feels toward a child who acts and thinks as he does.

Willie had his father's careful mind, a characteristic Lincoln quickly recognized in this incident, which took place shortly after their arrival in the White House.

One day at breakfast Tad was in tears. His father seemed unable to console him. Willie looked on disconsolately. He lapsed into a silence that lasted at least ten minutes, during which he was utterly oblivious to his surroundings. He was trying to think up a way to help, and eventually did. His absorption ended, "he clasped both hands together, shut his teeth over the under lip and looked up smilingly at his father." Lincoln, turning to the guest reporting this, said, "I know every step of the process by which that boy arrived at his satisfactory conclusion . . . as it is by just such slow methods that I attain results."

The shrieking of the engine's whistle and clanging of the big brass bell heralded a stop. The train eased its speed smoothly, the recently installed Loughbridge safety braking system helping to reduce the heretofore jarring operation of bringing a train to a halt. The slack in each primitive link-and-pin coupling, plus the need to set every brake by hand, made stopping a train a major task those days. The Loughbridge system, with which the Indianapolis and Cincinnati Railroad had recently equipped its passenger cars and engines, was one of the many improvements that had started to make their appearance in American railroading.

The first stop was Shelbyville. Next, Greensburg. Following that, Lawrenceburg, last stop in Indiana. The halts were for a few minutes only.

At Greensburg there was a glee club, a brass band and a huge crowd fervently rendering patriotic songs. Before Lincoln withdrew from the car platform, the town's most beloved citizen, eighty-five-year-old Reverend Mr. Blair, was assisted up by his friends. Shading his eyes with a trembling hand, he looked at the towering President-elect and extended the other hand in greeting.

"I shake hands with the President of the United States for the last time," he quavered. "May the Lord bless and guard you, sir. May He sustain you through the trials before you and bring you to His Heavenly Kingdom at last."

At Lawrenceburg, the Indianapolis and Cincinnati junctioned with the Ohio and Mississippi Railroad and ran into Cincinnati over the latter's roadbed by an ingenious arrangement. Track gauges of the two railroads differed. The Indianapolis track gauge was 4 feet 8½ inches (present standard gauge) and the Ohio and Mississippi, 6 feet. So it was impossible for the rolling stock of one to operate over the tracks of the other.

Different track gauges were common practice then. Cities and states franchised a new railroad with a view to strengthening the commercial position of their community or to weaken that of rivals. They didn't want the traffic interchange that is standard practice today; they wanted it all their way.

In the present instance no commercial rivalry existed. Rather, there was mutual profit to be gained by increasing the traffic between Indiana's land-bound capital and the river port of Cincinnati. They solved the gauge problem by laying down an extra rail, a third rail, on the same roadbed, thus providing two track gauges over the one road. By sharing the same right-of-way and terminal facilities, both railways reduced costs and improved service.

The Lawrenceburg stop was made at the gaily decorated Indianapolis and Cincinnati depot. Evidently Lincoln had been thinking about the locality. Saying he had no time to make a speech, he then gave his usual brief remarks.

"I suppose you are all Union men here." (Cheers and cries of "Right!") "And I suppose you are in favor of doing full justice to all, whether on that side of the river (pointing to the Kentucky shore) or on your own." (Cries of "We are.")

"If the politicians and leaders of the parties were as true as the people," he said, "there would be little fear that the peace of the country would be disturbed." (Cheers.)

"I have been selected to fill an important office for a brief while," he continued, "and am now in your eyes invested with an influence which will soon pass away. But should my administration prove to be a very wicked one, or what is more probable, a very foolish one, if you, the *people,* are but true to yourselves and to the Con-

stitution, there is but little harm I can do, thank God!"
(Applause.)

The eager crowd pushed forward to grasp his hand,
but the train was pulling away, picking up speed with
every chug and snort.

What did Lincoln's unusual comments portend? They
were so brief as to be cryptic. They might merely be a
glimpse into his thinking of the moment. Or they might
be a hint of what was coming.

Next was Cincinnati.

Before reaching Ohio's great river port, a touching
incident occurred just over the line at North Bend. This
was the home of William Henry Harrison, Ninth President, and here his remains were buried. Surviving members of the family had gathered at the gravesite that lay
a short distance from the railroad line. The Special
slowed as Lincoln stood with uncovered head, paying his
respects to the dead.

Then the Lincoln train entered the Queen City of
the West.

CHAPTER 6

The outpouring of Cincinnati citizenry was so great that the train was held up until the tracks were cleared by police and military personnel. It was a little after the appointed hour of 3:00 P.M. when the Presidential Special entered the Ohio and Mississippi Railroad depot at the foot of Fifth Street.

To the welcome of the reception committee chairman, Lincoln replied briefly. The crowd, seeing him enter the carriage and greet Mayor Richard M. Bishop, roared with enthusiasm. Also in the carriage, an open one drawn by six white horses decorated in national colors, were two Kentuckians from towns across the river. They were B. W. Foley, ex-mayor of Covington, and Mayor Robert E. Hawkins of Newport.

The pageantry was superb. Colorful banners reached across the streets. Windows were adorned with large portraits of Washington and Lincoln framed in evergreen. The buildings from the river up to Fifteenth Street, and many beyond, were festively garnished. A handsome house on Sixth Street carried a banner reading, WELCOME TO THE PRESIDENT OF THIRTY-FOUR STATES. The mayor's residence at Mound and Eighth Streets was attractively ornamented, and the next door waved a large flag with white letters on a blue ground carrying the word, UNION!

On Walnut Street the Gibson House drew the greatest attention. From its balcony a banner made of muslin stretched twenty feet high and sixty feet long. At one end was a portrait of Lincoln; in the center, Washington, over the federal coat-of-arms; and at the other end, Vice-President Hamlin. Between portraits were patriotic mottoes. Against a pink background along the bottom, the states were listed in alphabetical order, each encircled in evergreen. Under each seceded state was the caption, OUT ON PAPER. The transparency was brilliantly lighted at night, a difficult achievement in that era of kerosene and candles.

The President-elect was escorted by the Washington Dragoon Regiment. A detachment of police surrounded the carriage. The march lasted two hours. Heading the lengthy procession were eleven uniformed organizations. As Lincoln wheeled into sight from block to block, cheers were interspersed with shouts for the President, the Union, and the Constitution. A large group of ladies standing on the wide steps of the post office demonstrated their enthusiasm by concerted fluttering of large handkerchiefs.

Lincoln would rise in the carriage, uncover, and acknowledge the greetings with repeated bows. Some onlookers asserted that his lips could be seen saying, "Wonderful!" At the orphan asylum the assembled children sang a patriotic song to the tune of "Hail, Columbia!" waving miniature flags in unison. At the Banner Ward House, thirty little girls dressed in white stood on tables along the curb singing the "Star-Spangled Banner." Lincoln halted to accept a floral offering from a blushing emissary. Taking her up in his great arms, he kissed her on both cheeks and carefully set her down again.

At five-thirty Lincoln came out on the Burnet House balcony that overlooked Third and Vine Streets. Before him, and on all sides, extended an immense concourse of wildly cheering people. When he secured quiet he began:

"Twenty-four hours ago, at the capital of Indiana, I said to myself I have never seen so many people assembled in winter weather. I am no longer able to say that . . .

"My friends," he continued in his high-pitched voice that carried far, "I am entirely overwhelmed by the magnificence of the reception which has been given, I will not say to me, but to the President-elect of the United States of America. Most heartily I do thank you, one and all, for it."

It was not the military pageantry, not the stateliness of civil dignitaries, nor any other formal display that made the event a success, telegraphed the Associated Press correspondent to his newspapers, but the spontaneous turnout of 100,000 persons from rich merchant to humblest day laborer.

"But that is what might reasonably have been expected," Lincoln told the multitude, "that this great city of Cincinnati would thus acquit herself on such an occasion."

He did not exaggerate. Cincinnati, greatest inland city in the West, boasted a population of over 160,000, seventh in the nation, surpassing St. Louis, ahead of Chicago (109,000), Cleveland (43,500) and Pittsburgh (49,000). Named Queen City of the West by Longfellow, home port of river packet lines plying 250 boats to and from the city annually, Cincinnati ranked third in manufacturing, wholesaled a great variety of goods, and was the center of a fertile farming area.

"I have spoken but once before this in Cincinnati," Lincoln reminded the audience. That had been on September 17, 1859, when, campaigning for the party and not yet a presidential candidate, he had talked for over two hours. He predicted then the Republicans would beat the Democrats. Now he would recall to them what he had said. He would repeat those remarks.

"In a playful manner but with sincere words, I addressed much of what I said to the Kentuckians," he recalled. "I told them that after they were beaten they would be treated as Washington, Jefferson and Madison treated them.

"We mean to leave you alone and in no way to interfere with your institutions. We mean to recognize and bear in mind always that you have as good hearts in your bosoms as other people, or as we claim to have, and treat you accordingly.

"Fellow-citizens of Kentucky!—my friends!—brethen! may I call you in my new position? I see no occasion and feel no inclination, to retract one word of this.

"And now, my fellow-citizens of Ohio," he inquired of the vast assemblage before him, "have you who agree with him who now addresses you in political sentiment—have you ever entertained other sentiments toward our brethen of Kentucky than those I have expressed to you?"

To the thunderous *"No!"* that volleyed up, Lincoln replied that he took their response as the most reliable evidence that "we shall all be brethren again, forgetting all parties, ignoring all parties."

Just as in Lawrenceburg, so now in Cincinnati he was looking across the Ohio water to his native Kentucky.*

---

* For reasons never fully developed, Lincoln did not go into Kentucky as he had evidently planned. He never delivered or released for publication his Address to Kentuckians, which he so carefully prepared before leaving. He was vitally concerned with Kentucky, not merely because it was his native state but particularly because it was, in his estimate, the keystone of the border states. Later he explained this concern: "Kentucky gone, we can not hold Missouri nor, as I think, Maryland. These all against us, and the job on our hands is too large for us." Hence the appeal to Kentuckians contained in his Cincinnati speech.

He was telling Kentucky compatriots that he was as much their President as his distinguished predecessors had been. He was telling them they had nothing to fear from him despite all that had been said about him in the political campaign.

Kentucky was the immediate target of his remarks, but he was speaking also to the border states, Delaware, Maryland, Missouri. He was talking to the slaveholding states of Virginia, North Carolina, Tennessee and Arkansas that were voting in state conventions on whether or not to stay in the federal Union. He was talking also to the seven seceded states. "We will welcome them in every state of the Union," he said, "no matter where they are from."

He was speaking, actually, to Americans everywhere who disagreed with him politically; to those who disagreed on the vexing questions, and on all issues that had found political expression in the election campaign. For another of the objectives of his long trip was to try to bring greater patriotic harmony out of the political confusion.

It was easy for anyone to say, "Save the Union!" Easy to demand quick answers to insuperable problems, easy to insist that something be done. But what? What should be done? How to save the Union?

Could it be maintained without compromising the Constitution? Or would the decision have to be made by war? Could the end be reached by negative policies, by doing nothing, overlooking hostile acts against the government as Buchanan had been doing? If not by negative policies, then what positive measures would be effective? What could he do now, before taking office?

The passage of a hundred years makes clear that Lincoln's fortnight of travel, reaching the nation's important cities, was of inestimable importance in making him, an unknown factor in a new party, the coming leader of a politically distraught country. It was a master stroke. And it also represented courageous entry on the field of battle of the new Commander-in-Chief in person; deliberately exposing himself, his policies and his future to every crossfire and pot shot en route.

The journey also revealed Lincoln as a public relations expert, something unheard of in that time. The two-week trip turned public attention away from secessionists forming the cotton confederacy and from abolitionists who were saying, "Let them go, we want no slaveholders in *our* country." For too long the radicals of both sides had been monopolizing the news. For too long the President-elect had been silent. Now he was making headlines. Now his movements and his remarks were spread out that all might see. The eyes and ears of the world were focused on what he was saying and doing.

Moreover, the public, confused by a continual barrage of drastic charges and countercharges, was now being given reasoned appraisal of the vexing questions by its chosen leader; a leader who had been nominated by his party because he was a moderate, and elected because the people believed in what he stood for.

Additionally, there was daily evidence that the President-elect was enthusiastically received at every stop. The wide-spread acclaim could not fail to impress friend and foe. The so-called minority President had the backing of the people, a great many of whom had not voted for him. On the first day at Indianapolis, a city of eighteen thousand, a throng of nearly three times its population had come in the middle of winter to see and hear him. And next day, at Cincinnati, the turnout leaped to six figures. On that score alone the journey was proving a tremendous success.

Many of the things he was saying would be disclosed in the Inaugural Address as administration policies. His admonition to Kentuckians, for example, foreshadowed the first proposition of the Inaugural Address—that his administration would not directly or indirectly interfere with slavery.

After supper that night in Cincinnati, he held a levee, as a reception was then termed, in the hotel's main dining room. At eight o'clock he was called upon by several thousand members of the German Industrial Association. They had marched through streets still crowded, with bands playing, torchlights gleaming, cheers and shouts filling the cool night. Their committee conducted Lincoln to the hotel balcony where their appointed speaker, Frederick H. Oberkleine, an iron molder, declared to him before the assembled members,

"We, the Germans, free workingmen of Cincinnati, avail ourselves of this opportunity to assure you, our chosen Chief Magistrate, of our sincere and heartfelt regard. You won our votes as the champion of free labor and free homesteads . . . We trust you, the self-reliant, because self-made man will uphold the Constitution and the laws against secret treachery and avowed treason . . . If to this end you should be in need of men, the German free workingmen, with others, will rise as one man and at your call, ready to risk their lives in the effort to maintain the victory already won by freedom over slavery."

To this, and more, Lincoln replied,

"I agree with you, Mr. Chairman, that the working men are the basis of all governments, for the plain reason that they are the most numerous. . . .

"Mr. Chairman, I hold that while a man exists, it is his duty to improve not only his own condition, but to assist in ameliorating mankind. . . . I am for those means which will give the greatest good to the greatest number.

"In regard to the Germans and foreigners, I esteem them no better than other people, nor any worse. It is not my nature, when I see a people borne down by the weight of their shackles—to make their life more bitter by heaping upon them greater burdens . . . and if there are any abroad who desire to make this the land of their adoption, it is not in my heart to throw aught in their way. . . ."

The Lincoln-Oberkleine speeches may appear to be little more than a polite exchange of platitudes between a vote-conscious politician (Lincoln) and a favor-seeking group (the German workingmen). Until a more adequate understanding of the times is attained, one does not realize that Lincoln's favorable response to the immigrants' appeal meant taking his political life in his hands. A similar espousal of the foreign-born was an important factor that had cost Senator Seward the presidential nomination.

Immigration into the United States became a flood in the 1850's. A powerful political group sprang up called the American party. Its battle cry was "Americans must rule America." Foreigners threatening the security of native Americans became so potent a political issue that in Baltimore, for example, a municipal regime was voted into office by the burgeoning Know-Nothings, as the new nativist party was dubbed. It was a stunning blow to both Democrats and Republicans.

Hard times accentuated the political issue. Beginning in 1854, economic conditions in the country had worsened, and in 1857 the bottom fell out. To have one's job snatched away by a foreigner willing to work for lower wages, was a desperate matter for every native-born

American. Newcomers by the thousands were pouring in, many poverty-stricken, many hungry and jobless, some disease-ridden; the enormous total of 2,598,214 immigrants arrived in the ten years before 1860!

This posed a dilemma for the politicians. They were caught between their own kind—the natives—and the swelling mass of foreigners. Complicating matters still more, a temperance movement swept the country, supported by Americans and opposed by most aliens. Another political complication was land settlement. Immigrants wanted free homesteads; they wanted to settle down and develop "the land of the free and the home of the brave." The Republican party agreed, their platform offered "land for the landless." The Democrats disagreed. Dominated by the slaveholders, they wanted to settle the uninhabited acres with slaves and establish their own brand of aristocratic society.

A fitting symbol of Lincoln's difficult political position could be found on the parlor tables of that period in the stereoscopic view of Blondin, a tightrope performer, crossing the Niagara Falls gorge. A look through the stereoscope at a three-dimensional picture of this daring performer balancing himself on a thin wire over angry waters churning in the chasm far below, raised the hackles of every viewer. Lincoln was like Blondin.

The reply he made to the German free workingmen was not mere pleasantry. It could disturb his precarious balance on the political tightrope. Yet he welcomed immigrants, Germans, Irish, all newcomers, into the body politic. What he said was not offensive to nativists. He did not indulge in double-talk that meant little or nothing, but which was so common to rabble-rousers. His response was typically Lincolnian, simple and tactful. He also muted the drumbeats loudly resounding in

Wabash Railroad
Other railroads also is-
ed time cards and op-
ating instructions for
eir personnel, but this
the only one available.
ne correct corporate
me at that time was
eat Western Railway of
inois, now part of the
abash Railroad system.

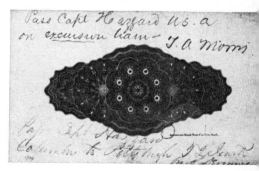

Library of Congress

Obverse and reverse of special pass issued by trip manager Wood to those authorized to ride with the President-elect. This one was issued to Captain George W. Hazzard, who joined the party at Indianapolis.

The only known photograph of the original one-story brick structure used by the Great Western Railway as their Springfield passenger and freight depot, from which Lincoln departed. A second story has since been added, but the architectural style has been retained. The enlarged building is used today as a freight station.

The railroad tracks cross the street at right angles. A freight car can be seen standing between the station and the house in the background. This photo is from the collection of Osborn H. Oldroyd, who lived in the Lincoln Springfield home from 1883 to 1893. His collection is now owned by the federal government and is on display at the old Ford Theater in Washington.

This old amateur snapshot is the only known photograph of the locomotive that hauled Lincoln's train out of Springfield on the first leg of the journey. The engine was built by the Hinkley Locomotive Works of Albany Street, Boston, in 1855, their 568th machine. It was named *L. M. Wiley* in honor of a director of the Great Western Railway, who was a cotton grower from Charleston, South Carolina. The photograph is here presented to the general public for the first time.

Oberkleine's remarks. The episode offered evidence of Lincoln's emerging statesmanship.

The greetings ended, he returned to the levee in the dining hall. Long, large and wide, the room was hung with national flags and patriotic festoons. At two-thirds of the distance from the entrance a square platform six inches high was placed, on which were two chairs. On the platform stood Lincoln. Behind him were Colonels Ellsworth and Sumner, Major Hunter, some of the local committee and the press. On one chair stood Mayor Bishop looking over the whole scene. Ranged around the platform was a cordon of policemen.

Meanwhile, Robert Lincoln was being dined and entertained by a group of Young Republicans that included Indiana's new governor and the escort committee. Mary had left to put the two younger boys to bed.

All sorts and all sizes poured in to shake the hand of the new President of the United States. An hour of it and his escort suggested that Lincoln stand on the chair beside the mayor, make a speech, and retire. Hand shaking was fatiguing work and he finally gave in. He said to those in the room that, although he would be happy to join hands with them all, he felt it would be wrong to attempt any more work like that and he would therefore bid them good night. A ring of police and soldiers formed to conduct him through the crowded room, through well-guarded corridors and up policed stairways to his suite.

Good old Cincinnati! The arrangements were well planned and carried out. No pushing, no shoving, no "hostile Injuns." The Lincoln-and-family reception day had been smooth and agreeable. Once-noisy streets were now clear of traffic. Quiet reigned. A good night's rest was in prospect.

One thing remained to be done. Little Taddie, fully dressed and dozing in a chair, was waiting up for his father. At home this evidently had been a ritual between them, for Lincoln now undressed his youngest son, silently and lovingly, half waking him to don his nightie, carrying the boy in his arms to join brother Willie, and tenderly covering the two sleeping sons.

Then, on this second evening of the journey into fame, and on the first night of his fifty-second year, the President-elect prepared to rest.

CHAPTER 7

T HE exact movements of the presidential party next morning at the Burnet House were detailed in the Cincinnati press.

The call to rise was made at six-fifteen on the floor assigned to the President-elect. A little after seven the entire company was breakfasting in the dining room. Here, Governor Morton and the Indiana delegation took formal leave. At eight-thirty the party was conveyed in eight carriages to the depot of the Little Miami Railroad, and at 9:00 A.M. the train took off, right on schedule.

The Presidential Special consisted of three coaches and a baggage car; the rear coach occupied by Lincoln and family; middle car by working staff and local committees; forward car by the press and railroad personnel; a total of a hundred persons distributed over the train. Western Union's superintendent, Anson Stager, came aboard bringing with him, as had his predecessors, special apparatus for making emergency connections.

A pilot engine appears to have preceded the Special, there having been disturbing rumors. One rumor had it that an attempt had been made to throw the train off the track near State Line, Indiana; another, that a grenade had been found on board before the train left Cin-

[59]

cinnati. Colonel Lamon tried to scotch the talk by saying no murderous doings had been heard of except in the newspapers.

The weather was glorious this first day of the Lenten season, Wednesday, February 13. Stops were made at Milford, Loveland, Miamiville, Morrow, Corwin, Xenia and London.

At each place Lincoln spoke briefly, but no speeches have been preserved except the one at London. Noticing the bright uniforms and shiny brass instruments, he said, after expressing his thanks, "I perceive a band of music present, and while the iron horse stops to water himself, I would prefer they discourse in their more eloquent music than I am capable of."

At Morrow, a junction point, Mrs. Lincoln was presented a bouquet of white camellias on behalf of the railroad president's wife. The Special hurried along at thirty miles an hour, halting for speeches and to water the iron horse. But no food was provided for the passengers. Xenia was reached just before one o'clock. The meal prepared for the presidential party had been gobbled up by the huge crowd that had stormed the depot dining room. Some of the train party were left behind trying to appease their appetites. Two baskets of cookies appeared on the train from somewhere and quickly disappeared under the onslaught of Bob and the boys.

Lincoln was forced to undergo the journey without food from early morning until supper.

He was very tired, limbs stiffened from the previous two days of vigorous handshaking, voice hoarsened from constant speechmaking. He seemed to be suffering from a severe cold, but laughed it off and presented an amiable demeanor. Mrs. Lincoln was charming, conversing with her guests in a lively manner. Bob didn't seem any worse from the sparkling wine he is reported to have been served the evening before. The two youngsters bounced around in juvenile delight at the excitement of the moment.

Lincoln avoided discussing political questions with press representatives who came aboard. They observed that he was a delightful talker and that his ability as a storyteller had not been exaggerated. He was always ready with an appropriate anecdote spiced with homespun humor.

Pressed into the subject of secessionist demands upon the federal government, he said it reminded him of a dispute between Willie and Tad. One had a toy the other wanted, who made his wants known in no uncertain manner, crying and demanding. At length the boy was told to let his brother have the toy in order to quiet him. "No, sir," came the sturdy response, "I must have it to quiet myself."

The train was entering Columbus when it was arranged for the President-elect to take the arm of Senator James Monroe, chairman of the legislation reception committee, and in this manner they were to walk together to the waiting carriage. Noting Lincoln's great height, six-feet-four, the senator remarked that "although it is etiquette you should take *my* arm, your stature makes that awkward so we had better reverse the order."

Accepting the senator's suggestion, Lincoln replied, "As for etiquette, I never was overburdened with it.

"Two friends of mine in Illinois were talking about me," he went on. "One said, 'Mr. Lincoln is a self-made man, isn't he?' to which the other said, 'Yes, but I didn't know that he ever took much pains about it.'"

Promptly at 2:00 P.M. the Special eased to a halt in the

Columbus railroad station. Waiting for the President-elect was another boy, a lad well up in his teens. School had been dismissed for the day—how could children be expected to study with Abraham Lincoln coming to town? He had maneuvered himself to where the rear coach of the train was likely to stop, having overheard comments in the crowd that the distinguished visitor would be in the last car.

There was no mistaking the great Railsplitter when he emerged and stepped down to an open carriage. Accompanied by the escort committee, he towered head and shoulders above them all. He smiled and bowed to the welcoming throng.

The eager schoolboy, who was to become a picked trooper guarding the President at the White House during the war, shouted himself hoarse. Threading his way along densely packed sidewalks, the youthful admirer, by the odd name of Smith Stimmel, kept abreast of the carriage. Up High Street to the Capitol grounds he followed the President-elect, who stood up in the slowly-moving vehicle and bowed to spectators who were jammed and perched everywhere. He watched Lincoln make his way through the mass of people up the long steps and into the Capitol.

Higher up the Capitol steps the earnest lad edged himself. It was said Lincoln was going to speak from the top when he finished with the legislature inside. While that was going on, the national flag was run up the Capitol dome amid rousing cheers.

Soon the great man was standing a few feet from him, thanking the people for their wonderful reception. The hero-worshipping youngster hung upon every word. One expression he never forgot.

"Boy as I was," he wrote years later. "When I heard

those generous words fall from his lips, my stock in Abraham Lincoln, already of high estate, went up five hundred per cent. . . . Not a word reflecting upon the political status of any individual or party fell from his lips that day," he wrote. "In the midst of great honors being shown him, Lincoln did not forget his competitor, though of a different political faith."

What the President-elect was saying on the west steps of the Ohio Capitol was this:

"I infer that you do me the honor to meet me here without distinction of party. I think this is as it should be. Many of you who were not favorable to the election of myself to the Presidency were favorable to the election of the distinguished Senator from the State in which I reside.

"If Senator Douglas had been elected to the Presidency in the late contest, I think my friends would have joined heartily in meeting and greeting him on his passage through your Capital, as you have me to-day. If any of the other candidates had been elected, I think it would have been altogether becoming and proper for all to have joined in showing honor, quite as well to the office, and the country, as to the man.

"I am doubly thankful that you have appeared here to give me this greeting. It is not much to me, for I shall very soon pass away from you, but we have a large country and a large future before us, and the manifestations of good-will towards the government, and affection for the Union you may exhibit, are of immense value to you and to your posterity forever. . . ."

He had expressed himself similarly in Indianapolis and Cincinnati; and he would repeat the theme in many journey speeches. He would remind audiences that their greeting to him was "not given by any one political party." The theme may seem too obvious for further comment, but it had special significance at the time. Special

[63]

meanings need to be examined here, even briefly, that a clearer concept may be gained of the significance of Lincoln's speeches en route. He had definite purposes for everything he said.

These purposes were political. Not, at this juncture, partisanly political. He had passed that mark. His aims, now that he had been elected President, were patriotically political—if the difference between partisan and patriot reveals the precise distinction. Transition from the part (partisan) to the whole (patriotism), Lincoln was endeavoring to bring about by transforming party feeling into national solidarity. He would elevate political competition into patriotic cooperation.

This sublimation constitutes the American political process. Citizens express their political will through partisan balloting and then accept the majority result of the balloting as total policy. The procedure was established by the Founding Fathers, deeded to the people in the federal Constitution. It formed the basis of American civil government.

Certain communities now were refusing to accept the long-established American process. Seven states had seceded from the legal decision of the body politic, claiming they had the right to do so. (The Constitution contained no such right.)

A reason each gave was that they could not be ruled by a sectional President who had been elected by sectional vote; meaning of course, Abraham Lincoln and the Republican ticket. Sectionalism was a partisan-political charge. Its purpose was to deny the fruits of the election to the winners. It is an old and effective political maneuver to accuse the opposition of one's own tactics and manipulations.

The Republicans had received votes from only four slave states, their party not appearing on most Southern ballots. In that sense Lincoln was sectional. Actually, Breckinridge and the "regular" Democrats were more sectional. They had polled a smaller popular vote (less than one-fifth of the total); had not carried all slave states (Bell had won three and Douglas one); and in four others had come through by an eyelash. Only in the deep South, and then excepting Louisiana, had they won substantial majorities. Bell and the Constitutional Unionists were also sectional, having carried the border states, no others.

Senator Charles Sumner of Massachusetts summed up the situation neatly when he said slavery was sectional, freedom was national.

Analysis of the 1860 presidential election returns discloses the astonishing fact that had the popular vote of the Democrats *as cast* been *combined* against him, Lincoln still would have won. Under that hypothetical circumstance he would have received 169 electoral votes, a majority of 35.

The three opposition parties did merge their differences and combined forces against Lincoln in four critical states. They fused their tickets in New York, Pennsylvania (partly), New Jersey, and Rhode Island in a desperate "stop-Lincoln" attempt. Against this combined opposition in these decisive states, without which states he would have lost the election, Lincoln won all except New Jersey, dividing that with Douglas.

Least sectional was Douglas the "independent" Demoocrat. He didn't miss getting votes in any state except Texas, where he was not on the ballot. Next to Lincoln he garnered the largest popular vote; almost twice that of Breckinridge. So widely scattered were his ballots, however, that he totaled the smallest electoral vote of all four contestants.

Douglas had said of "regular" Democrats in campaign

speeches: "I do not believe every Breckinridge man is a disunionist, but I do believe every disunionist is a Breckinridge man."

This summed up the situation from Douglas's partisan standpoint, but the issue had not been that clear-cut among the four parties. Each party had declared itself pro-Union. The Breckinridge ticket was dubbed "the seceders' slate," but outside of the cotton states some Democrats voted with the "regular" Democrats, since the platform promised to uphold the Constitution and to administer the laws of the land. (Meaning, no doubt, they would follow the Supreme Court's Dred Scott decision that a slave was property and could not become a citizen.)

From this summary it can be seen that the vote in favor of secession was much less than the total given the Breckinridge ticket. The "regular" Democrats had shrunk to a sectional party. Yet it was this pro-slavery minority that tried to break apart the federal Union.

To the charge of sectionalism they had hurled at the Republicans, secessionists now added a smear of the President-elect. They circulated the canard that they had to get out of the Union because of the election of the "black" Republican, Abraham Lincoln, thus throwing the onus onto him personally. The falsity of this was disclosed by the manifestoes each state issued when seceding, which set forth their reasons for the separation. The President-elect was not mentioned in a single one.

The Lincoln smirch, however, made splendid political propaganda. It swerved public attention to a gawky frontier politician and away from the conflagration they had ignited. The smirch implied he had achieved the high office by "dirty work at the crossroads," by vote buying, office peddling, land deals—how else could a poor country lawyer have attained it? The tale grew so tall gullible people were led to believe that Lincoln himself was responsible for the country's troubles and that if he were removed the turmoil would end. Hence, his continuing danger from cranks, party zealots and political anarchists.

The bitterness of the 1860 election campaign, the bitterest ever in American politics, was carried over by secessionists to justify their maneuverings.

That he was aware of his political position Lincoln made plain on many occasions. The plainness revealed how baseless were the smears. How could he have been responsible for the country's troubles when he had had no part in public life for more than a decade? Then they called him a nobody. He admitted he was a nobody. He talked about it frequently on the journey. He made it very clear in the speech to brother politicians of the Ohio Legislature.

"I cannot but know what you all know," he said to them, "that, without a name, perhaps without a reason why I should have a name, there has fallen upon me a task such as did not rest even upon the Father of His Country, and so feeling, I cannot but turn and look for the support without which it will be impossible for me to perform that great task.

"I turn, then, and look to the American people, and to that God who has never forsaken them. . . ."

He then concluded this first speech before a state legislature as President-elect.

The eager schoolboy by the odd name of Smith Stimmel did not hear these heartening statements. But it had been a wonderful day for the admiring youngster. Like thousands of fellow Ohioans, he would talk about it for the rest of his life. "I remember," he would reminisce years later, "how I thought at the time that Abraham Lincoln was the greatest man I had ever seen."

CHAPTER 8

FOLLOWING Lincoln's address from the Capitol steps, Governor William Dennison announced to the people that the President-elect would personally greet, in the Capitol rotunda, all who had been unable to hear him.

He took a position near the north stairs leading to the state library. The arrangement was that the public would come in through the south door, pass in front of him and exit through the north door. But when the doors were thrown open, instead of an orderly line forming, the rotunda was quickly crowded with pushing, pulling, jostling citizens, frantic to reach him and shake his hand.

A few Spartans bravely held back the mob from overwhelming him while he shook hands with great rapidity, to right, to left, overhead, with both hands at once, all the while replying cheerfully to greetings. The physical pressure was terrific. He had to retire from sheer exhaustion. Backing up the stairway to a safe distance, he saluted as the people moved past him. One fist fight and one fainting lady marred an otherwise perfect public reception. That he had been able to bear up under the strain since early morning without food or rest was remarkable.

At four-thirty that afternoon he was conducted to the

governor's room. Here Western Union superintendent Stager handed him a special wire from Washington. "The votes were counted peaceably," the dispatch read. "You are elected."

Lincoln stuffed the telegram into his pocket without making a sign. Looking up he saw everyone watching, and said: "What a beautiful building you have here, Governor Dennison!" At this there was general laughter and everyone moved off to get ready for supper, a meal sorely needed.

Despite his good nature, his smiles and his cheery greetings, Lincoln had been worrying. He had been deeply concerned about congressional confirmation of the electoral ballots as provided by the Constitution. The confirmation was necessary to make the election legal. Early in January he had written Senator Seward, "It seems to me the inauguration is not the most dangerous point for us. . . . On the second Wednesday of February the votes will be officially counted; if the two Houses shall refuse to meet at all, or meet without a quorum of each, where shall we be?"

Nor had the presiding officer of the Ohio Legislature joint session contributed to Lincoln's peace of mind that afternoon. When introducing him the first words had been, "Sir: On this day and probably at this very hour the Congress of the United States will declare the verdict of the people, making you their President." He had intended this to be a compliment, of course, and meant it was an honor to have their guest officially proclaimed President-elect while in their midst. He did not know secessionists had plotted that the election was not to be officially confirmed.

The plot was that Secretary of State Lewis Cass of Michigan, a staunch Unionist, was to be quarreled out of the cabinet (he was). President Buchanan, infirm and weakened of purpose, was to be controlled by secessionist cabinet members John B. Floyd of Virginia, Secretary of War; Howell Cobb of Georgia, Secretary of the Treasury; and Jacob Thompson of Mississippi, Secretary of the Interior. Under their orders as much national property was to be transferred to seceding states as possible, including arms and ammunition (some was). South Carolina was to secede at once (it did). The other slave states were to follow (six did).

The federal capital was to be packed with fighting seceders in civilian clothes (it was) who were to enter the House chamber and riot during the joint session. The Capital was to be seized along with government departments.

Hearing of the conspiracy, a Vermont delegate to the Peace Conference, then in session in Washington, went to the Army commander, General Winfield Scott.

"I have said," the general answered L. E. Chittenden, who would become Lincoln's Register of the Treasury, "that any man who attempted to . . . interfere with the lawful count of the electoral vote . . . should be lashed to the muzzle of a twelve-pounder and fired out of the window of the Capitol. I would manure the hills of Arlington with the fragments of his body!"

A senator from Texas hearing of the general's trumpetings wanted to know if he would dare to arrest a senator for high treason. Scott blazed, "No sir, I would not arrest him. I would blow him to hell!"

The wily Army chief had posted armed guards at all Capitol entrances. They stopped everyone, allowing only authorized visitors and members of Congress to enter the building. Credentials were again examined before entrance could be gained to the House chamber. Mingling with legislators and spectators were "minute men," a full regiment of picked men in civilian clothes ready in a minute to act as guardians of peace—with loaded repeating rifles. Guns and ammunition had been stacked in two connecting committee rooms on the north side of the hall. The general knew his business.

Credit also is due Vice-President John C. Breckinridge. A Kentuckian who subsequently became Secretary of War in the confederate cabinet, he was true to his oath of office. To the joint session of Congress he quietly announced the result of the electoral vote, declaring Abraham Lincoln elected President of the United States in conformance with the law.

"For a few minutes the tumult was so great it was impossible to restore order," related a spectator. "I thought I was in the midst of a revolution." But the Speaker finally gaveled unruly members back to order. Minute men were standing ready. The riot plot had failed.

Actually, a new conspiracy had been formed. Among top secession leaders the electoral day plan had already been called off. Too many things had gone wrong. On the night of January 5 at the Washington home of the senior senator from Mississippi, Jefferson Davis, it was agreed too many had been admitted to the counsel of the conspirators. Present at the caucus had been two senators from Alabama, Arkansas, Georgia, Louisiana and Florida, the junior senator from Mississippi and Senator James Mason of Virginia. They moved forward the date of rebellion to Inauguration Day, March 4.

Whether the new plot ever came to the attention of Lincoln or Scott is not disclosed in any of their writings. It is certain that following the electoral day fiasco, secession extremists let it be known that Lincoln would never reach the White House.

On this Wednesday evening in Columbus a reception was held in the governor's residence for members of the legislature, state officials, the city council, the press and special guests. Lincoln was attired in full evening dress. He appeared as fresh and unwearied as though he had not traveled a mile. After meeting him, guests moved to another parlor where, assisted by the governor's wife, Mrs. Lincoln received.

"She is a very pleasant lady," said the dispatches, "courteous, unassuming and with a smile for all," noting that she was dressed in a "very rich, dark-figured silk with headdress to match."

What pleased the press was a buffet supper served at eight o'clock with delicacies of the season and "sociable refreshments." After the supper, Lincoln and suite returned to the Capitol where the public, including the ladies, called on him. This continued until he was escorted, together with the governor, to Deshler Hall. Here the Governor's Guards were giving a grand military ball in honor of their distinguished guest. He was introduced to each member of the company and to the ladies by the captain of the Guards, and then was invited to lead the grand promenade. Accompanied by the captain's wife, Lincoln marched around the hall twice.

That night the Lincolns were house guests of the governor. What occurred at the hospitable gubernatorial mansion with the Lincoln family, that included three exuberant sons, was not reported.

Next morning Mrs. Lincoln and the two youngsters had to run for the Presidential Special as it pulled out of the Columbus depot a few minutes before eight o'clock. Somehow the engineer mixed his signals. No details are available except that Bob was safely aboard and so was the President-elect, he having been escorted from the governor's residence by the committee appointed to accompany him to the Ohio state line.

This day's Special was made up of two passenger coaches and baggage car. The locomotive was appropriately named *Washington City*. Experience of the previous days showed that the greater the number of coaches, the more committees, office-seekers and free-loaders came along for the ride. This had been made apparent on the trip out of Indianapolis. Without permission, the railroad had invited some two hundred excursionists who crowded into the cars including the one reserved for Lincoln.

This had caused considerable feeling and prompted the rule that none but those approved by manager Wood were to be allowed on the train. The information was released to the press, together with an admonition that political marching clubs such as "Wide-awakes," were unacceptable as escorts or in welcoming parades; and that while military formations were acceptable at stops and in parades, they were not to ride the train.

The weather this St. Valentine's Day morning was bad. Heavy clouds hung low as the train pulled away from Ohio's capital city. Half an hour later rain fell, first in big drops, then in torrents. The dreary dripping spread gloom over the party.

Few would be the audiences that day, it was felt. The young folks gathered in the forward car and amused themselves by singing songs. They joined in vocalizing the emancipation ballad, "Get Off the Track!", made famous by the Hutchinson family of singers. They sang Stephen Foster's latest ballad, "None Shall Weep a Tear for Me," and they harmonized the 1857 hit that the boys in blue and gray would soon make famous, the lilting "Lorena."

Colonel Lamon entertained with his banjo. He played "Bonny Eloise, the Belle of Mohawk Vale," destined to become the march tune of both armies. He strummed the novelty hit, "Sparkin' on a Sunday," and sang the widely-known spiritual, "De Gospel Train Am a-Comin'." All joined in singing Daniel D. Emmett's great minstrel hit, "Dixey's Land," later called "Dixie!"

In the rear car the President-elect and his lady entered into lively conversation with their more elderly companions. Stops were made at Newark, Frazeysburg, Dresden, Coshocton, Newcomerstown, Uhrichsville, Cadiz Junction, and the Ohio river port of Steubenville.

There was no denying the ardent Buckeyes. Undaunted by pelting rain above or oozy mud, large crowds had assembled at all stations, many under umbrellas, saluting the new President with patriotic choruses, bands, flying banners and artillery. Speeches were demanded and responded to. The size of the receptions was most remarkable under the adverse weather conditions. The Associated Press correspondent reported, "The yeomanry increases as the journey progresses eastward."

That word, yeomanry, sounds strange today when the term is applied only to the Navy, designating a petty officer aboard ship. Its social meaning has been lost in the march of the American Republic.

Back in the feudal days of England, yeoman denoted a small landowner, one who was a step up from a serf but a step beneath a gentleman. It represented sharp class distinction. Transplanted to America, the word had come to mean a landowner who cultivated his own land, a farmer. Then yeoman came to include any man of the common people. That is the meaning apparently used by the reporter in his dispatch.

That also is how the South looked upon the North;

a land of common people. To themselves, Southerners appeared of gentle birth; pedigreed, like a blooded mare or a prize bull. They felt they occupied a higher stratum in the society of mankind than did the shopkeepers, small farmers, mechanics, factory hands and the rag, tag and bobtail that made up the people of the northland. This class distinction, left over from the Old World, increased the political and economic antagonisms between slave-holding and free states.

Speaking in the Senate on the Lecompton constitution of Kansas, Senator James H. Hammond of South Carolina had drawn a fateful analogy. He had told of a structure being built on one of his plantations. Because of soggy ground the sills of the building had to be sunk in the mud. He gave that as an illustration.

The rough work of the world had to be done by unskilled labor directed by superior intelligence. Such was the state of the South, he said, under the slavery system. In the North it was the hireling system. Workers were the "mudsills" of society, and the only difference between them was in the terms of hire.

Hammond's picturesque phrase made perfect propaganda for the Republicans. They told the working people that slaveholders branded them as mudsills. The effect was terrific. At Galesburg, for example, when Lincoln had been debating with Douglas, a huge banner over the main street had proclaimed:

SMALL-FISTED FARMERS, GREASY MECHANICS,
MUDSILLS OF SOCIETY, FOR A. LINCOLN.

"Mudsill" became a dirty personal word. Little Tad, playing some months later in Lafayette Park across from the White House, was so called by a neighborhood boy. Washington society was Southern to the core and resented the Lincolns, snubbing their social affairs. They did not view Lincoln as the personality he is acclaimed today. Far from it. It is no exaggeration to say that the South looked upon Abraham Lincoln as white trash. His log cabin ancestry guaranteed this in their eyes.

By the same token, his log cabin ancestry guaranteed his endorsement by Northern mudsills. His rise from a lowly state in life to the highest office in the land was visible evidence of the great American dream. It *could* happen here. It did happen here.

The benefit to Lincoln from his mudsill position was incalculable. Public emotional response to it cannot be overestimated. Later, it even extended to the rush of war enlistments when the people would sing to him Stephen Foster's great tribute, "We Are Coming, Father Abraham, Three Hundred Thousand More!" So now, thousands of his neighbors poured out to get a look at one like themselves, a mudsill on his way to the White House.

Millions of Americans since that time, and millions more all over the world, have become familiar with the countenance of Abraham Lincoln. But in that day, when he was new and unknown, when photography had not yet reached the daily press or the magazines, he had to make his person known. The public was eager to find out what he really looked like. This was how a reporter, sitting on the train, sketched him from life.

"He has a large head with a very high, shelving forehead. He has thick, bushy, dark hair; a clear, bright, piercing, indeterminable-colored eye; a prominent, thin-nostriled nose; a large, well-bowed mouth; a round, pretty chin; a first crop of darkish whiskers; a clean, well-built neck; more back than chest; a long, lank trunk; limbs of good shape and extreme longitude; arms ditto; hands and feet symmetrical but unnaturally large. He wears a black silk hat (plug), a dress coat and pants of somber hue; a turndown collar, and other garments such as are usually found upon a gentleman. . . ."

The next stopping place, Cadiz Junction, consisting only of a small depot and hotel, blacksmith shop, livery stable and handful of houses, offered another surprisingly large crowd. The people shouted for a speech. Lincoln expressed his thanks for the warm reception and then was conducted to the hotel dining room.

Here occurred what all agreed was the most satisfying feature of the day. An elegant dinner was served under the sponsorship of Mrs. T. L. Jewett, wife of the president of the Steubenville and Indiana Railroad, which was host to the presidential party this morning. Mrs. Jewett was a spirited Republican and her husband a Democrat. Lincoln cordially invited both to accompany him to Pittsburgh.

The satisfying meal completed, the party returned to the waiting cars, the crowd again shouting for a speech. Lincoln responded by saying he was "too full for utterance" but that if there were time they would "canvass the train and pass a vote of thanks to the people of Harrison County for the wonderful dinner they had eaten, and especially to the lady of the house."

At Steubenville, the scudding clouds broke apart and the sun poured through. Some ten thousand Ohioans, and Virginians from across the river, were massed around a carpeted stage erected at trackside. Lincoln was escorted to it as a choir of young ladies from the seminary sang "The Red, White and Blue," and cannon boomed. Judge W. R. Lloyd (who would recruit the Sixth Ohio Cavalry Regiment), made the welcoming speech.

Unwittingly, the judge put Lincoln on the spot. He said Virginians and Ohioans were united in their welcome; that they were all attached to the Union and desired its maintenance; and that they looked to the President-elect for its support and restoration. He said the President who faithfully executed the laws in the discharge of his oath would receive the support of *both* sections. "To you, sir," concluded the judge, "we entrust our hopes with confidence."

Lincoln replied that the great confidence placed in his ability was unfounded. "Indeed, I am sure it is," he said. "But," he added, "nothing on my part shall be wanting if sustained by God and the American people."

Looking across the broad Ohio water to the rolling hills of Virginia, the state known as the mother of presidents, Lincoln declared, "I believe the devotion to the Constitution is equally great on both sides of the river. The only dispute is, 'What are their rights under the Constitution?'"

Replying to his own question, he asked, "To decide that, if the majority should *not* rule, who would be the judge?"

He answered that we should all be bound by the majority rule of the people. If that were not so, he said, the only alternative would be minority control, and that would not be just or generous. "Though the majority may be wrong," he asserted, "we must adhere to the principle that the majority must rule."

Here again he was foreshadowing his Inaugural Address, wherein he would state the same problem and offer the same solution. For this was the very basis of secession. Its final conclusion was fundamental to a continuance of American federal government. Thus, through the agency of his journey speeches Lincoln was endeavoring to clarify the vexing questions and to educate the people to his forthcoming policies.

CHAPTER 9

FROM Steubenville the railroad to Pittsburgh followed the Ohio River north, tagging along the water highway as it turned east and split into the Monongahela and Allegheny rivers, halting at Allegheny City across from the Golden Triangle. No railroad then bridged the Ohio at any point along its 980-mile course.

Water and roadways provided America's prime transportation, as they had for the world since the beginning of time. Watt's steam engine running on strap-ironed rails offered the world's first radical improvement in conveyance technique since the invention of the wheel, the first of modern improvements that would not end until man put himself beyond the moon. As of that day and date, however, he could not get himself over the Ohio River at Steubenville because the Commonwealth of Virginia would shout, "B and O!"

Virginia refused to charter a railroad to cross the few miles of its narrow panhandle from the Ohio River to the Pennsylvania state line. Reason: such a road would take traffic away from the Baltimore and Ohio line that ran for so many miles through the state and was doing so much to develop its western reaches. The Baltimore and

Ohio tapped the Ohio River at Wheeling and Parkersburg.*

The situation was not wholly of Virginia's making. When the Baltimore and Ohio was completing its main line to Cumberland, Maryland, it had sought a charter from the Pennsylvania Legislature for an extension into Pittsburgh. The petition had been denied, largely because of Philadelphia lobbyists who feared the western trade of their own state would bypass them and reach the seaboard via Baltimore—which was precisely why farsighted Baltimoreans were building their railroad.

The fact was, Philadelphians were late in recognizing the great potential of railroads. Like New Yorkers, who were also slow, their canal routes were bringing abundant commerce. But now the battle was underway among the seaports of New York, Philadelphia, Baltimore and Boston (through Canada) for trade by way of rail.

Pioneer lines had served only limited local needs. Seaports and river ports built them to develop trade with the nearby countryside, the lines fanning out like fingers on a hand, often ending nowhere. Others connected bodies of water such as the four-and-a-half-mile Pontchartrain Railroad, completed in 1831, to facilitate traffic between New Orleans and the lake. Lincoln probably saw this horse-powered affair as a young man on his second trip to the Crescent City. A railroad was the sensation of that day as a spaceship would be today.

From Cincinnati to Pittsburgh, the Lincoln train had to use six separate railroads. Out of Cincinnati it passed over the Little Miami Railroad to Xenia, thence to Columbus over the Columbus and Xenia Railroad, and east out of Columbus over four separate lines—Central Ohio, Steubenville and Indiana, Cleveland and Pitts-

---

* **West** Virginia would not become a state until 1863.

burgh, and Pittsburgh, Fort Wayne and Chicago. The beginnings of consolidation and merger were getting underway, however.

The change from a pioneering self-sufficiency to the interdependent economy of today was taking shape. Railroads, industry and finance were growing apace, each aiding the other in an expanding merry-go-round. The New World of magnificent distances and tremendous resources was being developed by these new techniques. As each technique expanded, the new nation-state profited accordingly, stimulated by the incentive of free enterprise.

Furnishing needed capital, eastern interests reached out for the little pioneer roads in Ohio, Indiana and Illinois, merging them into trunk lines. The Baltimore and Ohio and the Pennsylvania expanded west of the Ohio River from motives of civic and state policy. Concurrently, there had arisen in America the factor of finance capitalism. Railroad securities began to be purchased for earning power and appreciation value, not solely for indirect benefits that might accrue to the purchaser's community or his business. Of this finance type was the New York Central system, originally a merger of ten local lines across the center of the state, now expanding as a public investment. Investors were finding railroad securities a profitable repository for their capital.

Another factor tending to unify the fragmented rail lines of 1860 was the operating company. Such was the Pittsburgh, Columbus and Cincinnati railway; owning no right-of-way or equipment, it handled passengers and freight on through schedules between the named cities. The plan grew rapidly in expediting freight shipments, for railroads did not then handle through freight, having no organization for that purpose. Private operators purchased freight cars and ran them—fast freight, the green line, and other colors of the rainbow. The Pittsburgh, Columbus and Cincinnati Railroad was operated by officials of the Steubenville and Indiana, backed by the Pennsylvania Railroad.

Eventually, five of the six lines Lincoln traveled over were integrated into the Pennsylvania system. The sixth, the Central Ohio, joined the westward reach of the Baltimore and Ohio and was merged into that system. The iron horses had begun rolling across the nation in a transportation miracle—the miracle that made America.

Steaming out of Steubenville at 2:30 P.M., the Presidential Special was northbound on the Cleveland and Pittsburgh Railroad, river division. On board were the president of the road and the escort committee from Allegheny City. At Wellsville the Cleveland reception committee joined up. Here, Lincoln made his usual welcome-and-farewell remarks from the rear platform, and as he finished, a roughly dressed fellow pushed up, extended his hand and said,

"God bless ye, Misther Lincoln! I didn't vote for ye, sure; but I want to shake yer hand."

A good-humored shake was heartily exchanged, Lincoln asking for whom he had voted.

"Misther Dooglas," came the reply. The crowd laughed.

"Well, my friend," said Lincoln, leaning over, "let me tell you what, as a friend of Douglas, you ought to do. Just help us keep the ship of State together and right on her course for the next four years and then Mr. Douglas will have another chance. But if you let the good ship be broken up, he will never get to be President." The crowd applauded.

"That's so, Misther Lincoln," came the response. "I'm thinkin' meself you'll save the Union and we'll all help ye!"

Amid rousing cheers the train pulled out, Lincoln saluting with the tall plug hat.

The next stop was the first in Pennsylvania, Rochester, where entry was made to the tracks of the Pittsburgh, Fort Wayne and Chicago Railroad. Here the Pittsburgh reception committee came aboard, and from Harrisburg a joint committee of the Pennsylvania Legislature, to extend their invitation. Artillery boomed, flags snapped in the breeze, while the crowd shouted and cheered. Lincoln thanked the throng for the warm reception. He said he was on his way to Washington and that there on March 4 he intended to speak to all who chose to hear him.

"What will you do with the secessionists then?" asked a voice from the audience.

Turning in that direction, Lincoln replied, "My friend, that is a matter I have under grave consideration." And he bade them farewell.

Because a freight train had broken down near the hamlet of Baden, blocking the tracks, the Special could proceed only as far as the town of Freedom. Here it had to wait for hours while the track was cleared. It was apparent the 5:00 P.M. scheduled arrival at Pittsburgh would not hold.

While making his usual rear-platform talk Lincoln spotted an unusually tall coal miner in the crowd. Coming up, the big fellow said, "I want to shake hands with you; I can lick salt off the top of your head!" They shook hands and then measured statures to the huge satisfaction of the spectators (mostly miners) and to the subsequent sneers of the political opposition who strove mightily to make the friendly incident undignified. Short Colonel Ellsworth stood on the railing to decide the contest, so close were they; Lincoln had to stand straight and, as one friend put it, "use all his height" to get the edge. The audience applauded. Lincoln made the best possible use of such wayside encounters.

These homely incidents, trivial in themselves, contribute to an understanding of Lincoln's political philosophy. Since everyone was wondering what kind of person he was, and what he would do when he entered office, the small events represented steppingstones to larger acts, just as the journey speeches foreshadowed the Inaugural Address.

The episode of the Irishman who had voted for "Misther Dooglas," for example, specifically illustrated Lincoln's larger goal of turning partisan competitiveness into patriotic cooperation.

The measuring contest with the tall miner, seemingly devoid of political significance, was a gesture of good will and friendliness, to help make people feel he was one with them. It had the human touch, as did similar incidents such as the lagging horse tale begun in Thorntown and completed in Lebanon. These happenings went a long way toward winning the confidence of an audience. His rear-platform talks, his handshaking, his public receptions, his every contact with the people, added to his following. He was making himself a personal leader as well as a political one.

To generalize from a few small events of three days, Lincoln's political philosophy, adducing *a posteriori,* is not sound. Yet it is the specific that proves the general; the deed that reveals the thought. Understanding Lincoln's political principles is essential in illuminating this controversial journey. Fortunately, the distillate of the past hundred years has produced facts that can lead to sound conclusions. Many minds have probed the life and times of Abraham Lincoln—several volumes detail his life day by day—the sum of which limns the man.

From such sources and with the perspective of time, it is possible to say that Lincoln was a practical politician of high principle; that he was liberal in thought but conservative in method; that he was an idealist thoroughly earthbound; that he was guided by great shining lights, but practiced expediency.

"My policy is to have no policy," he would state. This is a political statement of the first magnitude. To have no policy is to have *that* policy. What he meant was that he allowed events to dictate the means to be used in achieving objectives, rather than imposing preconceived theories upon events, upon men, or upon himself. He would not try to force reality into a mold of his own making. Nevertheless, he had far-sighted goals that were present and operating at all times.

This may appear paradoxical, so let it be stated that the subject is a complex one, dealing with abstractions that intrigued the Greeks and plagued the Romans, and have bothered political men ever since. Moreover, Lincoln himself was a complicated subject.

An opponent might translate his "no-policy policy" into the Machiavellian alibi that the means justify the end, an unethical and unmoral procedure. Lincoln was both moral and ethical—a reason he is held in such high esteem. He did not traduce the *good* in order to achieve an objective called good.

Expediency in his hands became a way of harmonizing conflicting interests and sentiments. His political ideal was Henry Clay, a successful harmonizer, also a Kentuckian and a Whig. Like Clay, Lincoln spoke and practiced the spirit of mutual concession. "That spirit which first gave us the Constitution," Lincoln had declared in his famous Peoria speech. And years before, as a freshman congressman, he had described the yardstick for evaluating political action: "The true rule in determining to embrace or reject anything," he had stated in the House of Representatives in 1848, "is not whether it have any evil in it, but whether it shall have more of evil than good. There are few things wholly evil or wholly good."

What is good in reference to public affairs? What is good for the people as a whole, of course. Lincoln said it in his extemporaneous reply to the Cincinnati Germans: "I am for those means which will give the greatest good to the greatest number," he had asserted, thereby enunciating a political maxim that is as sacred to the conduct of American government as the principle of justice itself.

Greatest good for the greatest number—consent of the governed—rule of the majority—respect for the Constitution and laws of the land—love of liberty from the hearts of the people—these are political principles to which Lincoln subscribed and which motivated his decisions during his Presidency. Toward those ends he was preparing the people as he journeyed to take office.

The rain began again. It was coming down in torrents as the Special pulled into Allegheny City at 8:00 P.M. It had thinned the crowd that had been waiting long and patiently to see the man for whom the community had so overwhelmingly voted. Nevertheless, a hardy group acclaimed him as he detrained. Civic authorities of the two cities were present in strength, the Pittsburgh common council having voted to attend in a body.

The plan was for Pittsburgh groups to meet the President-elect at Allegheny City's Federal Street depot and act as an escort, the mayor of Allegheny City to accompany and introduce him to the Pittsburgh mayor upon arriving there. Citizens' committees from both places were to cooperate. Military escorts were to form a parade. The parade would wind through downtown Allegheny City, cross the St. Clair Street suspension bridge to Pittsburgh, and proceed via Smithfield Street to the Monongahela House where Lincoln would make an address.

To the mayor's welcoming speech at Allegheny City, Lincoln replied that owing to the lateness of the hour, caused by unavoidable delay, he would be unable to respond at any length, but that all would have an opportunity to hear him in the morning.

Thereupon the party ducked into carriages and was driven directly to the hotel. The heavy rain and late arrival had ruined plans of both communities for a rousing reception. Still, the streets were thronged and the excitement was tremendous. In Pittsburgh, across the river, masses of people blocked the avenues leading to the hotel; they cheered, they shouted, they vociferated. Lincoln finally had to respond:

"We had an accident upon the road to-day and were delayed till this late hour," he said, telling the eager throng he intended to say a few words to the people of Pittsburgh.

'I could not help thinking, my friends," he went on as the cheers subsided, "as I traveled in the rain through your crowded streets, on my way here, if all that people were in favor of the Union, it can certainly be in no great danger—it will be preserved. . . .

"I thank you sincerely for the warm reception I have received," he concluded, "and in the morning . . . I may have something to say of that 'peculiar interest' of Pennsylvania. . . ."

But the roaring crowd would not let him go. They demanded that he continue. Touched by devotion undampened by inclement weather, Lincoln succumbed. He said that if they would let him get some notes from his overcoat pocket he would have more to say. When he returned he told them:

"I have been prevailed upon by your committee to postpone my intended remarks to you until tomorrow when we hope for more favorable weather. . . ."

CHAPTER 10

A SEA of umbrellas confronted Lincoln next morning as he stepped to the balcony of the Monongahela House. The rain had not abated, but it had not deterred the largest crowd in Pittsburgh's history from assembling to hear him, nor had it dampened the President-elect's ardor in offering them the longest address of the entire trip. Introduced by Mayor George Wilson, Lincoln extended thanks for the flattering reception, touched on the national political crisis, and then launched into the main issue, the tariff:

"So long as direct taxation for the support of government is not resorted to," he said, "a tariff is necessary. The tariff is to the government what a meal is to the family. . . . It is a question," he explained, "of national housekeeping."

He did not enumerate what commodities to tax nor recommend how much to charge, matters of endless debate. He well knew that just as rain seems to the farmer, so a tariff always seems too little or too much. It never satisfies everyone, and is a source of constant political turmoil.

Back in 1832 the tariff had almost split the young

Republic when South Carolina, on the ground of harmful discrimination against its interests, declared the tariff law passed by Congress null and void and threatened to secede from the Union. President Jackson castigated the principal instigator, John C. Calhoun, as "heartless, selfish and a physical coward," proposing to deal with the South Carolinians by force. The nation at large had lauded the President's drum-beating, applauding what appeared to be his firm handling of an incipient revolt.

The dogmas of nullification and secession were part of the political scene throughout America's formative years. Lincoln was aware of the explosive political potentialities of the tariff. He was determined not to add fuel to the secession fire already raging.

Where he himself stood on the tariff he had made clear many times. He had summed up his position in a letter to Doctor Edward Wallace of Reading.

"I was once an old Henry Clay tariff Whig. In old times I made more speeches on that subject than on any other. I have not since changed my views. . . . Still, it is my opinion that just now the revival of that question will not advance the cause itself, nor the man who revives it."

He meant he would like to avoid the tariff issue altogether. In his Inaugural Address, he would pass it by as he would all problems save the burning ones. He would say, "I do not consider it necessary at present for me to discuss those matters of administration about which there is no special anxiety or excitement."

This he could not say in Pennsylvania, especially in Pittsburgh. What made the tariff so important here was that unemployment and hard times had begun in 1857, following the Democrat-controlled session of Congress that lowered tariffs on products vital to Pennsylvania's economy. Coal, iron, machinery and kindred articles were being imported to compete at low prices with American production. Believing a protective tariff benefited only manufacturing interests while hurting their own, the slaveholding states voted for low schedules.

Thus the Quaker State's sensational turnabout in the election, racking up Republican majorities after having elected native-son Democrat President Buchanan, was attributed in great measure to Republican tariff doctrine as against Southern-dictated dogma of free trade.

Following his nomination, Lincoln had received letters from Pennsylvanians on the subject. He answered another query from Dr. Wallace of Reading. He also replied to a G. Yoke Tams of Manayunk. Lincoln may have been prompted to write him as much because of the music of the name as by his place of residence.

Lincoln was a writer of great ability. The million words he left behind are as limpid today as they were when he set them down. His various styles, the despair of every writer, are melodious and distinctive; and that *desideratum* is not the result of chance.

The first thing Lincoln did upon reaching the office in the morning was to pick up a newspaper and read aloud. The habit annoyed Herndon beyond endurance, and often he had to leave. He asked Lincoln why he did so. "When I read aloud," Lincoln replied, "two senses catch the idea; first, I see what I read; and second, I hear it. Therefore, I remember it better, if I do not understand it better."

So unquestionably Lincoln heard from himself the musical tinkle of "G. Yoke Tams of Manayunk, Pa." And Mr. Tams's name will continue to tinkle in the files of Lincolniana for the Republican presidential nominee took his pen in hand and wrote:

"Your letter asking me, 'Are you in favor of Tariff and

Protection to American industry?' is received. The convention which nominated me, by the 12th plank of their platform, selected their position on this question and I have declared my approval of the platform and accepted the nomination."

To the Pittsburgh audience now before him, Lincoln made a similar statement. He asked his secretary to read the Chicago tariff plank,* and then said that as with all general propositions, doubtless there will be shades of difference in construing this.

"If I have any recommendation to make," he continued, "it will be that every man who is called upon to serve the people in a representative capacity, should study this whole subject thoroughly, as I intend to do myself . . . so that when the time for action arrives adequate protection can be extended to the coal and iron of Pennsylvania, the corn of Illinois and the 'reapers' of Chicago."

His recommendations did not involve details likely to stir up political antagonisms, yet gave sufficient guarantee to Pennsylvania interests. The address pleased the pro-Lincoln press. Opposition journals were critical as usual.

A Pittsburgh paper claimed the speech was a device to evade the basic issue of preservation of the Union. The Associated Press reporter, Henry Villard, gave his opinion

---

* Before the era of income taxes, personal and corporate, the main support of the central government was from levies on imports. Such taxes also helped to protect home industry, an especially important consideration then when young industrial America was getting on its feet. The tariff plank in the 1860 Republican platform adopted at Chicago read: "That while providing revenue for the support of the General Government by duties on imports, sound policy requires such an adjustment of these imports as will encourage the development of the industrial interests of the whole country; and we commend that policy of national exchanges which secures to working men liberal wages, to agriculture remunerating prices, to mechanics and manufacturers reward for their skill, labor and enterprise, and to the nation, commercial prosperity and independence."

[92]

that it was Lincoln's least creditable performance. "The crude, ignorant twaddle proved him the veriest novice in economic matters," he wrote, "and strengthened my doubts as to his capacity for the high office he was to fill."

Villard was referring particularly to what the anti-Lincoln papers gleefully pounced on—the several confessions in the speech:

"I must confess I do not understand this subject in all its multiform bearings," Lincoln calmly admitted, "but I promise you that I will give it my closest attention and endeavor to comprehend it more fully." Again he said, "I confess I do not understand the precise provisions of this bill (the Morrill tariff bill), and I do not know whether it can be passed by the present Congress or not. . . ."

There can be no doubt that Lincoln was determined not to stir up needless controversy; and it is difficult to see how he could have handled the delicate situation better. The *Pittsburgh Gazette* testified that "the impression he made upon our citizens generally, by his personal bearing and public remarks, was highly favorable; while his courteous and friendly manner captivated all who had intercourse with him."

The *Cincinnati Commercial* concurred, saying that the speech was received with frantic enthusiasm by the people of the Smoky City, and that it would doubtless produce a sensation throughout the country. "The temper of the remarks of Mr. Lincoln on the state of the country is that of a sincere, outspoken, honest man. He is not guilty of any diplomacy [double-talk] and does not understand why he should not in his own plain way tell the plain truth as it appears to him."

"The plain truth" did not make a hit in Washington. A dispatch published next day said that while his tariff speech tickled Pennsylvania Republicans, Lincoln was too unsophisticated and simple-hearted. "No man who wears his heart upon his sleeve," the dispatch concluded, "can pass as a statesman in Washington."

His forthrightness moved the *New York Times* to observe, "To these remarks at Pittsburgh, too great importance can hardly be attached. From this announcement of his intention to redeem all the engagements of the Chicago platform, we gain instruction as to the policy of the new President upon other questions of equally urgent moment."

The *Chicago Tribune* glowed pridefully. "Let the people shout! This time their hero is an honest man!"

Bringing his remarks to a close, Lincoln declared that tariff schedules were a question to be decided by Congress. "Permit me to express the hope," he said, "that this important subject may receive such consideration at the hands of your representatives that the interests of no part of the country may be overlooked, but that all sections may share in common the benefits of a just and equitable tariff."

The address had taken thirty minutes. Now it was time to leave for Cleveland. From hotel to depot, they drove through cheering crowds lining the streets despite mud and rain, pressing to get a closer look. At the railroad station Lincoln endured jostling and pushing without a sign of impatience, waiting for the Presidential Special to pull into the depot for its scheduled 10:00 A.M. departure.

So densely packed was the place that a determined father had to pass his little son over people's heads to reach the President-elect, by whom the youngster was heartily kissed. Three attractive young ladies managed to work their way to him and received the same salutation. Younger members of the entourage who tried to take the same privilege were indignantly repulsed, evoking general laughter in which Lincoln joined.

The two-car-and-baggage Special rolled out in a brisk shower to a farewell salute of minute guns. Proceeding slowly through the mass of cheering people lining the tracks, the train retraced its previous day's journey, going from Allegheny City by way of Rochester to Wellsville.

At the head was the locomotive *Comet*, designed and built by a Yankee mechanical genius, William Mason of Taunton, Massachusetts, who made fine engines and made them good-looking. Under engineer Williamson's direction, Bob Lincoln sat in the driver's seat and managed the controls, acting as assistant engine driver.

At Wellsville, a division point, another Mason-built locomotive took over—the *Meteor*—also decorated with bunting in national colors. Lincoln excused himself from speaking, reminding them he had spoken here the day before. As he stood on the platform, a man pushed up and handed him a rosy-cheeked apple. At this, a small boy's high treble cried out.

"Mr. Lincoln!" shrilled the voice, "That man is running for postmaster!"

The audience, including Lincoln, was convulsed with laughter.

Stops were made at Salineville and Bayard. Crowds had assembled in the mud and rain, but Lincoln limited his responses to bowing and saluting with the "stovepipe" hat. He told his entourage he intended to make as few speeches as possible for the rest of the trip for his voice had become so hoarse he could hardly make himself heard. He sat quietly, looking over newspapers, making notes and listening to the two younger boys.

At Alliance, the railroad's president, John N. McCullough, was host at a bountiful dinner at Sourbeck's noted hostelry. The press voted it the finest meal of the trip.

Excursionists had come over from Canton and Salem. An elegant company of Canton Zouaves stood guard during dinner, the band playing national airs. A salute was fired so close to the building that windows were smashed, including the one at which Mrs. Lincoln was sitting, which sprinkled her with flying glass. No one was hurt. After dinner Lincoln was escorted by the Zouaves to a temporary stand in front of the depot. Here he expressed his gratitude at seeing such an outpouring of happy people, thanked them for their warm reception, and excused himself from making a speech.

At Hudson another roaring mass engulfed the train. Nine carloads of people had made the trip from Akron and Cuyahoga Falls. Although the Special was running late, Lincoln felt he could not disappoint six thousand loyal constituents.

"You see by my voice that I am quite hoarse," he rasped. "You will not, therefore, expect a speech from me."

At Ravenna, last stop before Cleveland, the crowds were as dense as ever. The *Cleveland Herald* reported that Lincoln's journey through this land of native American pioneers, the Western Reserve, was a "continuous succession of ovations."

Clearly, these people of the Western Reserve saw more than a mudsill in Abraham Lincoln. They saw in him what was to them most characteristically American, the prairie pioneer. Back in colonial times the American hero had been the forest-and-mountain-man like Daniel Boone and Davy Crockett, the type idealized in Cooper's *Leatherstocking Tales* and in stories of the Appalachian country. The tide of empire had been moving westward, and the mythical center of United States population had jumped 350 miles west since 1790, from east to Baltimore to near Chillicothe, Ohio.

Now this tall, homely, hulking man from the western prairie personified the American hero of 1860. He was indeed the one they had voted for and had sung about. "Old Abe Lincoln Came Out of the Wilderness," they had chanted during the election campaign. And here, in person, was the great Railsplitter, the new President from out of their land, a prairie pioneer.

The three states had a common heritage. Ohio, Indiana, Illinois; each had been part of the great Northwest Territory, settled first in the extreme southern parts along the Ohio River by pioneers who had come from the limestone regions of Virginia, Kentucky and Tennessee. According to Herndon, they "were men of giant strength . . . mentally strong. They were individualists. The strong alone . . . could get here and the strong alone could survive."

Politically, each state was divided on a North-and-South basis, and continued to be until well after the war. The National turnpike west from Steubenville to Columbus to Indianapolis to Terre Haute to St. Louis roughly marked the division between New Englanders and other Easterners, who had settled the upper half, and the Southern pioneers of the lower half. Exceptions were the river ports of Cincinnati and St. Louis which were more cosmopolitan, having large foreign populations. Still, their economic faces were turned southward, down to New Orleans.

The railroads were changing this. Cutting across long-established water routes, opening new pathways to commerce, making possible development of new industries, and increasing trade whenever they touched, the busy iron horses were bringing a heterogenous population that would obliterate much of the early provincialism and create the America of the twentieth century.

[97]

The time was 4:20 P.M. on this rainy and blustery afternoon of February 15, 1861. The grinding of car brakes and crash of artillery indicated arrival at Cleveland. The train halted at the Euclid Street depot (now 79th Street and Euclid Avenue) of the Cleveland and Pittsburgh Railroad. A company of light artillery was energetically firing the presidential salute, and a great throng roared its welcome. The din was deafening.

Military and fire companies as well as gaily decorated omnibuses carrying workmen from local factories were drawn up for the parade into town. Young Republicans on horseback offered Bob Lincoln a splendid bay horse which he managed expertly. President-elect and party were escorted to waiting carriages, as Mary and the boys left directly for the hotel.

The patriotic procession moved along Euclid Street which was lined with cheering spectators, despite the deep mud. Lincoln stood and bowed in the open carriage. The party was landed safely at the Weddell House at Superior and Banks Streets in the gathering gloom at 5:30 P.M. Lincoln then stepped to the front of a platform built out from the hotel balcony and hung with colored lanterns. To J. E. Masters, president of the city council acting in the mayor's absence, and Judge Sherlock J. Andrews, acting for the citizens, both of whom gave welcoming speeches, Lincoln responded:

"We have been marching for two miles through snow, rain and deep mud. The large numbers that have turned out under these circumstances testify to your respect for the Union, the Constitution and the laws. . . ."

Then he launched into the subject that would make his Cleveland speech one of the most controversial of his public career; remarks that were later mutilated and misinterpreted.

[98]

CHAPTER 11

FREQUENT allusion is made to the excitement at present existing in our national politics, and it is well that I should also allude to it here," Lincoln said to the Cleveland audience.

"I think, that there is no occasion for any excitement. The crisis, as it is called, is altogether an artificial crisis. In all parts of the nation there are differences of opinion on politics. There are differences of opinion even here. You did not all vote for the person who now addresses you.

"What is happening now will not hurt those who are farther away from here. Have they not all their rights now as they have ever had? Do they not have their fugitive slaves returned now as ever? Have they not the same constitution that they have lived under for seventy odd years? Have they not a position as citizens of this common country, and have we any power to change that position? (Cries of 'No!')

"What then is the matter with them? Why all this excitement? Why all these complaints? As I said before, this crisis is all artificial. It has no foundation in fact. It was not argued up as the saying is, and cannot, therefore, be argued down. Let it alone and it will go down of itself," he counseled.

This was not the first time he uttered such sentiments. He had told the Ohio Legislators at Columbus Wednesday afternoon:

"It is a good thing that there is no more anxiety, for there is nothing going wrong. . . . We entertain different views upon political questions, but nobody is suffering anything. This is a most consoling circumstance. . . ."

That morning at Pittsburgh he made the point:

"Notwithstanding the troubles across the river (pointing south across the Monongahela), there is no crisis, . . . excepting such a one as may be gotten up at any time by designing politicians. . . . Let the people on both sides keep their self-possession, and just as other clouds have cleared away in due time, so will this, and this great nation shall continue to prosper as heretofore."

Was it to pour oil on troubled waters that he was enunciating "soft sentiments?" Was Lincoln a demagogue? Was he lying for the purpose of calming public fears?

Simple truth is often hardest to believe. That is so now. The simple truth is that Lincoln was not lying. Nor was he playing the demagogue. He was right in saying that "nothing is going wrong." He knew exactly what he meant when he proclaimed the crisis "altogether artificial." This, obviously, requires looking into. The inquiry in these pages must necessarily be limited.

The beginning was in the immortal American declaration that all men are created equal. The Constitution implemented the Declaration of Independence but failed to include involuntary servitude. Nor did it cover the subject of a state withdrawing from the federal Union. Yet these two problems, agitated for political purposes, had now become emotional issues.

The country had been growing prodigiously, leaping from a population of five million in 1800 to twenty-three million in 1850. Expanding geographically also, its eastern and western extremes, were the Atlantic and Pacific coasts, three thousand miles apart and separated by vast stretches of prairie and desert and high mountains peopled by hostile Indians. Transportation and communication had to be established; the nation must be developed, settled, unified.

The answer was a transcontinental railroad.

Numerous bills had been placed before Congress for a Pacific railroad. All had been stalemated as to where to locate the road. Southern states had killed Northern routes and vice versa, and both had killed central routes. It was a power struggle which no one seemed able to resolve; that is, until Senator Douglas, Illinois's "Little Giant," put his finger in the pie.

Speculative opportunities in those times were in land. Douglas had bought Chicago property, lots of it, along lake front and inland, wagering heavily on Chicago's future. Everybody could get on the bandwagon. Many did, and profited handsomely. The unhappy part was that Douglas's well-intentioned effort helped to tear the nation apart.

When Congress finally passed his Kansas-Nebraska bill, it lit the fuse that exploded the bomb that started the war. To intimate that Douglas's purpose had been to incite civil conflict is unfair. A more patriotic American did not live than Stephen Arnold Douglas, as much a self-made man as Abraham Lincoln, whose friend he was. That his endeavor to develop his country should blow up in his face was beyond his control. He cannot be excused, however, of a moral obtuseness and a single-minded cupidity that fatally obscured his political judgment.

He had framed the bill, introduced it into Congress, guided its passage through both houses, and outmaneuvered bitter opposition until it became law on May 30,

1854. Its purpose was to open for white settlement the wild plains region, the great Platte Territory, and to authorize formation of the two new territories, Kansas and Nebraska, through which a transcontinental railroad could be constructed.

Indian tribes then occupied the area, according to formal treaties. Federal laws imposed a fine of $1,000 and six months' imprisonment for settling treaty lands. But pressures had been mounting. This Indian country barred the way west. Ever since the rush for California gold in 1849, westward emigration had been gaining momentum. Fever of expansion was running high all over the nation. Prospective settlers waited impatiently along Iowa and Missouri boundaries for the Indian titles to be superseded and for civil government to be established, that they might take possession of the lush land.

To Douglas the role of state-maker was not new. As a raw congressman he had reported bills for admission of four states and three territories. He continued the work as senator. Winning of the West was his dream. Senator Bell of Tennessee said it was his mania.

"I tell you," said Douglas during the debate on his bill, "you must provide for continuous lines of settlement from the Mississippi Valley to the Pacific Ocean." But the long discussions in Congress drew away from constitional, legal and economic issues, and centered on the slavery issue. Where Douglas had seen dollars and a transcontinental railroad in his bill, others had seen votes and power. That is the way of public politics.

As finally passed, Douglas's Kansas-Nebraska Act repealed the 1820 Missouri Compromise which had prohibited slavery north of Missouri's southern boundary, but excluded that state. The question was now to be determined by the settlers. All the anti- and pro-slavery issues that had been laid to rest now sprang into life. Political battling obscured the overriding purpose of Douglas's measure. The Pacific railroad was forgotten. The issues of slavery and secession intruded. The struggle for power began.

To oppose the Kansas-Nebraska Act that would allow extension of slavery to any part of the nation, there emerged an anti-Nebraska group made up of former Free-Soilers, Know-Nothings, dissident Democrats, abolitionists and Whigs. By degrees they evolved into the Republican party. And lawyer Lincoln, lifetime Whig, retired from public life, peacefully riding a judicial circuit, was pulled back into a political war to stop the extension of slavery. Now came his most effective campaigning, his great Lost Speech, his eloquent House Divided Speech, his Cooper Union Speech, the New England tour, the famous debates, his answering Douglas's "popular sovereignty" manifesto with the retort that settlers in new territories wanted "clean beds with no snakes in them."

Now, Lincoln was declaring to his vast Cleveland audience that the crisis was artificial, "gotten up" he said.

Lincoln then said in his plain way that America was sound and prosperous and that this was apparent on every side. Look at the whole picture, he was pointing out, not just the political part. Observe the well-being of *all* the people. See how brightly the future is shining.

American inventive genius already had produced the Whitney cotton gin, Morse telegraph, Otis elevator, Goodyear rubber, Herring safes, Hoe printing presses, Howe scales, Singer sewing machines, Colt firearms, McCormick reapers and farm machinery that tripled the farmer's working output, to say nothing of automatic machinery that made shoes, scissors, fabrics, carpets, pins and watches.

The virgin American continent offered unequaled opportunities in agriculture, animal husbandry, mining, lumbering, fishing and trapping. Fifty million dollars annually were being added to American coinage from gold mining operations. The country had more railroad mileage than the rest of the world put together.

Output of manufactured goods was zooming. The capital invested in factories, shops and mills had doubled in a decade, totaling two billion dollars in 1860, a remarkable figure for the time. New farms and new businesses and new settlements were springing up like mushrooms. Farmers, planters, ranchers "never had it so good," with the price of wheat at the New York market soaring from ninety-three cents in 1851 to $2.50 a bushel.

The federal census of 1860 noted that the end of the ten-year period showed little trace of hesitations. The *American Railroad Journal,* January 5, 1861, reported "the most eventful year in American history as a nation had just closed. It has been marked alike by the most extraordinary commercial and political movements." The population was now thirty-one million.

Relations with foreign countries were amicable. The United States was at peace with the world. While the Old World continued to bicker and battle in its immemorial way, the New World was being left pretty much to its own devices.

A thousand churches were going up yearly in America. New hospitals were opening in the cities. The tax-supported primary school system was expanding. High schools were being established. A hundred new colleges were founded during the decade. Books and national magazines were flowing from the new steam presses. The lyceum and the theater flourished as never before.

Ann Sophia Stephens penned the paper-back thriller,

Maleska, the Indian Wife of a White Hunter, initiating the dime-novel craze. Herman Melville wrote *Moby Dick,* Longfellow, "The Children's Hour," and Stephen Foster, "Old Black Joe." The pony express carried the first overland mail between St. Joseph, Missouri, and Sacramento, California. Fitzpatrick and O'Neil fought the longest bare knuckle prizefight in four hours and twenty minutes. The Prince of Wales made a grand tour.

Such was the United States of America in the decade ending in 1860.

It was plain that there was nothing wrong with the national economy. The so-called crisis lay in one segment only, the purely political. Lincoln made this clear again and again. He introduced his Cleveland remarks by saying he would "allude to the excitement existing in our national *politics.*" He enunciated his initial "nothing-going-wrong" statement at Columbus, saying that "we entertain different views upon *political* questions." That morning in Pittsburgh he put his finger on the real cause, asserting "there is no crisis except as may be gotten up by turbulent men aided by *designing politicians.*" Now he spelled it out and counseled to let it alone and "it will go down by itself."

Everybody knows that it did not go down, but got progressively worse. The agitators would not let it alone. Thus it came about that Lincoln's Cleveland Address was characterized by his enemies as the high-water mark of his incompetence and blindness to the facts of life.

Few indeed were the commendations for the firm stand he took against the deadly trend of events. (The confederates were framing a constitution and appointing heads of government.) Was he supposed to condone or commend the seceders? There was no praise, either, for his courage in trying to explain the crisis to his muddled countrymen. Or was he supposed to beat the drums for war? (Secessionists were buying arms in the North and enlisting men in the South.)

How, in the face of all this, did he expect the thing to "go down?" He told how: "Let the people of both sides keep their self-possession, and just as other clouds have been cleared away in due time, so will this great nation prosper as before." How could this be accomplished? Like this: "The question which now distracts the country will be settled just as all other difficulties *of a like character,* which have originated in this government, have been adjusted."

How had they been adjusted? The American people were well aware of the two Missouri Compromises, the Fugitive Slave Law, the law prohibiting slave importation and other legislation, both federal and state, that had, since the founding of the nation, sought to ameliorate the problem. Lincoln's proposals of what could be done were based on what had been done. There was substantial ground for his recommendations.

His wise counsel was being bolstered by contemporary events. On the same day that the cotton states called their Montgomery convention, a Peace Congress was convened in Washington composed of delegates from nearly all non-seceding states. It was headed by former President John Tyler of Virginia, and it was in session as Lincoln spoke. Its purpose was to bring about settlement of the disputed issues.

Another current event was the series of special elections held in many border states to determine whether there should be a seceding convention. Pro-Unionists won hands down. Yet not one of these states had voted Republican. Arkansas, Missouri, Tennessee, Kentucky, North Carolina, Virginia (including what is now West

Virginia), Maryland and Delaware would have none of the secession business.

These elections were going on as Lincoln traveled. One by one the press was reporting victories for the Union. The outcome looked bright indeed. The fact of secession itself was not too disturbing. The cry of "Wolf!" had been throbbing throughout the land for years. Many Americans felt relieved when it finally did come. Now the worst was over, they thought. "Let the erring sisters go in peace," Greeley said in his popular newspaper. Many agreed.

Lincoln did not concur in that. His unalterable political objective was preservation of the Union. Nor did he believe in coercion—he was pledged not to use force. As a practical politician, he probably thought the seceders had made their drastic move to bargain for extension of slavery—secession being the political club with which to beat the opposition into submission. From the standpoint of economics, Lincoln may have felt the seceding states would soon be compelled to capitulate. They existed largely on the export of two crops, cotton and tobacco, and were almost without industry. Or he may have felt the new aggregation would make a fatal mistake which would lead them to negotiate.

There were other cogent reasons. Lincoln knew the slave states stood to gain more by remaining in the Union than by leaving. Through their political connections they dominated Congress. They would continue to do so after he took office. The Senate had a clear majority of Democrats. In the House, they and Southern Whigs combined to form a slaveholding block that controlled federal legislation. Lincoln could do nothing to injure their cause if he tried. And he didn't want to, stating repeatedly he had no intention of interfering with

Southern "institutions." He made this clear again in his Cincinnati Address on Tuesday.

Why, then, the question persists, did the seven states go out of the Union? One answer was provided by William G. "Parson" Brownlow, intrepid editor of a daily newspaper in Knoxville, the Tennessee citadel of pro-Union sentiment. Before he was ousted by the confederate government for saying he would "fight the secession leaders till hell froze over, and then fight them on the ice," Brownlow published this widely-quoted editorial in his *Knoxville Whig*: "I have considered the nature of many grievances we are told that we of the South have suffered at the hands of the North, and their effects upon the trade, commerce and religion of the South. They may be well expressed in the following words: The Democracy of the South have lost the offices of the Government and its immense patronage."

"Parson" Brownlow was not alone in his conviction. Other politically-wise journals noted the overthrow of the political party that had held national power for nearly three decades; that had, indeed, dominated the general government for sixty of its seventy-two years.

So long had the party been in power, avowed the *Cincinnati Commercial,* "as to have perpetuated its own means of existence by corruption and fraud." The reference was to wholesale fraud in the sale of federal bonds. The Secretary of War, a Virginian, had resigned under fire. The embezzlement had run into millions of dollars. Also uncovered were his secret orders to ship arms to various Southern arsenals.

The public had grown surfeited with the corruption and chicanery of the politicians in power. Voting them out of the federal government meant that thousands of party faithful would now be out of jobs.

Since civil service did not exist then, government positions were subject to political appointment, from mailman to cabinet officer. The Jacksonian policy of "to the victors belong the spoils" was in full force. The new administration appointed all new employees, loyal to their party. A Washington newsman covering the Montgomery convention reported that familiar party hangers-on were showing up there to pick a juicy job from the ripening political tree.

Turned out of office in a national election held under the provisions of the Constitution in the prescribed manner, the political leaders in the cotton states refused to abide by election returns. They repudiated the ballots of their fellow Americans.

"There was no sound of rejoicing here at Natchez, either on account of the formation of such a Southern confederacy or the appointment of such rulers," declared the *Natchez Courier*. "Are the people to have no choice? Can a convention alter Constitutions, impose taxes, inaugurate Presidents? Are they oligarchs and are we nothing? The consent of the governed is an essential element of government," maintained the *Courier,* reflecting the strong pro-Union sentiment prevailing in many parts of the southland.

The *New Orleans True Delta* called readers' attention to the fact that it had frequently asked them to bear in mind that the purpose of many politicians was to use the secession excitement as a pretext to take control of the government away from the people, and "to make such other disposition as will enable the few to rule at the expense of the many."

The cotton confederacy was a political oligarchy. It could lay no claim to having been endorsed or elected by its people.

CHAPTER 12

W<small>HEN</small> Lincoln finished
speaking in Cleveland, he stepped back to the balcony
proper, and there he was presented with an imposing
floral wreath. The presentation inspired the throng to
renewed cheers and applause.

A newly-elected member of Congress from Cleveland,
A. G. Riddle, said he saw Lincoln for the first time at the
Weddell House that evening: "He stood on the landing-
place at the top of a broad stairway, and the crowd approached him from below. Of the thousand times I afterward saw him, the first view remains the most distinct
impression.

"As I approached, someone whispered of me to him.
He took my hand in both of his for an instant and together we wheeled into the already crowded room. Mr.
Lincoln presented me to the gentlemen of his party . . .
and invited me to accompany him for at least a day on his
eastward journey. . . . Mrs. Lincoln impressed me very
favorably as a woman of spirit, intelligence, and decided
opinions, which she put very clearly. Our conversation
was mainly of her husband. . . ."

The brilliant reception kept Lincoln shaking hands
until he retired from public view at about ten o'clock.

A separate levee was held by Mrs. Lincoln. Then the Lincolns were interviewed in their suite by the editor of the *Cleveland Plain Dealer.*

Next day, the interview occupied the top of the editorial page. "We must confess to being most favorably impressed," wrote the editor and proprietor, J. W. Gray, who was anti-Lincoln. "If mistakes do occur in the Executive government of our country we are satisfied they will not be charged to design."

Next morning everyone seemed bright and cheerful. Overnight, the weather had turned sunny in the unpredictable manner of a Great Lakes winter. The departure was a gay one. From hotel to the Cleveland, Painesville and Ashtabula Railroad station, the presidential party was escorted by the Cleveland grays. At the depot Leland's brass band entertained with lively airs.

The press was well represented. The Weddell House register the night before showed: Henri Lovie, *Leslie's Weekly;* J. R. Drake, Associated Press; Henry Villard, *New York Herald;* O. H. Dutton, *New York Tribune;* J. Howard, Jr., *New York Times;* Henry M. Smith, *Chicago Tribune;* U. H. Painter, *Philadelphia Inquirer;* and W. G. Terrell, *Cincinnati Gazette.* Others must have stayed at the Angier House or elsewhere.

The schedule called for stops at Willoughby, Painesville, Geneva, Ashtabula, Conneaut, Girard, Erie, North East, Westfield, Dunkirk and Silver Creek, and would arrive in Buffalo at 4:30 P.M.

At Euclid William Hazen fired an artillery salute as the train passed, which cost him his arm. At Geneva Lincoln was exhorted by a voice in the crowd "to stand by the Constitution and the cause of liberty." At Ashtabula a huge turnout greeted his arrival. This was the home of a former congressman whose health had forced him to resign.

Lincoln would later appoint him Consul-General to the British North American Colonies, as Canada was then known. He was Joshua R. Giddings.

An energetic and well-liked politician, Giddings had represented the anti-slavery views of his district so ably as to have won repeated re-election. These anti-slavery people were now looking to Lincoln to back their sentiments. Radicals of the group were called abolitionists, since they subordinated every political consideration to total and immediate abolishment of slavery. Actually, they were the disunionists of the North; for rather than countenance slavery, they would prefer to separate from the slaveholding states.

Abolitionist feeling ran high in various parts of the land and was particularly strong in Massachusetts, where the left-wingers agitated unceasingly. "There is no reason for the Union!" cried an abolitionist spokesman at a Worcester rally. "We are essentially two nations!" And the meeting unanimously adopted a resolution saying the sooner the separation took place the more peaceful it would be, but, *"peace or war is a secondary consideration."*

The abolitionists would give Lincoln grave difficulty throughout his administration. They were vocal, persistent and demanding. Zealous crusaders, they sprang from every political faction. They were strong in northeastern Ohio. Lincoln was no abolitionist himself, and had been at pains to say so. His position was that slavery must not be extended (important at the time because new states and territories were being formed) but must remain restricted to areas where it was already established. This was the doctrine of George Washington.

Abolitionists had nowhere to go, politically, except to

the Republicans, for it was the only party taking a clear-cut stand on slavery. Lincoln had to walk his political tightrope between the unrelenting pressures of wild-eyed Northern radicals on the one hand and hotheaded secessionists on the other, a challenging task even for the most skillful politician.

The Ashtabula audience was in a gala mood. After listening to Lincoln rasp, "I can only say 'how-do-you-do and farewell,' as my voice you perceive will warrant nothing more," they called for Mrs. Lincoln to come out. Lincoln said he didn't think he could induce her to do so. "In fact," he wheezed, "I have never succeeded very well in getting her to do anything she didn't want to," which brought laughter and cheers as the train chugged away.

At Girard, back again in Pennsylvania, several baskets of fruit ("charming" apples, said one report) were presented as Lincoln concluded his rear-platform ritual. The sensation here was the unexpected appearance on the train of Horace Greeley, owner and editor of the *New York Tribune*.

Greeley had founded the penny morning newspaper after emigrating from the granite hills of Vermont, a green, country lad in Big Town. Now he was carrying a valise and red-and-blue blankets (for use on sleeping cars); he was wearing a long overcoat, collar partly turned in, pockets stuffed with papers. An old Quaker hat was pushed to the back of his head. What remains of him in public memory is his admonition, "Go west, young man!" Those days he was a power in politics. His newspaper commanded national circulation and attention. To use a favorite phrase of the era, he wielded a trenchant pen. He was conducted at once to the President-elect who introduced him to Mrs. Lincoln. A rival newshawk observed that "the broad-brimmed hat never once left the Horacian caput. We believe," the competitor snickered, "that politeness is not one of Mr. G's eccentricities."

Greeley rode the fifteen miles to Erie where he was to lecture that night. Then he would come to Buffalo where he expected to join the President-elect's party for Monday's trip to Albany.

Reaching Erie at 12:22 P.M. the Special was saluted by the Franklin Pierce Rifle Company, the roar of cannon, the shouts of an enthusiastic throng. The presidential party was conducted by the Erie escort committee through a bedecked depot to the upstairs dining room.

It was said that Lincoln was offered wine but declined, remarking he never indulged in liquor of any kind. On the other hand, an unconfirmed report stated he requested a second helping of mince pie baked by the wife of the proprietor, Mrs. Thomas B. Moore.

The meal finished, the east dining room doors were thrown open and Lincoln addressed the crowd below. Hoarse and fatigued from the heavy morning schedule, he thanked them for their warm reception and wonderful food. Asking to be excused for not expressing further opinions, he said he felt that when the time came for speaking he would not find it necessary to say anything that was not in accordance with the wishes of the whole people.

Returning to the cars, the party was now in the care of the Erie and Northeast and the Buffalo and State Line railroads. A patriotically-ornamented engine was coupled to the train. Named the *Rocket,* its throttle was controlled by Harvey Sales, an engine driver for eighteen years and reputed one of the ablest on the lines. Out of Erie, engines had been stationed every few miles, fired up, ready for instant duty. These emergency precautions had been prompted by a bitter railroad war that was still smoldering and that might explode at any moment.

Known as the Battle of the Gauges, fighting had broken out between citizens of Erie and railroad construction crews who had tried to re-lay the tracks to standard gauge. Powerful forces opposed the move, wanting the differing track gauges to stay as they were. Trade supremacy between New York and Philadelphia, economic survival of Erie itself, competition between struggling lakeports, marine traffic versus railroad transportation, and the political forces of both states, were factors involved in the rivalry.

Tracks had been ripped up time and again, bridges burned, militia called out, the city put under martial law, court injunctions defied, until the federal government threatened to send troops to prevent interference with the mails. Even then the conflict had not wholly ended. Trouble was still flaring intermittently when the Lincoln train came over the line. Fortunately, no violence occurred. The stand-by locomotives went unused.

At the town of North East, flags were flying, bands were playing and artillery was firing. A miniature Fort Sumter had been erected at trackside. Of this, Lincoln took no notice as he made his usual back-platform remarks.

At Westfield, New York, a large banner was stretched over the tracks inscribed, Welcome Abraham Lincoln to the Empire State. Westfield has achieved fame in Lincoln lore because of an eleven-year-old girl's letter to him suggesting he wear whiskers. He had replied at once. A facsimile of his letter follows on the next page.

Shortly afterward, Lincoln had begun his hirsute adornment, and now he was appearing with a full-grown crop. Concluding the platform remarks, he told the West-

Private

Springfield, Ill. Oct 19. 1860

Miss. Grace Bedell

My dear little Miss.

Your very agreable letter of the 15th is received—

I regret the necessity of saying I have no daughter— I have three sons— one seventeen, one nine, and one seven, years of age— They, with their Mother, constitute my whole family.—

As to the whiskers, having never worn any, do you not think people would call it a piece of silly affection if I were to begin it now?

Your very sincere well-wisher

A. Lincoln.

field audience he had a correspondent here. Her name he said, was Grace Bedell. Was Grace in the audience? She was; and she came up to the platform. Lifting her in his great arms, Lincoln kissed her, reminding her of her suggestion that he grow whiskers.

The incident produced a great sensation. Telegraph wires buzzed with the news. Headlines shrieked, OLD ABE KISSES PRETTY GIRL, WHISKERS WIN WINSOME MISS, and more of the same. As might be expected, political opponents twisted it to make Lincoln appear undignified.

The story of Grace's letter and Lincoln's whiskers appealed to people everywhere, telling, as it did, of two totally unlike persons who met for an instant and thereby gave the world a moment of pleasantry.

Whether Lincoln's appearance was improved by his beard is a matter of opinion. One thing is certain. Cartoonists had so exaggerated his salient features that the public, seeing him in the flesh for the first time, invariably remarked how much better looking he was than they had anticipated.

The dispatches going out of Indianapolis the first day had reported, "It is the general remark by all persons that he is a younger and nicer looking man than they expected to see."

At Cincinnati his physique had been freely discussed by the crowd, some expressing disappointment in not finding him so atrociously ugly as he had been represented. An opposition journal conceded, "His countenance was well enough to look upon."

Another pointed out, "He is not a handsome man . . . but there is an expression to the face that is pleasing."

Every man reaching the half-century mark has become aware (women long before that) of the effect his physical characteristics have upon others. Lincoln's must have impressed itself upon his consciousness early. His odd get-up was a political asset. Once seen, he could not be forgotten. No other President compares with him physically. That he, himself, realized the mixed reactions his appearance caused is indicated by his good-humored references to it. For Lincoln had the gift of humor. What is more, he had the common sense not to take himself too seriously. He was neither "stuffy" nor conceited. He could laugh at himself.

[117]

A recurring item in the brief back-platform remarks that tickled audiences concerned his appearance. A dozen instances are recorded, beginning at Newark, Ohio, where he said, "I stepped upon this platform that I may see you and that you may see me, and in this arrangement I have the best of the bargain."

Following his Cleveland visit a story made the rounds that would have amused him. A school principal, annoyed at the same excuse being brought in by so many pupils to explain their Friday afternoon absence, exclaimed, "The very idea! Tramping through mud and snow to look at a man, as if being elected President made him any different!"

"Oh, but it has," came a little voice. "He now has whiskers!"

Lincoln could be serious and thoughtful as the occasion demanded. He could reach into the hearts of his countrymen and stir them to the depths of their being. Such an occasion came at the very next stopover, the thriving lakeport of Dunkirk.

Dunkirk was the terminus at Lake Erie of the railroad that reached across the southern part of the state from New York City. Here a great triumphal arch had been erected, emblazoned with Union mottoes. Greeting the President-elect were military companies and military music, and fifteen thousand citizens, a good share of Chautauqua County. Lincoln stepped from the train onto a platform. Placing a hand around a pole from the top of which the national colors stood straight in the breeze, he said:

"Standing as I do with my hand upon this staff, and under the folds of the American flag, I ask you to stand by me so long as I stand by it!"

The effect was electric. "We will! We will!" shouted

the multitude. Lincoln stepped back to the train which moved off at once.

Following the next speaking stop, Silver Creek, it was arranged that Lincoln should rest in his private car, to be refreshed for the next big event which was Buffalo.

There he would be subjected to the worst buffeting of the trip. The knocking-about was not intentional and resulted from overenthusiasm. His life was endangered.

The episode was one of many along the way; and constant milling of many people, pushing and shoving and shouting, the long hours, strange food and incessant turmoil, finally moved a Cleveland reporter to begin his dispatch:

"We do not wish to be President!

"Whatever our ambition may have been heretofore," he wrote, "however our bosom may have swelled at the reflection that we should some day reach that exalted station, still we say that we no longer aspire to the office. We have seen enough of what it is to be President to effectually quench any ambition that may have been inspired by prophetic words of the past. This reporter declines to run."

If the pace was too much for the correspondent, what must it have been for Lincoln? Yet Lincoln was only at the halfway mark. Ahead of him stretched the same number of long days of the same grueling work; a deadly daily repetition of, as secretary Nicolay put it, "crowds, cannon and cheers."

CHAPTER 13

THE closer Lincoln's train came to Buffalo, the denser grew the crowds.

Puffing slowly into the Exchange Street depot, the rear car was brought to a stop opposite the main passenger entrance. As Lincoln emerged he was met at the car door by a welcoming committee headed by the Thirteenth President of the United States, Millard Fillmore, a resident of Buffalo. They shook hands heartily and stepped down into the narrow aisle being held open in the roaring throng by a file of policemen and Company D of the Seventy-fourth Infantry Regiment.

It was an historic occasion, this meeting of President-elect and former President. To better view them as they walked toward the street exit, the crowd pushed forward from both sides. Tremendous power was generated by the two masses of people pushing toward each other from opposite directions. It overwhelmed the scanty line of guards and pressed upon the two distinguished men. A scene of the wildest confusion ensued, heightened by the crashing of an artillery salute.

The disorder was so great that many were in danger of being crushed or trampled. The tall form of Lincoln and the white head of Fillmore could be seen swaying back and forth as the crowd surged first to one side and then the other. They were caught between the jaws of a power-ful human vise.

An old gentleman from Lancaster had his ribs frac-tured. Major David Hunter had a shoulder dislocated. Bob Lincoln and Neil Dennison, the Ohio governer's son, narrowly escaped being knocked down. The heavy portals of the depot entrance were broken apart. Dozens of per-sons reached the street scarcely able to stand from fright and exhaustion.

"The Pass of Thermopylae was a memorable perform-ance," said the *Buffalo Courier,* "but it was no such jam as the Pass of the Central Depot."

Only by the most desperate efforts of the presidential escort and the redoubtable Colonel Lamon were Lincoln and Fillmore extricated from the seething mass and taken to their carriage. The wild melee also broke up the line of waiting carriages so that many of the party, after fight-ing their way out of the depot, found that the carriages had departed or were occupied by local committeemen. It was digraceful mismanagement.

"We cannot cast reflections on the crowd whose action is so much to be regretted," stated the *Buffalo Express,* "because their conduct was no more than natural, how-ever improper." Decorous behavior can never be ex-pected from a mass of enthusiastic people, explained the editor, and in this instance their conduct "certainly signi-fied no disrespect towards the President-elect, but rather the opposite feelings."

Nor was it the fault of the soldiers and police. They were so outnumbered they had difficulty getting out themselves. Six times their number would not have been adequate. Where was the rest of the regiment? And why, in the first place, was the crowd permitted inside the depot?

Company D finally managed to line up on the street

for the parade, preceded by the Union cornet band and followed by the light artillery of the Sixty-fifth Regiment which had been firing the salute. Mrs. Lincoln and the boys were slipped out via Carroll Street and sent ahead to the hotel.

Up Exchange and over Main streets the procession made its measured way past gaily decorated buildings jammed with shouting spectators. The streets were solidly packed. It was a glorious afternoon. Under the mellowing influence of a springlike sun a blanket of soft snow that had fallen the previous night had melted.

Riding in the carriage with the two Presidents were Colonel Lamon, A. S. Bemis, acting mayor, and A. M. Clapp, chairman of Buffalo's joint committee that had escorted the President-elect from Cleveland. They disembarked at the American House located on Main between Court and Eagle streets. Police and militia formed a protective lane from street to hotel entrance, into the lobby and up to the balcony. This time the arrangement worked.

Out on the balcony Lincoln quickly appeared, and in a voice hoarse from his full day of speaking, responded to the acting mayor's welcoming remarks. His speech was disturbed by the sound of wood being sawed.

The sawing resulted from payment of an election bet —loser to cut half a cord of wood into stove lengths in front of the hotel. As Lincoln began, the sawing began, continuing during the speaking and not finishing until after it had ended. Someone in the lingering audience then suggested a subscription be taken up to buy the sawyer a medal inscribed: *Vidi!*

The interference did not faze an old campaigner like Lincoln. For years he had had to contend with hecklers, drunks and amen-shouters. The sawing act might seem inconsiderate or funny according to one's political preference, from this distance it appears discourteous. Granted, Lincoln had yet to be confirmed an official of the government and so might be construed fair political game, the sawing was still disrespectful of the office to which the people had elected him, and an affront to the audience. It should have been stopped.

Remarks of the acting mayor were well chosen, their sincerity helping to dispel this interference. The marked courtesy of Fillmore, noteworthy from the first handshake and continuing throughout the visit, more truly represented the hospitality of thoughtful Buffalonians. In view of the unfortunate events, Lincoln's response was most considerate.

"Your worthy Mayor has been pleased to mention in his address to me," he began, "the fortunate and agreeable journey which I have made from my home on my rather circuitous route to the Federal capital. . . . *It is true we have had nothing thus far to mar the pleasure of the trip . . . .*"

The sawing went on. Paying no attention, Lincoln continued. The substance of the address he embodied in this sentence:

"When I speak authoritatively [at Washington], I hope to say nothing inconsistent with the Constitution, the Union, the rights of all States, of each State, and of each section of the country, and not to disappoint the reasonable expectation of those who have confided to me their votes."

Here again he was foreshadowing the Inaugural Address. Into this sentence he compressed the fundamentals of his future policy, reassuring the people that they were to receive nothing but proper treatment at his hands and from his administration. The Buffalo speech brought much favorable comment, especially in view of the impending confederacy. (Jefferson Davis was arriving this day in Montgomery to be inaugurated on Monday). Lincoln took note of the event in these words:

"When we speak of threatened difficulties to the country, it is natural that there should be expected from me something with regard to particular measures . . . when it is considered that these difficulties are without precedent, and have never been acted upon by any individual situated as I am, it is most proper I should wait, see the developments, and get all the light I can, so that when I do speak authoritatively, I may be as near right as possible."

Even those politically opposed agreed it was prudent for him to remain silent on the national difficulties until he reached Washington. The *New York World,* which would make plenty of trouble for Lincoln in wartime, asserted there never was a greater mistake than to suppose he would violate the Constitution. "It will prove," the *World* prophesized, "that the sacred instrument of our fathers has never been in safer hands or will be more justly administered."

Re-entering the hotel after his speech, Lincoln was introduced to the thirty-four members of the Buffalo reception committee and to the governor's staff that would escort him to Albany. These ceremonies over, he retired for refreshment to the finest apartment the hotel could offer him and his family.

Beginning at seven-thirty that evening he held a levee, open to the public. A cold wind off the lake was bringing snow; but thousands of hardy citizens turned out for the ever-to-be-remembered pleasure of meeting their future President. Lincoln stood on a low platform in the second floor hall near the head of the right-hand stairway. The people filed up between a cordon of police and soldiers, passing in front of him, down the left stairway to the lobby, and out.

He had a greeting for one, a *bon mot* for another and a handshake for others. A large Rochester delegation, headed by the mayor, and representatives from Syracuse, Utica, and Albany were also greeted. To children who happened along Lincoln paid special attention.

Of a trio of ladies attended by their escorts, one, fired with sudden enthusiasm, turned to her companion and exclaimed over her shoulder, "I'd like to kiss him!" Overhearing the exclamation Lincoln smiled and said, "Come on, then!" And come she did, followed by her two companions.

Out of sight of her beleaguered husband, Mrs. Lincoln was receiving in another parlor where the guests were introduced by the chairman of the reception committee. The parlors were tastefully decorated in tricolored bunting. Mrs. Lincoln stood under a silk canopy draped with national colors and ornamented with national emblems. Robert stood by at various times, assisting in the ceremony.

"She is a lady who will preside over the hospitalities of the Presidential mansion with a grace becoming to that exalted station," one reporter wrote, and another said she was "a quiet, kindly-looking, elderly lady . . . with a sobriety and composure of mien which are perhaps desirable." The consensus was that she acquitted herself charmingly in a trying position.

To prevent a repetition of the depot fiasco, twenty soldiers from Company D and a detachment of police had been detailed to the hotel as house guards. But arrangements were faulty. Hundreds of canny visitors skipped through the hotel kitchen on Pearl Street and up the back stairs to meet the Lincolns.

The levee ended promptly at nine-thirty. At once Lincoln was waited on by a committee of twenty Germans, headed by ex-alderman Jacob Beyer. Beyer read a speech. He said the committee represented the Germans, of whom there were 25,000 in the city. (Buffalo's 1860 population was 81,000; tenth city of the nation.)

"Sir," concluded Beyer, "we wish you a pleasant and safe journey to the place of your destination and hope that your administration will alike be honorable and satisfactory and prove a blessing to the whole nation."

Lincoln replied: "I am gratified with this evidence of the feelings of the German citizens of Buffalo. My own idea about our foreign citizens has always been that they were no better than anyone else, and no worse. And it is best that they should forget they are foreigners as soon as possible."

Honest Old Abe! He never made a truer statement. Nor one more greatly needed by his fellow citizens. America should come first!

Lincoln's Response to Buffalo Germans, one of the most forthright public statements ever made, does not appear in a single collection of Lincolniana. Nor is it mentioned in a single biography. It is "lost." Newspaper accounts of the day barely mentioned the incident. One local paper, the *Buffalo Commercial Advertiser,* carried the verbatim transcript quoted above. So did the daily German newspaper, the *Buffalo Demokrat.*

Yet ex-alderman Beyer's speech was reprinted in full. Why? For the economic reason that newspapers, like all other means of public communication depending for existence on the good will of their subscribers, must cater to their buying public. News is slanted—altered, distorted—to pamper the prejudices and enhance the pride of readers. Lincoln's reply was patriotic and forthright. Yet it might be construed offensively by the foreign-born. In contrast, the ex-alderman's speech was local news. Readers would glow with pride perusing what "our man Beyer" had said to the new President.

Passing over the personal politics (an ex-officeholder looking for a job) it was clear that an ethnic group was being used for political ends. Lincoln recognized this.

Commenting on the situation, a writer in the *Rochester* (New York) *Union and Advertiser* said there was no objection to German meetings because many were not able to understand English. "But permanent political German associations, German wire-pullers, German ward politicians, Germans of so-called influence boasting that their countrymen will vote as they say to—such things are unnecessary. Abe Lincoln is right! Every distinction of nationality should be obliterated!"

For "German" in the above, substitute Irish, Jewish, Polish, Italian, Mexican, African, Japanese, Chinese, Burmese, or what are you? The Germans figure in the Lincoln story because, along with the Irish, they composed great waves of immigration at that time caused by political unrest in Europe and potato famines in Ireland. In 1861 the American population was about one-third foreign in birth, language and customs.

The Irish, whose poverty caused many thousands to settle where they landed in Boston, New York, Jersey City, Philadelphia and other ports, preferred to huddle in cities, and so came under the influence of city political machines. Except in Pennsylvania, the Irish voted for Democrats as a rule. In 1860 they went mostly for Douglas.

The Germans, strongly anti-slavery, were more inclined

to the Republicans because of the free land program. They wanted to settle down and help develop "the land of the free and the home of the brave." When war broke, they formed German-speaking regiments, brigades, and whole divisions.

Roughly, twenty-three out of every hundred soldiers in the Union army were of foreign birth. No greater tribute to this country can there be than this.

The welcome Lincoln gave to strangers to these shores is reflected in his granting posts of high command to foreign-born and foreign-trained officers. As Commander-in-Chief of the military forces, he appointed such capable commanders as Ferrero of Italy, Stolbrand of Sweden, Turchin of Russia, Schurz of Prussia, de Trobriand of France, Krzyzabowski of Poland, and others.

Lincoln's advice to the Germans to forget they were foreigners as soon as possible did not go unheeded. More quickly than any other group, they accepted the American way of life. A French observer prophesied that the blending in America of the Anglo-Saxon, nervous and irritable, and the German, heavy and rustic, should result in a better equilibrium of mental and physical qualities. In addition to the Old World culture that pioneer Americans needed, Germans also brought their friendly *Gemütlichkeit* to temper Yankee stiffness. Many German folk customs passed into American life, such as the Christmas tree with its joyous generosity and abundance of good cheer. Little wonder native Anglo-Saxons assimilated these hard-working newcomers, one of whose descendants —Dwight D. Eisenhower—occupies the White House as this is written.

Love of good music was another noteworthy Teutonic characteristic. As soon as Lincoln finished with the ex-alderman and committee he was serenaded by the

Saengerbund (choral society). Standing out in the blustery weather, they rendered a series of beautiful ballads. Hardly had they completed their repertoire than another group came along, the *Liedertafel* (glee club). Lincoln invited them in. Clustered in the hotel lobby, they sang a group of songs in the way that has made German singing societies famous the world over.

The song fest ended a long, arduous day. Lincoln turned to his apartment for rest. Out of a window he noticed across the street a banner on the Young Men's Christian Union building. Inscribed in reply to his Springfield farewell remarks, it read: We Will Pray For You.

CHAPTER 14

Sunday brought a blessed interlude in the week of exhausting activity. The weary presidential party took advantage of Buffalo's cold and windy weather to stay indoors—some to catch up on lost sleep, others to write letters and visit.

The President-elect went to church as the guest of the former President, attending service at the Unitarian Church on Franklin and Eagle streets. After hearing Dr. Hosmer's sermon, they returned to the hotel where they picked up Mrs. Lincoln and drove to the handsome Fillmore residence on Niagara Square. The Sunday dinner must have been especially enjoyable to Mrs. Lincoln, who admired the former President and had often spoken of him as a fine Chief Executive.

Meanwhile, private secretary Nicolay was trying to straighten out details and keep callers happy while allowing Lincoln time of his own. Not until late evening was he able to write his fiancée back home in Pittsfield, Illinois.

"Arrived at the hotel, all was confusion," he told her. "The committee not only did nothing, but didn't know and didn't seem to care, what to do. We took the matter into our own hands. . . . I don't know when I have done so much work as yesterday and I am feeling the effects of it today. The best criterion I can give you of my situation is the appearance of this letter. . . . Good night!"

Captain George Hazzard of the military escort wrote his wife and answered her question: "As to your joining us, I fear it will be impracticable, as Mr. and Mrs. Lincoln are worked almost out of their lives by visitors of both sexes. Every village sends a reception committee of twenty or thirty and some of them bring their wives, so that not only are all seats in the cars taken, but the pass way is filled with people standing."

Around two o'clock the Lincolns returned to the hotel. During the afternoon they received friends in the apartment, the boys coming in to be introduced on occasion. The family enjoyed supper together. Early in the evening Lincoln, escorted by Fillmore and acting mayor Bemis and others, attended Father John Beeson's meeting on behalf of American Indians in St. James Hall.

Father Beeson had lived and traveled among the Indians, particularly among the western tribes, and had been appalled at the inhuman acts committed against them. A band of musicians from a nearby Indian reservation entertained. The good Father had held a meeting Friday evening but it had been poorly attended. With the President-elect coming to town he decided to try again. Both Presidents listened attentively, and at the close expressed sympathy for the Indian cause.

Considering the merit of the cause, why had so little been done in the Indians' behalf? The treatment accorded them by the usurping immigrants is a black page in American history. The red men had rightfully defended their native land against interlopers. For generations the one-sided slaughter had gone on, guns versus arrows.

Resistance and torture had been the red man's mistake. He was a savage and made himself a menace, turning public opinion against him. For public safety he had to be relegated to reservations. Unlike every other racial and national group which, at some time or other, has organized political pressure for its benefit, the Indian cause passed away. Since colonial days the American aborigine has not constituted a political issue.

The imported African always has. Whether they wished it so or not, the Negro people have represented a political problem from America's very beginning. Their undigested mass in the body politic has afflicted it with severe bellyaches, one that was almost fatal. So severe was the conflict of 1861-1865 that it claimed the lives of a million citizens, the nation's greatest disaster, one that almost caused the death of the Republic.

At the masthead of the *Cleveland Plain Dealer*, as Lincoln passed through the city, this daily reminder appeared:

Epitaph for the late American Republic:
Here lies a people, who, in attempting to liberate
the Negro, lost their own freedom.

It was the moral issue of Negro slavery that had aroused Lincoln in 1854, triggered by passage of Douglas's political Kansas-Nebraska bill. But before he could take office as President, the slavery issue had been turned into a question of whether or not sovereign states could withdraw from the Union. Although secessionists maintained they would not fight over the Negro and that they were defending a political principle, this was patently a subterfuge. The emotional energizer, the moral motive, the political problem, was Negro slavery.

"All knew that this interest was, somehow, the cause

of the war," Lincoln would say in his second Inaugural Address, reiterating what he had said in his final debate with Douglas six years before, "the real issue was the wrong of slavery."

Lincoln would have to meet that problem as no other President had before him. He would become the Great Emancipator. In so becoming, he would not equivocate. As the question of emancipation reached a climax in 1862, he invited a group of Northern free Negro leaders to the White House. "You and we are different races," he told them. "We have between us a broader difference than existed between almost any two races." Painfully, he made clear to them the facts of life, explaining that freedom would not solve their problems.

These are not the pages in which to detail the difficulties of emancipation, nor to relate the causes of the Civil War, nor to discuss the myriad knotty problems with which Lincoln had to contend. But it is essential to realize what Lincoln was up against as President-elect in order to evaluate his inaugural journey.

He was up against deeper divergences in the body politic than those that caused the Revolution. These differences affected the entire populace and had become increasingly emotional year by year and month by month. They would eventually be agitated into the realm of violence, as is now known.

He was up against a nation-wide daily press that was more anti-Lincoln than favorable. This was understandable and not surprising considering the defection of Southern pro-slavery newssheets, the journals friendly to Douglas, the supporters of other defeated presidential hopefuls, and knights-errant like Bennett of the *New York Herald* and Greeley of the *New York Tribune* who played their own little political games.

Lincoln was up against his long obscurity. This was a

distinct handicap. He was not, in the national sense, a public figure. He was an unknown, a compromise candidate, elected in the face of great political turmoil and now charged with tremendous responsibilities. His nine months of self-imposed silence had magnified the uncertainties about him in the public eye.

As the new head of a new political party that had never before administered the federal government, and one that had promised to do definite things about certain political problems confronting the nation, he provided a personal target for all opposition. Not knowing his capabilities (no one could, not even himself), the public had to judge him in the context of the passing moment.

He was up against partisans within his own party, some of whom were as violent in their demands as the opposition. A leading Columbus banker, William G. Deshler, who had stood with him on the library steps in the Capitol rotunda, related that many of the crowd expressed disappointment at Lincoln's speech on the west steps. "Abe," one admonished him as they shook hands, "you've got to give them rebels a hotter shot than that before they're licked." The banker said the governor and other politicians also expressed disappointment.

Charles Francis Adams, whom Lincoln would appoint Minister to Great Britain, wrote that the speeches "have fallen like a wet blanket here. They put to flight all notions of greatness. . . ." Samuel Bowles, proprietor of the *Springfield* (Massachusetts) *Republican,* a staunch party supporter, asserted that Lincoln was a "simple Susan." Edward Everett, who would be the leading orator at the Gettysburg battlefield dedication, remarked that the "speeches thus far have been of the most ordinary kind, destitute of everything, not merely of felicity and grace, but of common pertinence."

A great Lincoln biographer quoted Everett and then commented that "in three days of speaking he had the country well baffled; at Indianapolis telling the Hoosiers to 'rise in mass'; at Cincinnati crying, 'Friends, brethren!' to the border state people; and in Columbus saying 'there is nothing going wrong!' "

The strangest and most astonishing fact in all Lincolniana is this: Not only was Lincoln villified for his lengthy inaugural tour by political opponents—which was to be expected—not only was he castigated by the radicals in his party—which was not unusual—and not only was he up against misunderstandings of friends and supporters —which was not expected—but what makes the whole situation utterly incredible is that the majority of Lincoln writers over the last ten decades have also downgraded the trip and disparaged the speeches. Biographers and historians for one hundred years, with but few exceptions, have condemned his "zigzag" travel and censured his speeches as among the worst of his career.

The first complete biography of Lincoln, published in 1865, was written by Josiah G. Holland, editor of the well-known *Springfield* (Massachusetts) *Republican*. A careful worker, he sought the aid of Herndon, Speed, and other intimate friends of Lincoln. Of the journey speeches, Dr. Holland commented:

"To talk when it was his impulse and his policy to say nothing, was the hardest task of his life. Hence, there never had been a passage in his life in which he appeared to such disadvantage as he did in the speeches during his journey. He could win the profoundest admiration of the gifted and the learned at the Cooper Union, but on the platform of a railroad car or before an august committee of city magnates, he was as much at loss as a schoolboy would have been."

Herndon was annoyed. He was annoyed by the poppy-cock quoted above and by the eulogistic content of the biography that tried to make a deity of his martyred law partner. More biographies, all eulogistic, continued to pour from the presses. Herndon scurried about, digging up documents, examining and cross-examining neighbors, writing letters to participants, neglecting his law practice to assemble a mass of data about Lincoln that has since proved priceless, despite his peculiar notions and unwarranted conclusions. His object was to produce a biography that would tell the *whole* truth. But he kept putting off the writing.

Along came jolly Ward Lamon, Lincoln's ex-Danville law associate, planning to turn out a Lincoln biography. He dickered with Herndon and bought $4,000 worth of Herndon's Lincoln notes (he paid half down and his father-in-law paid the rest when Herndon threatened to sue). Lamon, no writer, hired Chauncey S. Black, Democrat and son of President Buchanan's attorney-general, as a ghost writer. What Black did to the Lincoln story is heartbreaking. If Dr. Holland and similar eulogists are to be known as the angelic school of Lincolniana, then Herndon, Lamon and Black must be called the muckraker school.

The strangest thing was that regardless of whether the editorial approach to Lincoln's life was angelic or satanic, journey and speeches were given superficial mention or unwarranted criticism. The Lamon-Black opus repeated the strictures of Dr. Holland, claiming Lincoln regretted the long trip, convinced he had made a great mistake.

The erratic Herndon finally got himself a collaborator, and in 1889 produced the work that has grown into American folk literature, *Herndon's Lincoln, The True Story of a Great Life.* In it he spoke well of the journey, saying the speeches were "well timed and sensibly uttered." But to his collaborator he confided that he had been disgusted with Lincoln; that either Lincoln was "trying to cover up the seriousness of events, or he never fully comprehended the situation."

The "I-knew-him-when" writers were followed by the academicians, professional purveyors of history and biography who contributed much to the Lincoln story by their precise methods. But here again enters the strange and inexplicable fact that not one gave to journey and speeches thorough and careful investigation. Nearly all continued the same old catechism. Typical comments ranged from "he made of course many speeches, but none added anything to what was already known," to "The speeches . . . were appallingly unlike himself. His mind had suddenly fallen dumb."

Recent biographers have echoed the same theme. A former commissioner of education pontificated, "He spoke mainly in platitudes . . . he gave little sign of the man he had been or was to be." A scholar who penned the finest single volume biography said the journey speeches too often sounded trite, and that "Lincoln seemed evasive and uncertain of himself." A widely-known historian opined that the addresses were among the worst of Lincoln's career, maintaining "he was determined not to say anything that might be construed as a declaration of policy, so he spoke only a few banal words."

The most provocative opinion uttered by a living Lincoln commentator encompassed journey and speeches in one scathing swoop, to wit: "The triumphal progression from Springfield to Washington was a travesty, a fortnight of tense anxiety masked by levity and noisy orations, by cautious commonplace speech-making, the so-popular routine of measuring contests, the ordeal of social amenities, the incessant handshaking, and finally the nightmarish climax."

On the other side of the picture were those eulogists who could find no wrong with Lincoln. Among these were Lincoln's secretaries, Nicolay and Hay, who produced the monumental biography that is basic Lincolniana. Robert Lincoln threw open his father's papers to them on the condition that he see their manuscript. Despite their natural bias, their estimate of the journey is fair. They said, "Lincoln doubtless felt it would not only be a gracious act to accept as far as he could these invitations in which all parties had freely joined, and that both the people and their Chief Executive would be strengthened in their faith and patriotism by closer acquaintance."

Had Lincoln ever discussed his extended excursion, he would have settled the matter. He never did. With the exception of his acceptance letters to speaking invitations, no writings have been found that reveal his thinking or planning on this extraordinary event.

The most illuminating account, an on-the-spot report that can be accepted as authoritative, came from Henry Villard who had reported the Lincoln-Douglas debates for the *New York Staats-Zeitung*. On the strength of that experience he got himself assigned to Springfield for four months preceding the inauguration. Villard knew pretty well what was going on and enjoyed the confidence of Lincoln. On January 19, he reported:

"It was but yesterday that I had occasion to converse with Mr. Lincoln on the subject of his impending trip to Washington City. He stated that he had not as yet fixed the day of his departure nor selected the route, but that the former would probably take place on or about the 15th proximo.

"As to the latter, I think Mr. Lincoln's preferences are for a southerly route via Cincinnati, Wheeling and Baltimore, doubtless to demonstrate how little fear he entertains for his personal safety. But there is great pressure brought to bear on him in favor of a more northerly one via Pittsburgh and Harrisburg, and it is most likely that this will be ultimately detemined upon. . . .

"He knows those who elected him are anxious to see how he looks and hence is willing to gratify this, their excusable curiosity."

As to the speeches themselves—well, comparing Lincoln's major journey speeches with his Inaugural Address and with the Chicago party platform on which he was elected, provides a conclusion that is self-evident and inescapable. They are all tied together. The journey speeches form a bridge between them, the connecting link between party promise and administration policy.

A practical politician would say that Lincoln's journey speeches should have been exactly what they were.

In his letter accepting the presidential nomination, Lincoln had written: "The declaration of principles and sentiments which accompanies your letter [the Chicago platform] meets my approval, *it shall be my care not to violate it in any part.*" Nominated and elected on specific political objectives, Lincoln acknowledged them and adhered to them. He was Honest Abe.

Something of this was sensed by the *Cincinnati Commercial's* correspondent when Lincoln spoke in Columbus, and he observed astutely, "There was something Delphic in Lincoln's extempore speech in the Hall of the House. . . . But this may be speculative," he reflected.

[139]

"I remark here that the public ought not to be disappointed if Mr. Lincoln does not say anything in his reception speeches, since it is not reasonable to suppose he will expose his policy by driblets. . . ."

But that was exactly what Lincoln was doing. He *was* exposing his policies by driblets in the journey speeches. The keen reporter could not bring himself to say so because he feared it might not be true. That Lincoln was revealing his administration program bit by bit does not mean he labeled it as such. He gave not the slightest inkling that what he was saying would become official policy. That was good statesmanship.

This intrinsic evidence, the subject matter of the speeches, demonstrated their purpose in Lincoln's program. The fact is: Lincoln had prepared the journey speeches before he left Springfield. He did this as Thomas D. Jones, the Ohio sculptor, modeled a clay bust of him. The subsequent statue chiseled in Italian marble stands today in the rotunda of the Capitol at Columbus, at the head of the stairway where Lincoln shook hands with the multitude. His notes are preserved in the Library of Congress, manuscript division, and can be viewed by the general public in conformance with the Library's regulations.

For an hour each weekday, Lincoln sat in Jones's studio, a room in the St. Nicholas Hotel. A copy of his published speeches beside him for reference and a small portfolio on his knees, he wrote his notes on blue-ruled notepaper while the sculptor worked. When he had completed a composition, Jones related, "he would modestly read it to me." The sittings continued until the Saturday before the journey.

At the same time that he was fashioning the journey speeches in Jones's hotel studio, he was composing the

Inaugural Address in a dusty room over the store on the square belonging to C. M. Smith, his brother-in-law. Many persons knew he was working on the Inaugural Address as it was reported in the press, but only sculptor Jones seemed to have been privy to the writing of the journey speeches.

Didn't Villard know? On January 29 he sent a dispatch on the preparation of the Inaugural Address, "Knowing his present anxiety for privacy I certainly would not reveal his places of retreat. . . . One of his secret haunts," he went on to reveal, "is the studio of Mr. T. D. Jones, the Cincinnati sculptor, whither he repairs every morning, not for sittings, but to open and read his morning mail."

Was Villard covering up for Lincoln? Or did Lincoln cover his own tracks by allowing it to become known that he went there to read his mail? He did that also, the sculptor related. Villard never mentioned the preparation of the journey speeches until they were being delivered. His dispatch from Indianapolis the first day said the speech had been written in Springfield and carried along in manuscript. He reported also from Cincinnati and Pittsburgh that those speeches, too, were in manuscript.

How many journey speeches Lincoln wrote out or made notes for, never will be known. The miracle is that any at all have been preserved, evidence of the careful preparation he made for the journey.

Can it be said of Lincoln, who had made of himself in the first fifty-two years of his life a competent attorney and public servant, and who became one of the nation's greatest Presidents, that during his trip to Washington he was stupid, evasive, ill-informed and a purveyor of platitudes? Did this man who had, by the force of his character, lifted himself from a penniless backwoodsman

and uneducated flatboatman to state legislator, congressman, popular orator and party leader, suddenly, on his
way to enter the highest position in the land, grow dumb
and uncertain?

A British biographer answered these questions when
presenting to fellow Englishmen a thorough study of the
Sixteenth President. Godfrey Rathbone Benson, the first
Baron Charnwood, said of Lincoln's journey speeches
that "the intention of these much-criticised utterances
was the best proof of his statesmanship. He would appeal
to the steady loyalty of the North, but he was not going
to arouse its passion. He assumed to the last that calm
reflection might prevail in the South, which was menaced
by nothing but an 'artificial crisis.' He referred to war as
a possibility, but left no doubt of his own wish by all
means to avoid it."

Lord Charnwood observed that Lincoln was "mis-
understood and under-rated in his lifetime, and even yet
has hardly come into his own. For his place is among the
great men of the earth."

CHAPTER 15

THE earliest departure of the entire trip had been set for Monday morning at six o'clock. But the New York Central's division superintendent suggested stepping-up the hour still earlier in order to beat the crowd and avoid a repetition of Saturday's crush. Everyone approved. So the Lincoln party had to rise in the cold darkness of a winter morning to meet the new schedule.

Ubiquitous Company D, not to be daunted, appeared at the American House at four-thirty, the Union cornet band showed up shortly thereafter, as did a detail of local police. Downtown Buffalo was awakened at the unseemly hour of five-thirty on snowy and blowy February 18, 1861. A blast of patriotic tunes paraded the new President to the central depot. At Main and Swan streets firemen, attending the wake of the Townsend block that had burned out in the night, jumped into formation at the sound of bugles and drums. They saluted, then cheered along with a crowd of fire buffs.

Notwithstanding the hour and uncomfortable weather, several hundred hardy admirers were on hand to shout farewell. The Presidential Special took off as quickly as the party could be gotten aboard. Of the two-coach-and-baggage train, the last coach was a special sleeping car built for the occasion by Eaton and Gilbert, car builders of Troy. It incorporated a new system of ventilation in the ceiling, provided the most modern comforts, and was occupied by Lincoln, his family and suite.

The Special was under the command of John Corning, brother of the president of the New York Central. The locomotive was named *Dean Richmond,* for the road's vice-president. The face of its big kerosene headlight was covered with a lithograph of Lincoln. Sides of the lamp carried lithos of Richmond, much to the amusement of onlookers, for he was state chairman of the Democrats. Thus Lincoln, who had started the journey behind an engine named for a Southern cotton planter and secessionist, was now being pulled by one named for an opposition party official.

The single passenger coach was stuffed with the big Rochester delegation, and with delegations from Syracuse, Utica, the governor's escort, Buffalo's escort committee, local committees of other towns, the working press—and Horace Greeley. Greeley's dispatch in his *New York Tribune,* he modestly by-lined, "From Our Special Correspondent."

"The power of Mr. Lincoln," Greeley wrote, "is not in his presence or in his speech but in the honesty and gloriously refreshing sincerity of the MAN. . . . There is no guile in him, but he has not the weakness which is often the characteristic of what Yankees call cleverness. . . . His passage through the country has been like the return of grateful sunshine after a stormy winter day. The people breathe more freely and hope revives in all hearts."

Also aboard the train was E. C. Fellows, superintendent of the railroad's telegraph department. At that time

[144]

Timetable of the Presidential Special
February 18, 1861

Leave	Buffalo	5.48 A.M.	(Distance)
Arrive	Batavia	6.40	36½ miles
Leave	Batavia	6.45	
Passed	Byron	6.57	44½ miles
Passed	Bergen	7.09	51½ "
Arrive	Rochester	7.35	69 "
Leave	Rochester	7.40	
Passed	Fairport	7.52	79 miles
Passed	Palmyra	8.16	91¾ "
Passed	Newark	8.26	99 "
Passed	Lyons	8.35	104½ "
Arrive	Clyde	8.44	111¾ "
Leave	Clyde	8.49	
Passed	Port Byron	9.11	125¼ miles
Passed	Jordan	9.22	132¼ "
Arrive	Syracuse	9.52	149¾ "
Leave	Syracuse	10.05	
Passed	Chitenango	10.25	164¼ miles
Passed	Oneida	10.37	175½ "
Passed	Rome	10.54	188¼ "
Arrive	Utica	11.15	202¾ "
Leave	Utica	11.34	
Passed	Herkimer	11.55	216¼ miles
Arrive	Little Falls	12.05 P.M.	222¾ "
Passed	St. Johnsville	12.21	233¾ "
Passed	Palatine Bridge	12.44	242½ "
Passed	Fonda	1.05	254 "
Passed	Amsterdam	1.21	264¾ "
Arrive	Schenectady	1.50	280¾ "
Leave	Schenectady	1.55	
Arrive	Albany	2.20 P.M.	296¾ miles

Buffalo was the eastern terminus of the Western Union telegraph lines. It was also western terminus of the Central Railroad which ran east only to Albany. Mr. Fellows took over telegraphic responsibilities and turned in a most creditable job.

Commenting on the day's journey, the *Albany Journal* praised the railroad personnel, saying, "Within the past 24 hours every rail on the down track for the entire 298 miles has been sounded by hammer by hand-car parties." Of the management, the paper revealed they had arranged schedules of regular trains so that when the Special passed them, each locomotive had been detached, fired up, and located so as to be instantly ready in case of emergency. Trains and stations were in constant telegraphic communication, movements of the Special were marked to the second.

"Such achievements our railroading age has become accustomed to, and yet they are nonetheless marvelous," concluded the *Journal*.

Gray as was the dawn and deep as was the drifted snow, there had gathered at Batavia a sizeable crowd which greeted the President-elect with cheers and cannonades. Lincoln replied to their calls for a speech that he did not appear before them or the country as a talker, nor did he desire to obtain a reputation as such. He thanked them for their kind attention by rising at so inconvenient an hour and bade them an affectionate farewell.

The train sped across a white countryside dotted with farmhouses and villages where people waved hats and flags and lanterns. Suddenly a sharp odor of burning wood and oil permeated the speeding cars, and the train came to an abrupt halt at the hamlet of West Bergen. An axle-box on the forward coach had become overheated. Ten minutes were lost letting the "hot-box" cool off.

Rochester did not get to hear Lincoln as had been planned. Largely because of arrangements made and unmade, the majority of people waited for Lincoln at the wrong place.

The Waverly Hotel balcony had been selected by municipal and citizen committees for Lincoln to speak from. The railroad's division superintendent decided it was not feasible to move Lincoln safely within the allotted time from train to hotel and back again, especially through densely-packed streets. He so advised the committees, and a new program was announced in that morning's newspaper. Not enough people read the morning paper, said the evening rival smugly.

The Special halted just far enough inside the Rochester depot to permit the rear car to protrude into Mill Street. Lincoln appeared with the mayor on the rear platform. Noticing the immense crowd that packed all the streets, Lincoln began his remarks by saying: "I must confess myself overwhelmed, after having seen large audiences since leaving home, with the vast number of faces at this hour of the morning . . ."

The crowd stood quietly because they expected Lincoln to appear on the hotel balcony. When the three-car train moved out, they thought it was a pilot train. Disgruntled Rochesterians blamed the situation on the railroad. The *Rochester Express* reported that the railroad had provided a special car for the delegation to Buffalo and passed it over the line free of charge, commenting, "the Central railroad company and its officers are always generous to the people and authorities of this city."

As the Special rolled out of the decorated station, a small boy clambered up the back platform and said cheerily, "How do you do, Mr. Lincoln!" The tall man with the new beard reached down, shook the little fellow's hand, and in the manner of thoughtful fathers everywhere, admonished him not to get hurt.

A damp snow had fallen, adding to the Saturday storm that had blown into drifts several feet deep. "Sleighing is tolerable," said the weather reports. The Erie Canal had been frozen for months. From cleared surfaces occasional skaters waved at the passing train.

The next halt was at the important canal port of Clyde. All boats being iced in, the population turned out *en masse*. The editor of the local paper pushed up to the platform and told Lincoln he had been deputied by the people to shake hands, then distribute the handshake in tomorrow's edition. Saying it was a fine idea, Lincoln shook hands heartily.

While this was going on an enterprising artist set up a camera on a convenient woodpile and took pictures, reported the *New York Times* and the *Buffalo Express*. The *Times* said he got "pictures of the rear end of the car, of Mr. Lincoln, Mr. Wood, a brakeman and an unlucky reporter." (The last no doubt referred to the *Times* man himself.) The *Express* said the artist secured "pictures of the rear end of the car, of Mr. Lincoln, Mr. Wood and others."*

There was an interval of an hour after leaving Clyde before reaching Syracuse. The President-elect availed himself of the time and a sleeping compartment to get some rest. What was happening to Mrs. Lincoln and the younger boys is not related. Robert was riding the locomotive as assistant engineer. Whether the family had breakfasted before leaving Buffalo is not reported. In

*To the author's knowledge this Lincoln photograph has never come to light. The ONLY photograph of Lincoln taken during the journey that can be located is the one at the Philadelphia flag-raising ceremony. Any information about the Clyde pictures should be addressed to the author in care of the publisher.

those days there were no dining cars. Until the 1890's, train travelers were fed at "meal stops" which flourished in all parts of the country.

Food was put aboard at Syracuse, a bountiful lunch prepared under the direction of Dean Richmond (who joined the train at Syracuse), and consisted of various dishes including chicken, turkey, bread and cake, handed around by waiters. The "entertainment" was a distinct success, according to the report.

Syracuse's welcoming assemblage totaled ten thousand people. An elevated platform draped in national colors was set up in front of the Globe Hotel on Salina Street. On it waited the reception committee and, of all things, a live eagle. Lincoln told Syracuseans:

"I see you have erected a very fine and handsome platform here for me and I presume you expected me to speak from it. If I should go upon it you would imagine that I was about to deliver you a much longer speech than I am. I wish you to understand that I mean no discourtesy to you by thus declining. I intend discourtesy to no one. But I wish you to understand that though I am unwilling to go upon this platform, you are not at liberty to draw any inferences concerning any other platform with which my name has been or is connected." (Cheers and applause.)

Speaking platforms presented a recurring problem along the central New York sector that day. At Utica a fancy affair awaited, flag-draped, constructed atop a flat freight car. Upon it were official committees from the state, the city, and the citizens. The outfit was rolled up to the rear of the Special as it halted at the depot.

Before allowing Lincoln to go aboard, trip manager Wood inspected the arrangement carefully. He approved the structure, but ruled that individuals on the platform were not to be introduced until Lincoln had finished

[149]

speaking, so that the time at Utica should not be usurped by others. As it turned out, there was plenty of time. The train had come in ahead of schedule and had to lay over to cool off that overheated axle-box.

A heavy snow was falling. The Citizens Corps was firing the national salute. Despite the snowstorm, a huge crowd had assembled, including the senior student body of Hamilton College which had secured permission to come down from Clinton to attend the ceremony.

Lincoln stepped to the flat car and ascended the platform to be greeted by three committee chairmen. Following the mayor's introduction, he told the audience he had come out "for you to see me and for me to see you but as far as the ladies are concerned I have the best of the bargain." Shaking hands with committeemen all around he came to the north side and addressed that audience similarly. Not seeing as many ladies on this side, he added that "he did not make the same acknowledgment concerning the men" which brought hearty cheers. He re-entered his own car. The elevated affair with its cargo of committees was pulled to a side track. As the Special was about to leave Lincoln reappeared and bowed farewell.

On the trip so far, Lincoln had worn a weather-beaten "plug" hat and a thin worn-looking overcoat. Leaving Utica, Mrs. Lincoln decided something should be done about it. She gave an order to William Johnson, the Negro attendant, of whom it was said that "the untiring vigilance with which he took care of the presidential party is entitled to high credit." Presently William emerged from the baggage car carrying a handsome broadcloth overcoat and a hat box. The exchange was made, and the press reported that Lincoln's appearance improved fifty per cent thereby.

Like many people who live a great deal in their minds,

Lincoln tended to be careless about his personal appearance. He was not indifferent, however. His linen was clean —Mary made sure of that—and until he grew his beard he was always clean-shaven. He dressed in the manner of professional and businessmen of the day, a black broadcloth suit, a vest of satin in a conservative color and a buckram stock (neckcloth) covered with silk or other material. In summer he wore shoes known as the Wellington style, and in winter, boots.

His long, narrow frame made his clothes look as though they were hanging on him, and his large hands and feet contributed to the awkward ensemble. An enterprising reporter measured the calfskin boots Lincoln had set out by the hotel room door for polishing one night, and found they were exactly the length of foolscap, thirteen inches. His long shawl was regular winter attire for men those days.

Draping the shawl was an art. Ten feet in length, it was laid over the left shoulder so it dropped down the front just below the knee. The other part was draped across the back, brought over the right shoulder, thrown over the chest, and the free end put back over the left shoulder. At the point where the shawl crossed itself above the left breast, it was pinned with a large shawl pin, of ornate or expensive design. Lincoln's was plain and practical; the shawl material was a gray Scotch weave.

The new overcoat and hat may have been gifts, although this is not specifically stated. Since election Lincoln had received numerous presents. Titsworth and Brother of Chicago had sent a complete suit of clothes to be worn on Inauguration Day. They were put on display in a Springfield store window.

The oddest gift was a whistle made of a pig's tail, the donor a prominent Ohioan. After practicing on this masterpiece of human ingenuity, Lincoln declared he never suspected "there was music in such a thing as that." Little Taddie inherited the instrument.

Samuel Alschuler of Chicago sent handsomely-framed portraits of Lincoln and Hamlin. Abraham Kohn, Chicago's city clerk, painted a watercolor of the American flag inscribed with Biblical references in Hebrew. Daniel Ullman of New York presented a bronze medal of Henry Clay, the great Whig leader. A Californian forwarded a gold-headed rosewood cane. The workmen of a Cleveland rolling mill gave him a model T-rail, that structural shape being new in those days. Mrs. Lincoln was presented with an ornamented sewing machine. Other tokens of appreciation appeared on the trip, fruit and flowers predominating.

The next stopping place, Little Falls, made the prettiest picture of the entire excursion. Here in the picturesque valley of the Mohawk, the frozen canal and river, the encircling hills, the warmly-lighted homes and buildings, were covered with a light blanket of snow. The brightly-colored train rolled into the storybook village as church bells pealed a welcome on the frosty air. On the hotel veranda a group of ladies applauded Lincoln's pleasant remarks, and waved their kerchiefs to the tune of "Hail, Columbia!" as the train wound its way down the valley. The colorful scene must have looked like a picture post card.

At the next halt, Fonda, Lincoln was again offered a platform on which to stand. He told the hearty crowd that although he would not get upon the structure, he wished it to be understood that he would never shrink from the one upon which he properly belonged. At Amsterdam and Schenectady next in order, record crowds welcomed him. Entering Schenectady, the train was fired

The only known photograph of Lincoln on the inaugural journey was taken in front of Independence Hall at sunrise on February 22, 1861. The Philadelphia photographer, F. D. Richards, took several views. The one above shows the President-elect most plainly. Towering above the others, he can be easily identified. Slightly to his left stands the Reverend Henry S. Clarke (white bib), who is uttering a prayer. Note that Lincoln and the others on the platform stand uncovered.

Under his right arm, Lincoln is clutching the folded flag that he will raise to the top of the Hall's flagstaff. It was the first one with thirty-four stars to go up there.

A guard of honor, facing the platform, wearing white Sam Browne belts and white gun slings, is made up of veterans of the Mexican War from Scott's Legion.

This is credited with being the first photograph ever to show a President-elect or President speaking to an audience.

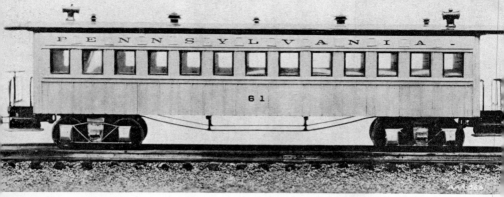

Pennsylvania Railroad

The early type of coach such as carried Lincoln on the first leg of his inaugural journey. For some twenty-five years it was the common passenger carrier. It had from twelve to twenty transverse, double, reversible-back seats upholstered in plush or straw matting, and at either end of the car were lengthwise seats or sofas. A single stove often completed the equipment. Night lighting was by candles held in sockets, or whale-oil lamps. A good photograph of this type of coach is so rare the Pennsylvania Railroad had the above wash drawing made.

New York Central Lines

The locomotive *Dean Richmond* headed the Lincoln train on the first of the three laps over the New York Central Railroad from Buffalo to Rochester. Note the lithographed portrait of Richmond on the side of the big kerosene headlight. He was vice-president of the railroad. The front of the lamp carried a campaign poster of the President-elect.

Four years later this same engine pulled the Lincoln Special in the opposite direction.

on directly by saluting cannon which burst open a door of the forward coach and broke windows. No one was injured. Introduced at Schenectady by Judge Platt Potter of the New York Supreme Court, Lincoln repeated his Fonda remarks, for here again he was confronted with a platform. The noise of the reception prompted the local paper to say, "We were able only to obtain a few disjointed sentences of what the President-elect said."

On the heights above Albany, watchers signaled the approach of the Special to waiting artillery, and the thunder of cannon announced its arrival in the capital city of the Empire State. The gaily-festooned locomotive, *Erastus Corning, Jr.,* which had taken over at Syracuse, added to the din by shrieking its way through the multitude that blocked the Broadway street crossing. At the crossing, a platform had been built between and alongside the rails. Here the train stopped.

And here it waited. From the rear platform manager Wood looked over a concourse of people cheering, shouting, and yelping for Lincoln. The wait offered a fine opportunity for crowd and police to demonstrate their relative muscular prowess in a contest for possession of the track-level platform. The mob pushed. The policemen pushed back. The mob carried the police forward. The police transformed themselves into human levers, planting their feet on the rails, their heads against the mob, jacking the mass of humanity back into place. The general battle was enlivened by personal spats between bluecoats and individualists. All was confusion, commotion and mud.

The object of the commotion wisely stayed put in his car.

Finally, Albany's intrepid mayor, George H. Thacher, showed up on foot. He had tired of waiting for the military escort. Hearing the racket he slogged over from his office. Jostled and bumped around like any spectator, he pushed up to the train platform and asked Wood, "How about getting started?" Wood answered he wouldn't budge until reinforcements arrived. Crowd and police continued their gymnastics. Minutes ticked by.

From one end of the state to the other daily papers had been full of controversy for a week. The governor, Edwin D. Morgan, wanted to dine Lincoln at the executive mansion and select the guests. The legislative committee objected. They wanted Lincoln for a banquet with their own guests. The argument dragged on until, in the interest of public harmony, the governor was conceded his dinner with Lincoln.

Then commenced a struggle between senators and assemblymen as to which body and, of the selected committees, who would be first to welcome the distinguished visitor. Debate waxed long and acrimonious, dragging in all manner of political dead cats. It was still going on that forenoon when guests began to arrive in the assembly chamber.

Meanwhile, back at the Broadway crossing, a good half hour went by before Company B, Twenty-fifth Infantry Regiment, finally marched up, accompanied by a band, a barouche and extra carriages. The military at once joined their blue-coated colleagues in opening a space on the platform about ten by six feet in area. Into this trap stepped Lincoln and Thacher, greeting each other in brief speeches, then climbing into the waiting carriages.

Along jam-packed Broadway the procession moved, band blaring "Hail to the Chief," turning at State Street to go up the steep grade to the Capitol.

A resident of New York State ought to write a book telling all about what happened to Lincoln in Albany.

Someone should reveal that the struggle between the governor and the legislative committee started because Governor Morgan wanted Lincoln alone so that he might find out if Lincoln were going to compromise or if there would be war. He could then confidentially advise his cousin and partner in the brokerage business whether to sell or to hold their supply of Missouri bonds. Energetic Ed Morgan was born on a Massachusetts farm, and became governor, United States Senator, a founder of the famed banking house of Morgan. The story would show that, whether New England farm boy or Kentucky backwoodsman, America offered equal opportunity to all; the land where, as Lincoln said, "Every man can make himself."

CHAPTER 16

O<small>N</small> this day, Monday, February 18, 1861, the nation was formally divided into federal and confederate states, and the American people began to be ruled by two separate national governments.

The extraordinary event was chronicled by the press in parallel columns. One column told of Lincoln in Albany. Alongside, ran the account of the Montgomery inauguration. Proclaimed Jefferson Davis: "We must prepare to meet the emergency and maintain by final arbitrament of the sword the position which we have assumed among the nations of the earth."

Lincoln pleaded: "If we have patience, if we restrain ourselves, if we allow ourselves not to run off in a passion, I still have confidence. . . ."

The contrast between the two addresses inspired editorial comment. A New York journal declared, "Mr. Davis' idea is to fight . . . to baptize his principles in blood. . . . He talks of fighting with entire impunity and without a breath of censure," and said this could not be reconciled with the fact that when Lincoln asked questions at Indianapolis, a torrent of execution had been showered upon him.

"There is something very curious in the reception which these two men meet with," continued the editorial. "The President-elect is bound by his oath to execute the laws of the land but he must not hint of such, whereas entire tolerance is extended to threats of resistance by parties who are openly rebellious."

But in the end it was Davis who complained. In his subsequent apologia, "The Rise and Fall of the Confederate Government," he charged that Northern newspapers twisted his speeches into warmongering. He cited in rebuttal his farewell remarks to the United States Senate and his Inaugural Address. The latter, a curious blending of propriety and insincerity, contained such statements as "mutual interest will invite good will and kind offices on both parts," which were nullified by his haughty "arbitrament of the sword" challenges.

Davis further revealed his intransigent attitude by declaring, "I was not one of those who believed there ever could be peaceful separation of the States." And again, "I knew secession meant war."

If these were not warlike statements, nothing could be. They also contravened the basic purpose of secession, which was peaceful separation. Secession was claimed by its proponents to be an inherent right of a sovereign state. That secession was the remedy for any evil that might arise in the government was stoutly denied by "Parson" Brownlow in that famous *Knoxville Whig* editorial: "The right of Revolution I admit," wrote Brownlow, "but I deny such remedy is called for in the present crisis of our affairs."

Lincoln would stress this point in his Inaugural Address. He would say: "This country, with its institutions, belongs to the people who inhabit it. Whenever they shall grow weary of the existing government they can exercise their constitutional right of amending it, or their revolutionary right to dismember or overthrow it."

Revolt meant forceful change. Revolution carried the factor of violence while secession could be construed as peaceful change. Circumstances in 1860 did not warrant a drastic course. Secession was a *political* maneuver; a maneuver of which the South Carolina politician, John C. Calhoun, long had preached. Moreover, if peaceful separation via secession was not successful, resort could always be made to force. Indeed, the secession maneuver might compel the established government into violent action. The crisis thus became exactly what Lincoln said it was, "gotten up by turbulent men aided by designing politicians."

As to Davis's parting remarks to the Senate, they must be weighed against his actions. Mississippi seceded January 9. Davis did not voice his Senate farewell until the twenty-first, and he lingered in Washington until the twenty-fifth. Most congressmen left for home when they learned of their state's seceding, as was proper. Davis said that he was waiting for "official" notice from his state, meanwhile doing what he could in Washington to "avert the impending calamity." What he was doing was indicated by his wire to Governor John J. Pettus: "Judge what Mississippi requires of me and place me accordingly."

When Davis did reach his state capital he found Pettus had placed him in the position he most desired, namely, major general in command of the Republic of Mississippi military affairs. He at once held military conferences and said that a seventy-five thousand stand of arms was needed. The governor demurred. Davis replied that the limit to the number of arms purchased should be only the ability of the state to pay. A special tax increase of fifty per cent

[158]

on real and personal property was imposed for "defense" purposes.

After a week of making military preparations, the new general returned to his cotton plantation, "Brierfield," which had been given him by his elder brother Joseph on the occasion of his first marriage in 1835. He had been developing the land with Negro slaves. The following Sunday afternoon, February 10, in a garden blooming with violets and camellias, while he was helping his wife Varina with her prized rose bushes, a messenger on horseback galloped up and handed him a telegram.

Montgomery, Alabama, February 9, 1861.

Hon. Jefferson Davis,
Jackson, Miss.

Sir:

> We are directed to inform you that you are this day unanimously elected President of the Provisional Government of the Confederate States of America,* and to request you to come to Montgomery immediately. We send also a special messenger. Do not wait for him.

R. Toombs, R. Barnwell Rhett, Jackson Morton.

Davis was disappointed. He wanted to be commander-in-chief of the confederate armies. He had dropped hints to that effect, and friends had assured him of the place. Before leaving Washington he had received confirmation from Governor Francis W. Pickens of South Carolina, who wrote him that "as soon as the states meet in Montgomery they should elect a commander-in-chief. . . . Allow me to say I think you are the proper man to be selected at this juncture."

---

* Davis was "unanimously elected" president by a total of thirty-eight delegates representing six cotton states. The organizing convention at Montgomery was composed of that many delegates, ranging from three for Florida to ten for Georgia, all appointed by their respective state legislatures. The people of the South had no voice in the proceedings. Politicians in power organized the confederate government.

On assuming the confederate presidency, Davis, professional soldier and war veteran, took upon himself active command of the confederate armies. He would run out to battlefields, intrude himself into military affairs and administrative details and, worst of all, keep in command incompetent West Point classmates he should have booted into obscurity. An able man, Davis failed to see that he should devote his limited energies to building up the new nation-state he had helped to create. In this, his prime task, he fell down completely.

The consequence of his myopic autocratic rule was that the second confederate congress (1863) was almost entirely against him. He had lost the confidence of his own people. He antagonized his cabinet and changed members frequently. The vice-president, Alexander H. Stephens (Little Alec) quit in disgust and went back to Georgia muttering that Davis was a "humbug." Davis's personal tragedy was that he could not manage men; and he would not let others manage him. He felt his greatness was so apparent that when anyone disagreed with him he was personally insulted. He had little political skill, in contrast to his opposite number in the White House. Only when the confederate cause was about to go under in 1865 would he appoint a chief of the armies with full power over the gray soldiers, and then only because of insistent public demand. He appointed that great Virginian, Robert E. Lee, who would become America's greatest military hero.

Next morning at the Davis plantation the bell tolled, bringing the slaves to the big house to receive the master's farewell. Then Davis set out in a rowboat oared by a young slave, Isaiah Montgomery, to reach a nearby landing from which he would catch the New Orleans-Vicksburg steamboat. The *Natchez*, Captain Tom Leathers commanding, picked him up in mid-river.

Thirty-five miles upstream a great crowd waited at Vicksburg, saluting with cannon and musketry as the boat hauled in, greeting their distinguished neighbor with an array of civic and military pomp. To the mayor's welcome Davis replied briefly while the afternoon train was being held for him. In this, his first speech to the public as president-appointee, he alluded to bloodshed.

"I hope our separation may be peaceful," said Davis. "But whether it be so or not, I am ready as I always have been ready to redeem my pledges to you and to the South by shedding every drop of my blood in your cause."

At Jackson that evening, a tremendous demonstration greeted him. Borne in the procession and surrounded by former comrades was the tattered flag of the Mississippi Rifles, the regiment he had commanded in the Mexican fracas. "When the warrior-president stepped from the cars," read outgoing dispatches, "he was welcomed by loud, long cheers mingled with the rattle of musketry."

Escorted to the House of Representatives and introduced by the governor, Davis held his packed audience spellbound for half an hour, reviewing the secession cause.

"It may be that we will be confronted with war; that the attempt will be made to blockade our ports, to starve us out. But they know little of the Southern heart—of Southern endurance. No amount of privations could force us to remain in a Union on unequal terms.

"England and France will not allow our great staple [cotton] to be dammed up within our limits. The starving thousands in their midst will not allow it. We have nothing to apprehend from blockade; but if they attempt invasion by land, we must take the war out of our territory.

"The land fighting shall be upon Northern soil and not upon Southern. If they provoke the contest we must carry it into their midst and make them support the contending armies and endure the evils of civil war."

The next day he was at the governor's office resigning his commission as major general, conferring with the other generals on military preparations. A wire from Montgomery requested his immediate presence there. At 5:43 P.M. on the afternoon of February 13 he boarded the New Orleans, Jackson and Great Northern passenger train going north. He was accompanied by Ethelbert Barksdale, editor of the Jackson newspaper, *The Mississippian,* and C. R. Dickson, the Jackson postmaster.

Montgomery, Alabama, his destination, was only 250 miles due east of Jackson. But no railroad connected the two, and to go direct would have meant a series of short hauls by way of stagecoach, steamboat and railroad. Davis chose to go around three sides of a square, all by rail, which totaled 800 miles. Perhaps he saw in the circuitous itinerary an opportunity to rival the Lincoln expedition then being reported in newspapers all over the land.

At Canton, he dined and changed to the Mississippi Central line. All night long he made speeches and greeted crowds. Since no sleeping car was available a cot was set up for him upon which he reclined fully dressed. North through Vaughan, Winona, Grenada, Oxford and Holly Springs, he reached Grand Junction, Tennessee, fifty-two miles east of Memphis, at 9:45 A.M. Here the Memphis and Charleston Railroad carried him eastward, dipping back into Mississippi and through Corinth and Iuka; then through the Alabama towns of Tuscumbia, Decatur, and Huntsville to Stevenson.

Jefferson Davis arrived at Stevenson, Alabama, at 10:00 P.M., February 15, en route to Montgomery. He was saluted with guns and fireworks and the houses were illumined. In his speech he said, "You Border states will gladly come into the Southern Confederacy within sixty days as we will be your only friends. . . ." He said he hoped for peace but was prepared for war.

The *Nashville Banner* wanted to know if Davis had forgotten what he had said at the public dinner given to himself at Vicksburg about the gallant Tennessee regiment at Monterrey. If he had, the people of Tennessee had not. He had said that "we did not have so many reported killed or wounded as others, the reason being we were so far in advance that the enemy's shot, aimed at the body of the army, passed over our heads" "No sir!" exploded the *Banner,* "We Border states never will 'gladly' come into the Southern Confederacy!"

Writing to his wife a few days later, Davis told her that "all along the route, except when in Tennessee, the people at every station manifested goodwill and approbation by bonfires at night and firing by day; shouts and salutations at both."

A hiatus occurred over the Nashville and Chattanooga line between Stevenson and Chattanooga. Press reports said there were heavy floods and that trains were delayed because of washouts, a likely cause since the railroad here ran alongside the Tennessee River. The upshot was that Davis missed his connection at Chattanooga for Atlanta and had to wait for the evening train.

Again it was an all-night up-and-down affair, leaving Chattanooga at 6:30 P.M. on the Western and Atlantic, the railroad owned by the state of Georgia. Through a countryside soon to be consecrated by the sacrifice of men in blue and gray, through towns and hamlets that would witness brave deeds, Ringgold, Dalton, Resaca, Kingston, Big Shanty, Allatoona and Marietta, Davis reached Atlanta at dawn. He went at once to the Trout House across from the depot.

At 7:30 A.M. a "national" salute of seven guns by the Atlanta grays announced the presence of the president-appointee. While a procession was forming he held a reception in the hotel parlors. Atlanta wanted to see him.

At nine o'clock the mayor introduced him from the hotel veranda. The crowd waiting in the cold rain saw a man of medium height, weight about a hundred and fifty pounds, clad in a full suit of blue-gray, apparently home-made but fitting perfectly, hair of light color, mouth well cut, chin decisive, features sharp and well defined, and a thin, bold nose coupled with a high but deep forehead.

"His features in calm repose, he seems not the man for the occasion," asserted the *Charleston Mercury*. "But hark! he speaks, and like trumpet notes ring the words, 'Georgians and Fellow-citizens!' The windows of his soul are opened and forth from his eyes flash the power to light up his placid and stern features, and his sonorous voice penetrates where the flash of his eyes cannot reach, stirs the blood of his listeners. . . ."

He spoke of the South's glorious future, that posterity should see a great nation, homogenous in nature, stretching from the Atlantic to the Pacific, with northern portions of Mexico forming a part of the broad domain. He desired peace with Northern people, but if needs be war he was willing to meet the issue and would "provide our foes with bloody graves ere their hostile steps should pollute our soil."

The time for departure at hand, the honor guard of firemen and military faced inwards, forming a passage from hotel to depot through which Davis was escorted to the train. It was 10:10 A.M. as the Atlanta and West Point cars carrying Davis moved toward Montgomery.

Montgomery newspapers reported, on February 17, that the president of the confederate states arrived there from his home in Mississippi. His long trip had been one continuous ovation. At twenty-four different places along his route he had been called out and made speeches in return for complimentary greetings. At various depots, salutes were fired by local military companies. The committee of congress and the Montgomery authorities met the president about eighty miles off and formally received him. Two fine military companies from Columbus, Georgia, joined the escort at Opelika. They all reached Montgomery at ten o'clock the night before amid shouts from the enthusiastic populace and firing of cannon. A large crowd assembled at the depot called upon the new president to speak.

To the depot audience Davis proceeded to vent his most warlike sentiments: "The time for compromise has passed!" he declaimed to the hurrahs of his hearers. "Our only hope is in a determined maintenance of our position, and to make all who oppose smell Southern powder and feel Southern steel! We will maintain our rights of government at all hazards. We ask nothing, want nothing, will have no complications. . . . Our separation from the old Union is complete. No compromise, no reconsideration can now be entertained."

He and his enlarged entourage proceeded up to the Exchange Hotel. Here he appeared on the balcony and again rattled the sword.

"It may be our career will be ushered in in the midst of storm . . . we shall show that Southern valor still shines as brightly as in 1776, in 1812, and in every other conflict. If, in the progress of events, necessity shall require that I again enter the ranks as a soldier, I hope you will welcome me there."

Then followed William L. Yancey, the bell-tongued voice of secession, who had secretly hoped to be in Davis's place as president. He now lauded Davis—"the soldier distinguished upon the field of battle, wise in council, terrible in the charge. . . . The man and the hour have met!"

So came Monday, fateful February 18. Davis took the oath of office on the front porch of the Alabama Capitol at about the same moment that Lincoln was speaking at Fonda, New York. Davis read his inaugural address avowing that "our present position has been achieved in a manner unprecedented in the history of the nation."

Then followed the signing of the confederate constitution, an imitation of the federal document with a few minor changes and written up in five days by vice-president Stephens. A grand ball was held in the evening at Estelle Hall, complete with fireworks, booming cannon, dancing and general jubilation. The Confederate States of America was in business.

Unprecedented? Davis was right. Never had the world witnessed so smooth, so speedy, so complete, a change of government affecting so many people. In the seven weeks after South Carolina had pulled away, federal forts in seven cotton states (except Ft. Pickens at Pensacola and Ft. Sumter at Charleston) were taken. So had other federal property been seized, except post offices which went undisturbed for the sake of convenience.

Two weeks after the six seceding states opened their Montgomery convention on February 4, Davis was inaugurated confederate president. On the third day, the provisional government had been formed: the oath of allegiance was taken on the fifth day; the president and vice-president were appointed on the ninth day. Committees were selected while Davis was en route, to organize an army and navy, and to impose taxes. By a stroke of the pen on the hurried-up confederate inauguration day, five million Americans, slightly more than two and a half million whites and slightly less than two and a half million Negroes, were removed from the authority of their original government and taken over by a small group of self-appointed rulers.

Unprecedented? It was fantastic. Obviously, it could only have been brought about by expert organizing. No amateur job this. It had been carefully planned and deliberately timed. Writing to Davis in Washington, South Carolina's governor had advised, "We must have all the organization and form of government in full operation before March 4."

So it came to be that a fortnight before the legally-elected President of the United States could be sworn in, he was confronted by a rival "republic," a government *de facto* and *de jure*. Gloated a dispatch in the *Charleston Mercury*, "The United States of America are dissolved forever! 'Alas, poor Yorick! I knew him well!' But what a sad rogue he was!"

Now thousands of party faithful would be taken care of. There would be jobs for all. Ministers, consuls, chargés d'affaires, attaches, couriers, clerkships, to represent the confederacy around the world. At home there would be generals, colonels, captains, sergeants, and many, many privates; senators, congressmen, department heads, postmasters, mailmen, judges, bailiffs, assistants and clerks by the thousands; the whole alphabet of big and little politicians who go to make up the machinery of a national government.

The political significance of secession would not soon be recognized by the man on the street. Not until hostilities assumed a gory impasse would an awakening come to the South. Then the blueblooded Carolinian, Mrs. James Chestnut, Jr., wife of the former United States senator who became an aide to Davis, would lament in her *Diary from Dixie* that the people were saying, "New Orleans has gone and with it the Confederacy! The Confederacy has been done to death by the politicians!"

And the political oligarchy that gripped the cotton states would not be removed except by military defeat.

CHAPTER 17

AT the same time that the political partition of America was taking place, Lincoln was delivering two scheduled addresses in Albany; one to the public from the steps of the Capitol and the other to the legislature in joint session. He dined at the executive mansion with the governor *en famille* and then held two levees at the Delevan House; first a reception for the public on the main floor, followed by one for the ladies in an upstairs parlor.

This reception for the ladies had been originally scheduled for Tuesday morning, following which Lincoln was to leave for New York City. The arrangement had to be changed.

A midwinter thaw had released great masses of ice that had hurtled down the Hudson River, demolishing the State Street bridge and partly carrying away the Hamilton and Columbia Street bridges. Ice jams had piled up below the city causing overflow into the lower streets and making the ferry inoperable. Those best qualified to judge said the damage exceeded the floods of 1839 and 1857. The "freshet at Albany" worked such havoc that a new route for New York had to be found. The railroad bridge to East Albany was not built until after the war.

So it was that at 7:45 Tuesday morning, the Lincoln party, accompanied from hotel to depot across the street by the mayor and other civic dignitaries and escorted by the corps of burgesses, boarded the same cars they had used the day before. The train headed north on the Albany and Vermont Railroad. Passing through the towns of Watervliet and Cohoes, the Special crossed the Mohawk River to Waterford Junction, entered the tracks of the Rensselaer and Saratoga line and turned south to Waterford, recrossed the Mohawk River, passed again through Cohoes, and thence to Green Island. From Green Island the direction was easterly over the only railroad bridge spanning the Hudson River and into Troy on the Troy Union tracks. These roads are now part of the Delaware and Hudson Railroad.

At Cohoes Falls, Lincoln viewed the ice-gorged river from the train platform. At Waterford Junction a carload of Trojans was coupled to the train as escorts into the city. At Troy, an unexpected host, a throng of ten thousand welcomed the distinguished guest despite the short notice and early hour.

Stepping to the platform alongside the train, Lincoln spoke to the enthusiastic crowd, remarking: "Since I left my home it has not been my fortune to meet an assemblage more numerous and more orderly than this. . . ." He shook hands with all on the platform and bowed farewell, descending on the other side into the waiting cars of the Hudson River Railroad. It had been a happy arrangement.

The Presidential Special provided by the Hudson River Railroad which Lincoln now entered was headed south for the run to New York City. It was an all-new train; even the locomotive was new, appropriately named *Union*. Its twin, *Constitution*, would take over at Poughkeepsie. These two engines were reported to be the road's first coal-burners. At the throttle was William Buchanan, master mechanic at the East Albany shops.*

The special coach the railroad built in its shops expressly for the President-elect was so unlike anything ever seen that the metropolitan press gave it extended mention. Its exterior was finished in narrow perpendicular panels painted a deep orange relieved by ornamental flourishes in dark brown and black, all highly varnished. Inside, crimson plush walls were offset by blue silk panels studded with silver stars. The light tone of the tapestry carpet contrasted with black walnut furniture upholstered in blue mazarine cloth trimmed in tricolored gimp braid and tassels. Four splendid lounges, and four each of arm and reading and parlor chairs, offered luxurious comfort. An oblong table of ebony stood as a centerpiece. This handsome ensemble was enhanced by special wall decorations in national colors. The car was equipped with patented heaters and ventilators. For night illumination there were four wax candle chandeliers with cut-glass globes.

On duty along the line, as flagmen and track guards, was the entire personnel of the railroad. Stationed within signaling distance of each other, each flag section was in the charge of a foreman. Track was patrolled. Switches were spiked. A pilot engine ran ahead, the wood-burning *Young America* minced down the line by herself.

---

* William Buchanan was no relation of President James Buchanan. But he deserves notice. He was to develop and patent important interlocking devices that would form the basis for the Union Switch and Signal Company of Pittsburgh. He was to become superintendent of motive power for the merged New York Central and Hudson River lines, and would build the world's most famous passenger engine, the "999," that whisked the Empire State Express at the incredible speed of 112½ miles an hour between Batavia and Buffalo.

Timetable of Presidential Special
February 19, 1861
Hudson River Railroad Company

East Albany	Leave	10:00 A.M.
Castleton		10:16
Schodack		10:22
Stuyvesant		10:36
Coxsackie		10:41
Stockport		10:56
Hudson (stops)	Leave	11:10
Oakhill		11:12
Germantown		11:28
Tivoli		11:39
Barrytown		11:47
Rhinebeck (stops)	Leave	12:00 Noon
Staatsburg		12:10 P.M.
Hyde Park		12:18
Poughkeepsie (stops)	Arrive	12:29
	Leave	12:40
New Hamburgh		12:55
Fishkill (stops)	Leave	1:08
Cold Spring		1:20
Garrison		1:25
Peekskill	Arrive	1:41
	Leave	1:44
Sing Sing		2:02
Tarrytown		2:12
Dobbs Ferry		2:20
Yonkers		2:30
Manhattan		2:45
52nd Street		2:52
30th Street (new depot)		3:00

On board the Special were Samuel Sloan, president of the line, and D. T. Vail, vice-president. Also aboard was William Creamer, inventor of the safety braking mechanism with which the train was equipped. The telegraph department kept accurate tab on the train's movements.

It was 10:00 A.M. when the handsome Special reached Greenbush opposite Albany, only half a mile from the starting point, but separated by the gorge of ice which had necessitated the two-hour detour. Lincoln came out and shook hands with a score of ladies nearby.

At Hudson another platform was offered but Lincoln declined, saying, "You must not on this account draw the inference that I have any intention to desert any platform I have legitimate right to stand on." At Rhinebeck, William Kelley, Tammany candidate for governor in the last election and a director of the railroad, came aboard for a chat. As the Special wound along the frozen Hudson River with its frequent expanses of smooth ice, skaters with flags waved and shouted.

At Poughkeepsie a large basket of flowers, choice at any season of the year, was presented to Mrs. Lincoln. When she opened her window to return the neighborly welcome, the crowd called for the children. She had them come to her window and introduced them. Except Tad who flattened himself on the floor, face down. The more his mother persisted in trying to get him up the more he resisted. Tad won.

Meanwhile, Lincoln had come out. The crowd shouted for him to take the special platform. The train had not proceeded far enough. Evidently Buchanan had missed his cue. Since the engine had been detached, a group of husky spectators took hold of the five cars and, with a mighty heave-to, "spotted" them precisely.

Lincoln's speech reiterated the theme that, even though they could not all hear him (the long hill was dense with people), their numbers indicated that "the whole people were willing to make common cause" for the object of saving the country's institutions. When he concluded president Sloan had the two new locomotives run by the platform that he might see them.

Gaily bedecked, flags flying, name banner displayed from a bowsprit flagpole, first came the *Union* and then the *Constitution*—first coal-burning engines to head up the Presidential Special on the journey. Use of coal for locomotive fuel was as momentous a development then as atomic power is today. Coal marked a new era in railroading.

Lincoln's appraisal of the new coal-burners was more than that of a mere bystander. He appreciated their merit from his special experience as a successful railroad attorney. Of his many legal actions on behalf of railroads, two have been made widely known by biographers; not so much to show his connection with the railroad industry as to illustrate his forensic skill. One, popularly known as the Rock Island Bridge Case, attracted attention because of the basic principles involved. Lincoln's charge to the jury was reported in full, an unusual circumstance, by the *Chicago Press* on September 24, 1857.

Powerful forces had been engaged in the struggle. Mississippi River towns including St. Louis were bitterly opposed to having a bridge that would interfere with their navigating "rights" flung across the 1,932-mile navigable river. Marine interests made common cause against the bold railroad trespasser. Cutting through bitter charges and voluminous testimony, Lincoln summed up the situation in a typical sentence: "One man has as good a right to cross a river as another has to sail up or down it," he said.

So the first railroad bridge over the Mississippi River at Rock Island became a forerunner of railroad crossovers spanning navigable waterways. The case was significant also in illustrating Lincoln's stature in the legal profession. Out of all legal talent available in Chicago, in Illinois, in the nation, he, a small-town circuit-riding lawyer, had been selected to manage this highly important federal court case.

He was invited by the Rock Island Railroad's general counsel, Norman B. Judd, a shrewd judge of men and talents; this was the same Judd who later would help him get the presidential nomination and who was riding the train at this moment. Judd's invitation came, it must be noted, before Lincoln's debates with Douglas and before his famous Cooper Union speech, two events that helped catapult him into the national spotlight. Judd picked Lincoln because of his professional reputation and his ability, especially with juries.

An earlier action for a railroad by Lincoln had contributed greatly to his reputation. It has become his best known railroad suit, largely because so many writers mention it. Popularly called the "big fee" case, legally it is indexed *The Illinois Central Railroad Company v. The County of McLean and George Parke, Sheriff, et al.* After winning, Lincoln had to sue the railroad to collect his $5,000 fee which he divided with Herndon.

Some Lincoln biographies relate only this one legal action of his for a railroad, giving the impression he had no other railroad cases, making this one seem like a windfall. Other accounts imply he "soaked" the railroad.

[174]

Or that the railroad would not pay his price. All are untrue.

The case has been reviewed so often over the years, suffice it to state here that critical evaluation of available facts indicates that both Lincoln and the railroad were justified in the positions they took. The final outcome also appears to have been satisfactory to both. This is not as paradoxical as may appear. Lincoln's fee was infinitesimal compared to the many millions of dollars he saved the railroad.

Here is his own explanation of the controversy, his reply to the charge made by Douglas in the 1858 senatorial campaign that Lincoln had accepted the "people's money" in taking the big fee:

"The railroad company employed me as one of their lawyers in the case," he explained, "the county having declined to employ me. I was not on a salary and no agreement was made as to the amount of the fee. The railroad company finally gained the case. The decision, I thought, was worth half a million dollars to them. I wanted them to pay me $5,000 and they wanted to pay me about $500. I sued them and got the $5,000. This is the whole truth about the fee; and what tendency it has to prove that I received any of the people's money or that I am on cozy terms with the railroad company, I do not understand." Another court action Lincoln won for the Illinois Central, which yielded even greater savings to the railroad than the so-called "big fee" case, but which is known to few outside the legal profession, is the Charter Lines tax case; indexed, *State of Illinois v. Illinois Central Railroad Co., 27 Ill. 56, and 27 Ill. 64.* Just as the county of McLean had sought to take from the railroad its pound of tax flesh (in the "big fee" case above), so now the state reached for its full share. Through skillful handling and legal acumen, Lincoln was able to have the state's demands restrained, saving the railroad from near-bankruptcy.

His final action in court for a railroad was also for the Illinois Central. It too has become famous. *Johnson v. Jones and Marsh* is widely known as the "sand bar" case. Tried in the United States Circuit Court at Chicago, it was Lincoln's last railroad case, because in the month following its conclusion he was made presidential nominee. His final court action seems to have been in the United States Circuit Court at Springfield on June 20, 1860. A plow patent case ended his notable law career.

Lincoln's first railroad suit was on behalf of the Alton and Sangamon in 1851, which later became the Chicago and Alton and is now part of the Gulf, Mobile and Ohio system. Fairly complete records in McLean, DeWitt, and Champaign counties reveal Lincoln representing the Illinois Central in fifty court actions between April, 1853, and October, 1859. On a single day, May 16, 1854, he appeared in seven cases for the railroad in DeWitt County Court at Clinton.

Evidence has been offered to the effect that Lincoln entered into the Central's charter legislation of 1851, but the material must be regarded as dubious. There is no question, however, that in his single term as a congressman he introduced twelve memorials from constituents on the subject of the Central Railroad; and in his second speech in the House, December 22, 1847, he proposed a land grant for the projected line.

As to why he had not engaged previously in railroad work, the reason is that Illinois had no railroads. It was the "wild west" of the era.* By 1850 there were only three partly-built roads in the entire state; the longest, fifty-eight miles, was a remnant of the disastrous "internal improvement" schemes that had swept the country in the thirties and in which Lincoln had had a hand as a state legislator. Named the Northern Cross Railroad, it was to cross the state at what was in that early day the northern limits of settlement, although actually the geographical center. Later, privately financed and rebuilt, it was renamed the Morgan and Sangamon from the two counties through which it ran. Extended eastward to the Illinois-Indiana state line, it became the Great Western Railway; and it was over this road Lincoln commenced the inaugural journey from Springfield. Today, Illinois's first steam rail line is part of the Wabash system.

Lincoln put in more time—eight years—in the service of the Illinois Central Railroad than with any other employer. He received from them not only the single biggest fee of his career but more in fees than from any other source before becoming President.

Railroads represented the first sizable corporations in America involving large sums of money. The concept of corporation in those days was that, being a creature of the state, a corporation was to be formed only upon approval and vote of the state legislature. Daily the press printed as news lists of corporations that had been granted state charters. There were no great manufacturing, proc-

---

* In 1849 one could stand on a knoll in the village of Peoria and gaze northward over an expanse of green prairie as far as the eye could reach, a howling wilderness containing a few Indians wandering in search of game. To get to Chicago, then a town of 27,000, required a stage ride of three days and cost twelve dollars. When the Lincoln family arrived the entire state contained but 157,000 persons (1830 census). Thirty years later, when Lincoln left, the population totaled an unbelievable 1,711,455. All Illinois indicators leaped upward when the railroads arrived. For the United States as a whole the gain in railroad mileage during the decade 1850-1860 was a tremendous 300%; but for Illinois it was 3000%!

essing, extracting or service corporations as there are today. The coming of the railroads, the rise of corporations, and the growth of Abraham Lincoln, were contemporaneous.

As a successful railroad attorney Lincoln demonstrated his ability to handle large affairs. The Illinois Central, when completed in 1856, was the longest railroad in the world and the largest corporation in Illinois. Lincoln was a forerunner of what today is known as a corporation counsel; the term designating a legal counselor who goes beyond the confines of the law in guiding the management of a company, handling legal action as needed, conferring with all manner of men to insure the competitive success of the enterprise.

In addition to railroads, Lincoln numbered among his clients growing corporations such as public utilities, insurance companies, manufacturing and commercial concerns, his practice extended from Chicago to St. Louis to Columbus and involved court actions in many parts of expanding young America. His ability and reputation resulted in his being retained on behalf of municipalities and counties and for the state auditor, state hospital, office of public instruction, and secretary of state.

The above recapitulation of Lincoln's corporation experiences, abbreviated though it is, evidences the high position he achieved in his profession. He had become a leading member of the bar.

Lincoln's law career extended over nearly a quarter of a century, beginning March 1, 1837, when he was enrolled by the court and received a license to practice. Twice a year, spring and fall, he made the rounds of the Eighth Judicial Circuit, handling a variety of cases. Some were criminal, like the "Duff" Armstrong homicide case, in which Lincoln showed that the moon was not shining as a witness had testified; the little-known murder case of "Peachy" Harrison, grandson of one-time political rival Peter Cartwright; the murder cases of Isaac Wyant and William Fraim. Mostly he handled civil actions; trover, tort, assumpsit, replevin, chancery and the like.

As his reputation for honest dealing and sound counsel grew (he often counseled compromise rather than court suit) he increased in professional stature. He became a lawyer's lawyer. Local attorneys prepared the facts, drew up the legal papers, and retained Lincoln to advise and try the case. In such a manner he came to have numerous partners and associates.

In this way, too, he learned to think on his feet and to speak tellingly on the spur of the immediate situation. Day upon day and year upon year for twenty-odd years, Lincoln stood before juries, convincing them with his pleadings, examining and cross-examining witnesses, refuting opposing arguments, summing up testimony, preparing briefs for higher courts. He had contact and collision with every possible type of person. He was up against able opponents, the roarers and the bulldozers, the untrustworthy and the unscrupulous, those who work with disarming softness to gain their ends by indirection, as well as the straightforward and the broad-minded.

Contrary to the opinion of law partner Herndon that he disregarded the niceties of legal form, Lincoln knew his law. But he made little use of technicalities in the law to gain a case; "pettifogging" it was called. A circuit associate related how Lincoln constantly developed himself; how Lincoln had become puzzled by the word, *to demonstrate;* the meaning of which he had found to be given as, *of certain proof beyond the probability of doubt.*

"But," demurred Lincoln, according to this friend, "I could form no idea of what sort of proof that was. I consulted reference books with no better results. . . . So I worked until I could give any proposition of the six books of Euclid at sight. I then found out what 'demonstrate' means."

Many a schoolboy, painfully sweating through the Euclidean propositions to reach each tantalizing *Q.E.D.*, has wondered what earthly use it was. The mature Lincoln, successful attorney and public man, memorized these ancient Greek demonstrations of what proof is, that he might make his legal presentations irrefutable and advance himself in his chosen profession.

For Lincoln practiced law not only in courts of the first instance, then called *nisi prius* courts. He appeared also before the state supreme court, where close reasoning and clear proof were essential. Available records show him before the state's highest tribunal in 178 cases, a total rarely equaled by any lawyer even today. He handled all manner of clients, not only on behalf of railroads but also against them.

Take the case of Mr. and Mrs. Joseph H. Dalby. The Dalbys wanted to take the train to a point for which the station agent had no ticket on hand at the moment. In lieu thereof the agent gave Dalby a note to that effect. The train conductor, however, demanded the extra fare for selling the ticket. Dalby refused to pay it. He was, with Mrs. Dalby, forcibly put off the train. The understandably angry Dalbys sued the railroad and won. The road carried the case to the Supreme Court. Under Lincoln's guidance, Dalby won again.

What is more, the Dalby decision was subsequently cited in cases by the Supreme Courts of Colorado, Indiana, Minnesota, New Hampshire, Georgia and Mississippi. This points to an extraordinary aspect of Lincoln's supreme court work. Of his 178 cases, 99 were cited by other supreme courts or federal courts. Nine were cited by the United States Supreme Court.

Other little-known facts about Lincoln's legal life include his practicing before the nation's highest tribunal. Admitted to the bar of the United States Supreme Court on March 7, 1849, he personally appeared in two cases.

Knox College, one of the nation's finest small colleges, located at Galesburg, Illinois, conferred on Lincoln the honorary degree of Doctor of Laws, July 3, 1860. This was followed on June 26, 1861, by a similar degree from Columbia University. The College of New Jersey, now Princeton University, did likewise on December 20, 1864. The great Daniel Webster was a Lincoln client. A small town, circuit-riding lawyer? Lincoln certainly was that—and a great deal more.

In the little black gripsack Robert was now guarding so carefully reposed the Inaugural Address Lincoln would soon deliver and which would become world renowned. In that address he would render an opinion on behalf of his new corporation client, the American body politic. He would declare to a world jury:

"I hold, that in contemplation of universal law and of the Constitution, the Union of these States is perpetual. . . . It is safe to assert that no government ever had a provision in its organic law for its own termination. . . .

"Again, if the United States be not a government proper, but an association of states in the nature of contract merely, can it, as a contract, be peaceably unmade, by less than all the parties who made it?

"It follows from these views that no state, upon its own mere motion—can lawfully get out of the Union, that resolves and ordinances to that effect are legally void. . . .

"I therefore consider that, in view of the Constitution and the laws, the Union is unbroken. . . ."

CHAPTER 18

DID you see the Railsplitter?" "No, but I saw his hat!"

A quarter of a million New Yorkers witnessed passage of the President-elect through their streets on a sunny Tuesday afternoon. Anti-Lincolnites maintained that a mere hundred thousand paid any attention to the fresh-whiskered Republican. Those who didn't catch a glimpse of him in the flesh, saw his hat, as the two-line conceit had it.

He arrived right on schedule, at 3:00 P.M., after making speaking stops at Fishkill and Peekskill and bowing from the back platform as the train slowed at other points. Detraining at the Hudson River railroad's new Thirtieth Street depot, he was accompanied by Judge Davis and Colonel Sumner, and guided by alderman Charles G. Cornell, chairman of the common council committee. Lincoln was also accompanied by the railroad's officials as he walked through the brand-new passenger station—so new that it had to be hurried to completion so that he might be the first passenger.

The depot, located between Ninth and Tenth avenues, was not intended to replace the main passenger station at Chambers Street, but was built to accommodate those wishing to "take the cars" uptown. Substantially constructed of brick, two hundred feet long and twenty-five feet wide, the railroad track ran along the rear, the roof projecting so as to protect passengers from the weather. The site is now occupied by the Morgan Annex of the United States Post Office. A bronze tablet commemorates the only occasion when a President-elect helped to dedicate a railroad station.

Emerging from the building, Lincoln was met by superintendent of police John Kennedy, who escorted him to a handsome carriage, an open barouche drawn by a spanking team of six black horses. The conveyance was built especially for the occasion and was not, as erroneously reported, the same as that used by the Prince of Wales the year before.

The order of procession was as follows: first, a squad of mounted policemen followed by a platoon on foot extending from curb to curb; and then a carriage containing Superintendent Kennedy and Police Inspectors Leonard and Dilks. Next the carriage of the common council committee, all of whom had gone to Albany Saturday and escorted the President-elect back to the city. So had the chairman, Alderman Cornell, who took his place in the third carriage with Lincoln, Davis and Sumner. Then followed twenty-five carriages carrying the presidential party and local celebrities.

Bringing up the rear was a large Wescott and Dodge express wagon piled with baggage and drawn by six bay horses smartly ornamented with plumes. Closing the procession was another foot platoon reaching from curb to curb, and finally another mounted squad of New York police. There was no military escort and no uniformed organization other than the police, no band, not even a bugle corps. Mrs. Lincoln and the boys were driven directly to the hotel.

The route of the procession was from Thirtieth Street to Ninth Avenue, down to Twenty-third, over to Fifth Avenue, down the avenue to Fourteenth Street, over to Broadway, and down to the Astor House at Broadway and Vesey streets.

The condition of the area around the railroad's bright new Thirtieth Street depot prompted the New York press to give it special mention. "Some portions of the city west of Broadway, notwithstanding their historic freshness, are not particularly remarkable for their beauty, elegance, or odor," apologized the *New York Herald*. When the presidential procession moved into Ninth Avenue it encountered the outpourings of that section, an *olla podrida* of humanity such as is usually to be found, chirruped the reporter, in what Mrs. Partington called the "outsquirts" of the city.

Thus, the President-elect was compelled to look upon a picture in which "all stages of dirtiness entered as the component feature," moaned the *Herald*. "Heads unkempt, faces unclean, bare arms fresh from the washtubs." Men without coats, women without bonnets, small boys in tattered clothes, shouting and whistling, babies screaming in the first stage of infant eloquence all added to the applause that greeted Lincoln, loud and prolonged.

The *New York Tribune* also noted that this part of the city skirting the North River was not distinguished by magnificent mansions. It was low, lumbery, muddy and noisy. It was fragrant, to be sure, but the perfume was not that of orange blossoms. The scent defied hasty and correct analysis by an ordinary nose, but from a prolonged smell of three hours duration, we were enabled, testified

This photograph, taken in 1858, shows the New York Central passenger station in Rochester as it was when the Lincoln train came through. The engine *Dean Richmond* was uncoupled and replaced by Number Eighty-four, engine-driver John Duff at the controls. The change was made inside the station. The public was prevented from entering the depot at trackside, so the reception went off smoothly. For further reasons why, see text.

The *William Mason*, Number Twenty-five, was a typical 4-4-0 American-style engine in widespread use during the latter half of the nineteenth century. Along with its twin, Number Twenty-six, it was put into service in August, 1857, and was used on the regular runs between Baltimore and Washington. The Baltimore and Ohio train that carried Lincoln into Washington might have been powered by any one of a dozen similar engines. The name, *William Mason*, was in honor of its builder located in Taunton, Massachusetts.

As an historic memento of railroad pioneering, the Baltimore and Ohio Railroad maintains this century-old wood burner in tiptop shape. It operates as well today as ever.

A rare view of the old Washington passenger station of the Baltimore and Ohio Railroad, the only rail line then entering the national capital. Through this depot passed President-elect Lincoln on Saturday morning February 23, 1861, at approximately 6:00 A.M. The photo was taken after the street level had been raised. Part of the present Union Station Plaza, this ground has now been filled in and is no longer occupied. This depot stood at the corner of New Jersey Avenue and C Street, just to the north of what is now the new Taft Memorial.

Waiting room of the old Baltimore and Ohio's Washington depot through which Lincoln passed. When he went through the double doors at the far end, it can be said that his rail journey from Springfield to Washington had come to an end. This photograph was taken at a later date, but its furnishings are substantially as they were at the time of Lincoln's passage.

the reporter, to say that pig-flavor predominated. There were other pungent flavors difficult to classify but the overwhelming odor was that of pig.

Turning into Twenty-third Street the spectacle assumed a more cheerful aspect. The crowds were not as dense nor as vociferous, but the neighborhood embraced elements of greater refinement. Near Eigth Avenue a banner over the street proclaimed: "Fear Not, Abraham, I Am Thy Shield, And Thy Exceeding Great Reward." (Genesis 15:1). The demonstrations of applause, especially those by the fairer part of the population, were enthusiastic. Lincoln responded by bowing from side to side and often rising to his feet.

Flags were flying, and banners with special messages appeared in conspicuous places. Business houses, residences, hotels and newspaper offices were all patriotically adorned. Church bells heralded the passing procession. Doors and windows of the Church of the Messiah on Broadway were open and filled. The chimes pealed out a warm welcome.

The sight, sound and smell of the largest city in America (population 805,650) spanned the spectrum from sublime to farcical.

Thirteen hundred Metropolitan police, only two hundred less than the entire force, lined the three-and-a-half-mile route, beginning inside the railway depot and continuing to the hotel. One hundred and fifty men each were distributed under seven captains. Two details of twenty-four men under two sergeants, one from the harbor police and one from the third ward, guarded the hotel itself.

Captain Hopkins and two hundred men from the Sixteenth Precinct held open the street in front of the Astor

House where the Woolworth building now stands. Spectators were permitted only on the opposite side of the street, even with the curb. Barnum's famous museum, gaily decorated, band playing on the roof, located diagonally across from the hotel at Broadway and Ann Street, had sold out all its windows and balconies. Enterprising bus operators parked their vehicles on nearby streets and sold space on the roofs.

On such a bus-top seat sat a man who would become known in later years as the "good gray poet," Walt Whitman, contemporary of Lincoln, who would pen the most revered of all Lincoln elegies, "O Captain! my Captain! our fearful trip is done." Of the moment now before his eyes he would write:

"I shall not easily forget the first time I ever saw Abraham Lincoln. It was rather a pleasant afternoon in New York city. . . . I saw him on Broadway, near the site of the present Postoffice [now removed]. . . . The broad spaces, sidewalks, and streets in the neighborhood [City Hall Park], and for some distance, were crowded with solid masses of people, many thousands. The omnibuses and other vehicles had all been turned off, leaving an unusual hush in that busy part of the city. . . .

"A tall figure stepp'd out of the center of these barouches, paus'd leisurely on the sidewalk, look'd up at the granite walls and looming architecture of the grand old hotel—then, after a relieving stretch of arms and legs, turn'd round for over a minute to slowly and good-humoredly scan the appearance of the vast and silent crowds."

As the procession reached the hotel entrance the police platoon split into two sections between which Lincoln's carriage drew to the curb. He alighted, and the silent crowd which Whitman noted, surged forward for a closer look. The police held firmly though with difficulty. Through a gauntlet of blue-coats guarding the doors, garrisoning the stairways and investing the halls, Lincoln was guided to a room on the second floor reserved for receiving visitors.

This was room number forty-three, a large chamber richly but not ostentatiously furnished. On the center table the day's mail was piled awaiting attention, flanked by several boxes of troches—a thoughtful touch in view of the President-elect's hoarseness. Next door was a private dining room. The south room of the suite, thirty-seven, toward St. Paul's Church, was designed as a lady's chamber. It was reserved for Mrs. Lincoln. Another bedroom was between it and the dining-room. The four rooms fronted on Broadway and were directly over the main entrance. They had been occupied by several of Lincoln's predecessors and other eminent guests.

Standing with his back to a crackling fire in the hearth, shaking hands vigorously, Lincoln was introduced to members of the city council and others who had been riding in the procession. Alderman Cornell made the introductions. When Superintendent of Police Kennedy was introduced, Lincoln complimented him on the excellent police arrangements. Kennedy replied that he had done his duty; to which Lincoln responded, "Well, a man ought to be thanked when he does his duty right well."

The throng outside, now filling all streets solidly, kept shouting for a speech. Going to the window, Alderman Cornell opened it and Lincoln stepped out to the narrow coping of the ornamental front entrance. Looking over the cornice, he spoke as well as his hoarseness would allow:

"Fellow-citizens! I have stepped before you merely in

compliance with what appeared to be your wish and with no purpose of making a speech this afternoon. I could not be heard by any but a small fragment of you at best; and what is still worse than that, I have nothing just now to say that is worth your hearing." (Cheers.) "I beg you to believe that I do not now refuse to address you from any disposition not to oblige you, but the contrary. At the same time I beg you to excuse me for the present."

He stepped back through the window and resumed the reception. A few minutes later he ended the ceremony and retired to freshen up for dinner.

Dinner was served at six o'clock in the private dining room to a select party of ten. The service was exquisitely set on a round table in the center of the room, a nosegay of flowers at each place. In the center had been placed a floral mound of white camellias, red roses and violets set in a bed of yellow pansies and green fern trimmed with tricolored satin ribbons, the presentation of a Broadway florist.

A side table was heaped with a tempting display of assorted fresh fruits ornamented with flowers. The buffet carried a handsome new silver service, never used before; and underneath were the wine coolers. A coal fire sparkled in the grate. Above the mantlepiece hung a large painting of Washington crossing the Delaware set in a massive gold frame. The festive scene was brilliantly lighted by a cut-glass chandelier.

The menu was sumptuous. For the first time on the journey, after nine days of travel, it is possible to make known what Lincoln was offered to eat.

Though Cleveland and Albany news accounts mentioned menus being printed, none can be located. Nor was anything obtainable on Sourbeck's at Alliance, Ohio,

Reception of

Hon. Abraham Lincoln

President-elect

Soup
Julian

Fish
Boiled salmon, anchovy sauce

Cold Dishes

Tureen of goose liver   Boned turkey with jelly

Relevés
Fillet of beef, larded, with green peas
Larded sweetbreads, tomato sauce
Fillet of chicken, truffle sauce
Shrewsbury oysters, baked in shell

Vegetables

Boiled potatoes   Turnips, cream sauce
Baked mashed potatoes   Green peas
Beets   Lettuce   Celery

Game
Roast canvas back duck   Roast stuffed quail

Pastry

Charlotte russe   French cream cakes
Champagne jelly   Claret jelly
Cream cakes   Ladies' fingers
Cup custards   Kisses

Fruits
All kinds in season

Ice cream

This menu was printed in black on scalloped note paper with a gold
border on a white ground. It was oval in form and the outer part was
pink and "other soft colors." (The above menu was taken, not from the
original itself, but from the *New York Herald* of February 20.)

or other hostelries along the way. The lack was the more astounding when it is recalled that there were no railroad dining cars then. Three times each day the presidential party had to stop somewhere for meals.

Perhaps little was said about the food on the journey because victuals exerted little influence on Lincoln. Partner Herndon revealed, corroborated by others, that Lincoln was indifferent to food; that he would eat what was set before him and not be able to tell at the end of the meal what he had eaten. Seldom did he comment on food or cooking, even the atrocious meals he encountered on the circuit.

For this reason the item at Erie which stated that Lincoln called for a second helping of mince pie, was labeled "unconfirmed." The fact was not related by a participant. Nor did it sound like Lincoln. It was included, however, for although not like him gastronomically, it could be Lincoln politically.

While Lincoln is enjoying the splendid Astor House dinner in the privacy of his family and friends, an important question may be disposed of, the question of finances. Who was paying the expenses of the long trip? Before leaving home Lincoln had drawn four hundred dollars from his bank account. He hardly needed to. Railroads supplied the special trains without charge. Other transportation was also provided, such as carriages. Handling of hotel bills and meals varied.

The invitation of a municipality or state carried the same implications as a social invitation—the invited guest would be cared for by the host. In authorizing such expenditures, a political wrangle sometimes ensued. The mayor and the common council, the governor and the legislature, each wanted precedence. Or there would be disagreement over protocol—those first in the political world were given social precedence. On occasion a citizens committee had to take over from the warring politicians. In no case was a partisan political group permitted to intervene. The time for partisan politics had passed.

New York provided a case in point. The common council voted to extend Lincoln an invitation, beating out the county board of supervisors. A reception committee of the common council was appointed, which in turn elected a chairman. This committee assumed supervision of all arrangements, providing the carriages, paying the hotel expenses, securing police cooperation, charging the bills to the city treasury. The chairman of the New York reception committee being Alderman Cornell, he appeared frequently on the scene. Whoever picked up the tab got to be first with the invited guest.

Personally, Lincoln was put to no expense on the journey except family incidentals, tips and so forth.

One may have wondered what was happening to other members of the authorized presidential group who had left Springfield with him. Unless cited in dispatches as being involved in the day's events, nothing has been said of them here. Space limitations prevented. The focus was on Lincoln.

All of the originally named Springfield party reached New York. Of Major David Hunter, some reports had it that he stopped here because of his injured shoulder. Other reports contradicted this. Such discrepancies were not uncommon during the journey and remain unresolved because of conflicting testimony.

There was no question about Henry Villard. He said he didn't want any more of the "traveling show" and that he was sick and tired of the "wearisome sameness of the performances." By giving up in New York he was to miss the most extraordinary part of the whole trip.

For some reason Villard didn't like Bob Lincoln* and smeared him to such an extent in his dispatches that by the time the party arrived in New York Lincoln had to ask friendly newspapers to counteract the reports. The following is taken from the *New York Evening Post* of February 21, 1861.

"Personal—Robert T. Lincoln is a student at Harvard and is a young man of fine abilities and much dignity of character. The reports in various papers intimating that his course of life is what is popularly dominated as 'fast' are strictly erroneous, and no less painful to him than to his parents."

The delightful dinner party finally came to a reluctant end at half-past seven. Meantime the reception parlor next door had been filling up with visitors. Shortly before eight o'clock Lincoln entered the parlor, greeting many local celebrities including Mayor Fernando Wood who had come to extend his personal welcome preceding the official ceremonies scheduled for the next morning at city hall. The introductions were made by one of America's great poets, then a newspaper editor and publisher, William Cullen Bryant.

At eight-twenty the informal reception ended and Lin-

---

* Villard didn't like the President-elect either. "I must say frankly that although I found him most approachable, good-natured and full of wit and humor," wrote Villard in his memoirs published in 1904, "I could not take a real personal liking to the man owing to an inborn weakness for which he was even then notorious and so remained during his great public career. He was inordinately fond of jokes, anecdotes and stories."

Unbelievable—but there it is in his own words. He disliked Lincoln because Lincoln was "full of wit and humor." Nor was it a passing fancy. Villard first met Lincoln during the Douglas debates. He also covered the Chicago nominating convention, and that Lincoln won the presidential nomination disappointed him. "I had not got over the prejudice against Lincoln which my personal contact in 1858 imbued me," he declared, saying it was incomprehensible to him that "the uncouth, common Illinois politician . . . should carry the day over the tried and true statesman."

There is probably no clearer instance of an otherwise able man (Villard later became president of the Northern Pacific Railroad) failing to recognize greatness when it was thrust upon him.

coln was conducted to a larger reception on the floor below. Today the place would be called a parlor on the mezzanine floor. At that time it was called the "gentlemen's ordinary," from its use as a dining place for men only. The tables had been pushed aside and it was now full of noisy gentlemen from the metropolitan area, including a delegation from Kings County headed by Brooklyn's Mayor Samuel S. Powell, and one from Queens County.

The exuberant affair might be termed a victory celebration. At Lincoln's request the area's electoral college members had been invited as well as a big slate of committees, numbering some four hundred. They had assembled at the Young Men's Republican headquarters on Broadway and marched to the hotel, a happy group of campaign workers come to pay homage to their successful candidate. There were officials from the various Wideawakes, central campaign clubs, neighborhood committees, and federal, city and county employees.

Into this ebullient gathering that jammed the gentlemen's ordinary, Lincoln was conducted by E. Delafield Smith, chairman of the Republican central committee. Unable to make himself heard above the clamor, he mounted a table, Lincoln with him. Hushing the gabble in stentorian tones, Smith welcomed the President-elect.

"It is a remarkable incident," he noted, "that there should have been but two receptions in this room. One was to Daniel Webster, the other to Henry Clay, and a third is now to Abraham Lincoln." (Cheers.) But, Mr. President, we meet you tonight, not as partisans, but as Americans and as citizens of the greatest and most glorious Republic. . . ."

Lincoln responded in an impromptu speech that caught the flavor of the festive occasion yet recognized the serious political situation—a short speech that went straight to the heart of the matter with a smile in the telling. It was typically Lincolnian.*

Dismounting from the table, he was surrounded at once by a self-appointed bodyguard including a dozen policemen who hurried him toward the hallway. Many wanted to shake his hand and said so as he passed by. Asked if he would, Lincoln said he was perfectly willing and would like to. So the operation commenced.

The police formed the crowd in a single line and passed the line before him. Lincoln shook the hand of each cordially, accompanying the act with a hearty greeting that varied with each person. "How are you, sir!" "Glad to see you!" "I hope you are well, sir!" He would grasp the hands of those with whom he had previous acquaintance in both of his and make an appropriate comment. Everyone got a genuine handshake, western style, no dainty finger tipping.

Several times he was asked if he would like to retire. "Bring them along!" he replied. "If the policemen will pass them quickly, I'll empty the room!" And he did. For he wanted to meet all the party workers and express to them his personal appreciation for the efforts they had made against great odds. The worker was due his credit.

At ten o'clock the affair came to an end, and he bade

---

* Here are two paragraphs from the speech—first the smile and then the telling—both demonstrating Lincoln's great impromptu oratorical ability.

"I have been occupying the position, since the election, of silence—of avoiding public speaking. I have been doing so because I thought, upon due consideration, that was the proper course for me to take. (Applause.) I am brought before you now to make a speech, while you all approve, more than anything else, that I have been keeping silence. (Laughter as the audience caught the drift of his remarks.) It seems to me the response you give to that remark ought to justify me in closing just here. (Cheers and laughter.)

"I have not kept silence since the Presidential election from any party craftiness or from any indifference to the anxieties that pervade the minds of men in this country. I have kept silence for the reason that it was peculiarly proper for me to wait until the time should come when, according to the custom of the country, I would speak officially." (Applause.)

his friends good night. He was conducted to his suite by police detailed to his person. All night a strong cordon of Metropolitans surrounded the hotel, and inside they patrolled hallways and stairs. The other members of the presidential suite were roomed on the same floor.

Of the day's events, the *World* said they were worthy of the great city of New York. "There was not the slightest insult either by word or action offered to the distinguished guest. This is remarkable when the state of political feeling existing all over the country is considered . . . and is in marked contrast with the disturbances in European capitals in times of great political excitement."

What impressed *Harper's Weekly* was that this man, head bared, riding quietly in a carriage, accompanied by no soldiers, no martial music, no pageantry, could elicit the cheers and applause of thousands. "A simple, earnest, sincere-looking man bowed at intervals with natural dignity as if instinctively conscious, as he had so frequently said, that it was not he but the majesty of the nation visible in his presence that aroused the profound interest of the people."

CHAPTER 19

A T half-past eight the next morning, the carriages of Moses H. Grinnell and William H. Aspinwall drew up at the Astor House main entrance to fetch the President-elect to the Grinnell mansion located on Fifth Avenue near Fourteenth Street facing Union Park.

Here Lincoln breakfasted with a group of leading New Yorkers that included John Jacob Astor, Jr., Hamilton Fish, Robert L. Stevens, Robert E. Minturn, James Gallatin, Simeon Draper, James Watson Webb, Thurlow Weed, William R. Evarts, and others of the solid merchant class rather than the politicians.

The host was a successful merchant and ship owner, youngest of three brothers from an old Huguenot family (Grenuelle) who had fled religious persecution in France and had emigrated to Massachusetts from England. Each brother had subsequently come to New York City; and each made a fortune, starting with ships and whale oil for the lamps of America; then branching into new enterprises. Brother Henry was an original incorporator of the Illinois Central Railroad. So was Will Aspinwall; also famous for his daring construction of the Panama Railroad. As directors of the Illinois Central, both Aspinwall and Henry Grinnell were well aware of Lincoln's work for their company.

Breakfasting with these successful American businessmen, capable, hard-driving men building a greater future and bringing fame and fortune to the old Dutch settlement of Nieuw Amsterdam, one would give his right arm to know what was said between them and Lincoln. It is possible to conjecture that they wanted to know from him, as Governor Morgan in Albany had wanted to know, what he was going to do? Would he compromise on Negro slavery extension? Or would there be war?

Well might they be concerned, for the South was in debt to the North to the extent of $211,000,000, a tremendous sum in those days. According to R. G. Dun and Company, $170,000,000 was due in New York City— to the firms and banks these men represented. No report of what went on at the breakfast, however, has turned up. The affair was described as "social and pleasant." From the standpoint of money, these men did not want war. Yet when war did come, they rendered services beyond price to the nation.

Two hours at the breakfast table, then Lincoln returned to the hotel, with several guests, only to find his reception room filled. He greeted the visitors as secretary Nicolay introduced them. Among them was the Honorable Joshua Dewey of Brooklyn.

If any man was entitled to have the distinction of "Honorable," that man was Joshua Dewey. The Lincolns gave him their undivided attention. He gave them a picture of himself. He was ninety-four years of age; had cast his first ballot for George Washington and had voted in every presidential election since, the last time for Honest Abe. At the tender age of fifteen he had enlisted in the revolutionary army. Subsequently he had held responsible positions and had entered the New York Legislature of 1799. He was the oldest Yale graduate; and he was the last of that great generation of Americans who pledged "their lives, their fortunes and their sacred honor" in defense of their civil and religious liberties.

Precisely at eleven o'clock Alderman Cornell and the common council committee appeared in Lincoln's reception room. They conducted the President-elect, by way of carriage, to the city hall and into the governor's room where the entire council, city officials, and members of the press were waiting. The mayor stood behind President Washington's rosewood writing desk and in front of a large portrait of former Governor Seward. He extended the city's greetings in a prepared speech. Lincoln, listening intently, responded in a few words.

At the conclusion Mayor Wood stepped forward, shook hands with Lincoln and introduced him all around. Arrangements were then made for the public reception. Lincoln was placed in the angle of a window looking toward the balcony. Finding the light in his eyes, and that the people would be passing from the right to left, he pointed to Houdon's bronze statue of George Washington.

"Let me stand there with my back to the old General," he suggested to the mayor. Taking the position, he remarked, "Sustained by Washington, I shall get along better."

"You have a hard task before you," replied the mayor, standing to his left, Colonel Lamon and Norman Judd to the right.

"How long will it last?"

"Till one o'clock. Nearly two hours."

"Two hours of manual labor?" queried Lincoln cheerfully. "I am used to fourteen hours a day."

Double lines of policemen arranged by superintendent Kennedy reached from incoming door to Lincoln and then to outgoing door. When all was ready the outer door was opened and in poured the eager crowd. A dozen or more would shoot through the line, then a few would dribble along, and then they would roar through like a prairie wind. The doughty Metropolitans had a hard time controlling the throng.

"I have been told I look like you," said a tall, skinny, weasened-faced man with New Jersey mud on his boots, sticking out a horny hand.

"Then it's all settled," responded Lincoln, vigorously shaking the hand, "you're a handsome man!"

A large lady with a faded umbrella pulled along a jaded-looking male. "This is my husband," she said proudly, "and you must shake hands with him for he is a member of the Indiana Legislature."

"He might have come from a worse state," answered Lincoln, taking the man's hand and pumping it up and down, "but he could not have a better half."

"How is your wife and family?" inquired another visitor very soberly.

"Able to be about," replied Lincoln, also very soberly, passing the man along. He turned to the mayor, "That fellow is from the country and meant to be polite," he said.

When two persons happened to reach him at the same instant, he would hold out both hands. The work grew so hot that, assisted by the mayor, he removed his overcoat. Wood suggested halting the ceremony.

"Let them come on and I will shake hands until twelve o'clock," replied Lincoln. "After that I will be satisfied if they pass by."

Thirty veterans of the War of 1812 came in a body,

their colonel presenting Lincoln with a sheaf of resolutions which he promptly tucked into his left coattail pocket. Shortly after, another old 1812 veteran who had been lost in the shuffle, came by, advising Lincoln, "We are the old boys and you must not forget us when you get into your station."

Bells rang out the hour of noon. At once visitors were forbidden to shake hands with the President-elect, policemen instructing the crowd outside. But Lincoln could not help making exceptions—to the ladies, of course. And to special guests, like ex-Mayor Harper, ex-Governor Clark, the port health officer, Commander Breese of the Brooklyn Navy Yard, and Navy Captains Foote and Gansevoort whom he invited to come to the hotel.

Requests to shake his hand he met by saying, "They won't let me." A white-haired, ruddy-cheeked man made no attempt and said, "I came forty-mile to do it, but never mind." Unable to resist the appeal, Lincoln reached after him and gave him a hearty handclasp.

A cadaverous individual of melodramatic look intoned, "God bless you, sir; the flag of our country is looking at you."

"I only hope it won't lose any of its eyes," rejoined Lincoln.

"You must shake hands with me," declared a tall man from the Green Mountains. "I'm as tall as you are." Lincoln wheeled about, "Let's measure," he said. Surveying the two standing back to back, the mayor said to Lincoln, "You're an inch taller." "I give in," muttered the disappointed Vermonter, starting away. But Lincoln shook his hand nevertheless. Turning to Wood, he said, "I saw he was stretching himself to make the question, so I thought I would try it."

Another visitor described himself as being from Canada and Lincoln observed, "I suppose I must shake hands with representatives of foreign nations." He repeated the operation when another came along saying he was from South Carolina.

His affability and his agility in handling all comers kept the mayor and attendants in a continual state of merriment. Two hours passed quickly enough. Doors were shut promptly at one o'clock. The throng at once let out a roar. Stepping to the balcony, Lincoln gave a friendly speech.

Before leaving the governor's room, Lincoln had some sight-seeing of his own to do. He passed around the gallery of portraits of Americans celebrated in the history of state and nation, including Presidents Washington, Monroe, Taylor and Fillmore. Then through a roaring crowd, in company with city officials, he walked down the driveway to the waiting carriage. As he shook hands with the mayor he leaned forward and expressed his thanks for the kind attentions extended by the city. A city father said he overheard Lincoln telling Wood that without intending disparagement of others, he considered his (Wood's) speech the most appropriate yet made on a like occasion and he endorsed every word of it.

This contrasted with published reports which tried to make their meeting look like a personal vendetta. There was, indeed, a difference between these two politicians as individuals—a difference that was not petty. Fernando Wood was in politics to put as much as he could into his pockets. His personal fortune had risen $250,000 from political manipulations. Only corrupt courts saved him from convictions for forgery, perjury and related crimes.

When the war began Wood openly advocated that New York secede and establish itself as a city-state, thus enabling it to maintain "uninterrupted commerce with all sections of the country." Lincoln retorted that "the front door would have a hard time setting up housekeeping by itself."

Returning to the Astor House, Lincoln retired to his suite for refreshment and rest. His reception room had filled up again. Alternating between interviews and periods of rest, he greeted some two hundred persons, including notables like ex-Mayor Kingsland, Postmaster Taylor, officers of the Seventh New York Regiment, the venerable Reverend and Mrs. Lyman Beecher, and a second visit from the Brooklyn common council committee who had come the night before to arrange a visit to the City of Churches. Lincoln was distressed that the schedule could not be stretched to accommodate this trip to Brooklyn.

The previous afternoon Phineas T. Barnum, self-styled Prince of Showmen, had waited upon Lincoln and invited him to visit his museum. Lincoln said he would try. Barnum kept bobbing in and out of the reception room, importuning Lincoln to come over. "Don't forget," Barnum adjured, "You're Honest Abe and I rely upon you." His newspaper advertisements repeated twenty times: PRESIDENT LINCOLN VISITS THE MUSEUM, stating that "Those who would see him should come early. Visit the Museum this day." The advertising kept appearing but Lincoln did not. He could not be put on exhibition for a twenty-five cent admission charge.

Bob went over in the morning to view the oddities. At two o'clock in the afternoon Mrs. Lincoln and Willie, accompanied by a nurse and Officer Dolan, sat in a box with Barnum viewing the Wilkie Collins play, *Woman in White,* a feature attraction. Little Tad refused to go. He said he could see plenty of bears in his own country and didn't need to go to Barnum's.

The Lincoln visit to commercially-minded New York

presented opportunities to turn a fast dollar. An advertisement offered Bellingham's Stimulating Ointment. Stimulating for what? The headline made it very plain: "Do you want whiskers? Or a mustache?" Even Lincoln's beard was put to profitable use. A Greenwich Street firm advertised, "Excursion Trip to Washington City and Return to New York on the SS. *Coatzacoalcos*," offering sleeping accommodations for one thousand persons, and stopover for the inauguration. Stateroom each way, eight dollars. Forward cabin, five dollars. The New Jersey Railroad put on sale excursion tickets to Trenton and Philadelphia in "trains to accompany the Special Train with President Lincoln." Fare, New York to Trenton and return, two dollars. To Philadelphia and return, five dollars.

Hardly had Barnum finished making his final plea than Lincoln was waited upon by Knox, the hatter, who presented him with a beautiful silk topper. Half an hour later Leary, the hatter downstairs in the hotel, sent up for Lincoln's measurement. Trying on different headpieces, Lincoln sent down the new Knox hat with a message that it was the best fit. Quickly it came back accompanied by one of Leary's best. Lincoln was much pleased.

A reporter asked, in the manner of one who has a public man in a tight fix, which hat he preferred. Such a dilemma was "old hat" to a skilled politician like Lincoln. He replied that they mutually surpassed each other.

The police detail at the Astor House had been receiving contradictory orders as to whom they were to let into the Lincoln reception room. They just could not seem to get it straight. So at five-thirty they made doubly certain by clearing all the corridors. At ten minutes to six the Vice-President-elect and Mrs. Hamlin drew up to the main entrance and he alighted.

The carriage was driven around to the Vesey Street

entrance where Mrs. Hamlin was greeted by the hotel manager and the special assistant in charge of the ladies, Mrs. Follansbee. The Hamlins freshened up in their suite and then entered the Lincoln's reception parlor.

It was seven o'clock, an hour late, when they all sat down to dinner in the private dining room. Room and table were tastefully decorated as they had been on the previous evening. Fresh bouquets of flowers graced each of the eleven places. The ladies included Mrs. Ninian W. Edwards of Springfield, Mrs. Lincoln's sister Elizabeth.

With her was her daughter, also named Elizabeth. They had arrived the previous night and would continue to Washington to assist in the social ceremonies at the White House. Who the others were at the dinner, in addition to the Lincolns and the Hamlins, is not reported. One would judge it was more personal than a state affair.

For the second time during the journey there is a record of the food served. This time the Astor House made its offerings in French. From soup to ice cream, the menu was in the language of the gourmet. It would be interesting to know what Lincoln selected from the gargantuan menu, but it is not reported. Even more, it would be interesting to know what he said when it was handed to him. His response will have to remain in the imagination.

Hamlin would relate in later years that when oysters on the half shell were served, Lincoln looked at them quizzically as if he had never partaken of such a dish before. "Well, I don't know that I can manage these things," he said solemnly, "but I guess I can learn." That put everyone at ease and provided a delightful conversation piece.

The serenity that so far characterized the New York visit was rudely disturbed by sensation-loving editor James Gordon Bennett, quoting the *Lafayette* (Indiana) *Journal,* in his *Herald* under the startling headline: AT-

CARTE DU DINER

Huitres en coquilles cru

— Potage —
Potage Brunoise, aux oeufs pochés

— Poisson —
Alose farcies, braisées, sauce au vin de Champagne

— Piéce Froide —
Pain de gibier, en Bellevue

— Relevés —
Duides bouillie, aux Huitres

—Entrées—
Cailles, farcies, aux Champignones
Côtelettes d'Agneau, aux petites pommes de terre frites, au Beurre
Timbale de Volaille, à la Toulouse
Arcade de Perdrix, à la financer

— Légumes —

Pommes de terre, bouillies	Pommes de terre, au gratin
Epinards, aux oeufs	Petits Pois à la française
Navets, au lait	Betteraves
Celeri	Laitue

— Gibier —
Canard de Canvas Back

— Patisseries —
Gâteaux, à la Française

Charlotte Russe	Marigner Suisse
Gelée au vin de Champagne	Gelée au vin de Bordeaux

Macarons, aux Amandes
Gâteaux de Lafayette

— Fruit —
Glacé, à la Vanille

Maison d'Astor, 20 Fevrier, 1861

The copy read as follows: "We were on Saturday night placed in possession of the astounding information that an attempt was made on Monday last to wreck the train bearing the President-elect and suite about one mile west of the State line. The particulars as given us by Mr. Rich of the Toledo & Western railroad were, that a short time before the train was due at State Line city, an engineer who was preparing to take out a train, found it necessary to run out to the wood yard for fuel. Running at a moderate speed, he noticed an obstruction on the track and, stopping his engine, he found that a machine for putting cars on the track had been fastened to the rails in such a manner that if a train had struck it at full speed, engine and cars must have been thrown off and many persons killed.

"It is almost impossible," the report continued, "to think that anyone is so thoroughly depraved as to attempt so damnable a deed, but we are assured by our informant that his information comes from undoubted authority. The matter would have been made public before but it was hoped that the perpetrator of the dastardly outrage could be detected and brought to justice. The whole thing was admirably planned; the obstruction was near a station and on a straight track where it would not be deemed necessary to exercise any great degree of caution."

Since New York City had opposed Lincoln in the presidential election, many expected the worst to happen when he arrived in person. (The state as a whole had given him a handsome majority.) Some metropolitan newspapers tried to stir up the political pot by playing up trivial items such as the mayor giving Lincoln "the eye" as they traded speeches. Even Walt Whitman, from his seat on the omnibus, cooked up a strange tale.

In the lecture that he would give annually in later years, Whitman would tell of his seeing Lincoln arrive at the hotel this day, and would then comment, "But it was evidently tacitly agreed that if the few political supporters of Mr. Lincoln would entirely abstain from any demonstration on their side, the immense majority, who were anything but supporters, would abstain on their side. The result was sulky, unbroken silence, such as certainly never before characterized so great a New York crowd."

Whitman failed to mention the enthusiastic outburst a few minutes later which brought Lincoln out of the hotel window for the short speech that was received with such vociferous acclaim. Nor did Whitman mention the ovations given later that same night and again the next day.

The fact was, Lincoln, visiting this community politically opposed to him, was greeted by many spontaneous demonstrations. New Yorkers gave him a welcome that derived from the heart, as will be witnessed again.

CHAPTER 20

T HE New York Academy of
Music publicly announced that President-elect Lincoln
would attend its Wednesday evening performance, the
sixth in the current production of *Un Ballo in Maschera,
A Masked Ball,* advertised as Giuseppe Verdi's "last and
most celebrated work."

The academy, located at Fourteenth Street near Lexing-
ton Avenue, was filled at seven-thirty with an audience
of three thousand, the elite of the metropolis. The curtain rose at eight. At quarter past the hour Lincoln
unobtrusively entered the right-hand proscenium box,
second tier. He was accompanied by Judge Davis and
Alderman Cornell. Others in the party, including two
ladies, took seats behind them.

The opera continued uninterrupted. Many in the audience kept scrutinizing the various boxes in search of the
distinguished visitor. At last a view of the sunburned face,
rimmed with bushy dark hair and whiskers, and the good-
humored expression on a countenance absorbed in the
stage proceedings, left no doubt that Abraham Lincoln
of Illinois was present. The news was whispered from one
person to another and there followed much head-turning
and nodding until the buzz was audible. As the curtain

fell on the first act, the audience burst forth with such vigorous applause the cast took six curtain calls. The applause increased as the curtain stayed down, and it was evident the President-elect had been discovered.

At first he bowed from his seat. Shout followed shout. He rose. His tall and sinewy frame was to be seen in full proportion, towering above the friends beside him. His rising touched off a tumult that reached a deafening apogee. Gentlemen waved hats wildly and ladies fluttered handkerchiefs. The sound ascended and receded and ascended again.

Then the curtain rose on the full company assembled on the stage singing the "Star-Spangled Banner," the two feminine leads taking the verses alternately. At the end of the first stanza a magnificent American flag was dropped behind the singers. The rendition had brought every person in the auditorium to his feet, shouting and singing at the top of his capacity. Facing the flag, Lincoln sang along with the audience.

The demonstration of respect and reverence was one no man could fail to feel inspiring.

The orchestra played, "Hail, Columbia!" and the curtain fell. The opera continued in a few moments. At the close of the second act Lincoln and party departed quietly and returned to the Astor House, where he retired for the night.

The two youngest Lincolns, accompanied by a nurse and Officer Dolan, had gone out at eight o'clock to Laura Keene's Theater to see *The Seven Sisters* and the added patriotic tableau, *Uncle Sam's Magic Lantern*. Tad was so anxious to go that long before the nurse was ready he was telling her "it will be all over before we get there, so make haste."

Mrs. Lincoln did not accompany her husband to the

[209]

opera. She came into the reception parlor with Mrs. Hamlin at about eight o'clock. After greeting the roomful of guests, she took the arm of "General" James Watson Webb (publisher of the *New York Courier and Enquirer*) and, together with her sister, Mrs. Edwards, and Mrs. Webb, went to the ladies' parlor on the first floor where some five hundred guests were presented. The affair lasted until about ten o'clock.

A society reporter described Mrs. Lincoln as about forty years of age, below medium height, of full form and face, brown hair and blue eyes, nose rather retroussé, lips thin and compressed, manner and carriage graceful and pleasing. "She was a lady who would be pronounced fine-looking but not beautiful."

She was dressed in steel brocade trimmed with box quilling of ribbon edged with lace which extended from the waist to the lower part of the skirt where it ended in a neatly gathered bow. Flowing sleeves with point lace undersleeving added to the pleasing arrangement. A point lace collar secured by a fine diamond brooch encircled her neck. She wore diamond earrings to match. Her headdress was of chenille and gold. Another eye-witness described Mrs. Lincoln as wearing steel-colored silk, made high in the collar with a trimming of box-plaited satin ribbon, small lace collar fastened with a diamond brooch and matching eardrops.

Mrs. Webb, who had come to town just before the reception, wore a dark French merino dress, cashmere shawl and black velvet bonnet. Mrs. Edwards had on a dark silk dress sprigged with small, bright flowers. The ladies held bouquets of flowers and Mrs. Lincoln also carried a small ivory fan.

A less public reception was held by Mrs. Hamlin in her parlor, and many of those who had been presented to Mrs. Lincoln were received there. It was observed that Mrs. Hamlin was about twenty-five years of age, taller, and not so full in form as Mrs. Lincoln, with auburn hair, a mild blue eye and rather sharp features, but a gentle expression of face. Having arrived recently from the train, she was still wearing her traveling dress. This was the second Mrs. Hamlin, the young half-sister of the first wife who had died.

And that is the way New York glimpsed the ladies of the President-elect and Vice-President-elect, Wednesday evening, February 20, 1861.

A considerable stir was made when the Quartette Club of Hoboken, a group of twenty-two singers, took position in the hotel corridor and rendered a program of beautiful songs, "The Day of Our Lord," "Hymn on Music," "Goodnight," and others. Mrs. Lincoln emerged from the reception parlor with her attendants, complimenting them and excusing her husband's absence, saying he had retired for the evening. The stir was occasioned by many who thought this was the midnight serenade, an event that had been widely announced.

By the time the Hoboken serenaders finished, the fifty-four-piece band of the famous Seventh Regiment was setting up instruments in the street in front of the main entrance. The band had marched from Republican central headquarters at 618 Broadway escorted by 150 Wide-awakes drawn from ward Wide-awake companies and headed by General J. H. Hobart Ward. They were accompanied by a detail of fifty policemen who opened a semicircle in the crowd that had been gathering since early evening. Inside the police semicircle the Wide-awakes took position to assist the musicians. They set up four large lanterns on stands to add to the light of the street lamps.

The streets were solidly packed. Hotel windows and surrounding buildings were filled. Barnum's was overflowing. Promptly at twelve o'clock the midnight serenade commenced.

The band played selections from the operas *Nebuchadnezzar* and *Il Trovatore,* interspersed with such popular numbers as "The Lucien Quickstep" and the "Ypsilanti Gallop." Between pieces the crowd shouted lustily for Lincoln and Hamlin. Their urgent and prolonged calls finally brought the Vice-President-elect to a window where he was introduced by General Ward.

"Fellow-citizens," began the stocky senator from Maine, "I am gratified to hear these generous tones that come from the honest hearts of the men who occupy the Empire City of the old State of New York. They speak as if devoted to a principle in which all have a common interest. (Cheers.)

"They give evidence of the love they bear to a common country; they satisfy me here, even in this great commercial mart, that the heads, the hearts, and the hands of our people are ready to vindicate the Government under which they live, and which they received from their fathers. (Cheers.)

"They show how truly a Government like ours may repose upon the popular will, They tell me how truly the great and good and honest man whom you have elevated to the first position that Americans can bestow, will receive in all times that loyalty which the citizen owes his government, (applause) and that with your heads, your hearts, and your hands, you will rally to its support in sunshine and in storm."

The immense applause was heightened by the band rendering popular minstrel ballads and a series of patriotic pieces. The Wide-awakes joined to sing the spirited

"Yankee Doodle," concluding the program with a touching "Auld Lang Syne."

The midnight serenade was ended. By one o'clock in the morning the once-crowded streets were deserted. Big Town rested from its labors and its excitements. Inside the hotel enthusiasm had not ceased, the manager, Charles A. Stetson, having invited members of the band and the committee, to be his guests for refreshments. The Astor House rotunda and its hospitable brass rail were renowned as a convivial meeting place.

The Hamlins, in the parlor of their suite, continued to receive friends and guests until an early-morning hour. Hamlin was a good mixer and liked people.

Born six months after Lincoln, August 27, 1809, at Paris Hill, Oxford County, Maine, Hannibal Hamlin was a farm boy whose paternal ancestors had been early settlers of Massachusetts. His grandfather had commanded a company of minute men in the Revolution, in which five sons were active. Like Lincoln, Hamlin had to make his own way in the world early in life. His father, a country doctor, died suddenly when the boy was eighteen years old. (Hannibal was named after his father's twin brother.)

Admitted to the bar in 1833, he set up an office in Hampden, near Bangor, and soon acquired an enviable reputation in the practice of law and as a public speaker. Elected to the state legislature in 1835, he was re-elected five succesive times, made speaker three times. In 1840 he was nominated for Congress, introducing in this campaign for the first time in Maine the custom of joint debates between rival candidates for office. He was a congressman from 1843 to 1847 and then was elected to the Senate, serving until 1856. Although a Jacksonian Democrat, he could not stomach the Kansas-Nebraska bill. His speech of June 12, 1856, renouncing his party allegiance, was widely quoted and became one of his most effective utterances. That same year he was elected governor of Maine, the first of a long line of Republican governors. But he resigned a month after being inaugurated to re-enter the Senate, from which he would now resign to be sworn in as Vice-President.

Personally, Hannibal Hamlin was a likable man, a politician of the best type, honest, forthright, with attractive qualities that held the loyalty and affection of a host of supporters. He was an inveterate smoker and card player, a witty conversationalist. He had a powerful frame and great muscular strength. His complexion was so swarthy that in the 1860 election campaign the story was circulated in the South that he had Negro blood and that was why he was so strongly anti-slavery. Actually, his paternal ancestor, James Hamlin, had arrived from England in the second boatload of Pilgrims; went back for his family, and settled on Cape Cod in 1639.

Following the election in November, Hamlin came to Chicago at Lincoln's invitation. Reaching Lincoln's room in the Tremont House, he knocked on the door and a voice called for him to come in. It was Lincoln, alone. Greeting his teammate and taking his hand, Lincoln asked if they had ever been introduced. Hamlin replied they had not.

"That is also my impression," said Lincoln. "But I remember distinctly while I was in Congress to have heard you make a speech in the Senate. I was very much struck with that speech, Senator, particularly struck with it, for the reason that it was filled, chock-up, with the very best kind of anti-slavery doctrine."

"Well, now," laughed the affable Hamlin, "That is very singular, for my one and first recollection of yourself is having heard you make a speech in the House, a speech so full of good humor and sharp points that I, together with your other auditors, was convulsed with laughter."

The friendship thus cordially begun continued throughout the turbulent years. Lincoln reposed the utmost confidence in his teammate, often seeking his advice and counsel. Indeed, it was for that purpose Lincoln had invited Hamlin to meet with him in Chicago. But rumors of their being together in the hotel quickly got around and their privacy was soon invaded. They escaped next day to the Lakeview home of Ebenezer Peck on Chicago's north side.

Lincoln told Hamlin, "I shall accept, and shall always be willing to accept, in the very best spirit, any advice that you may give me."

Hamlin replied, "Mr. Lincoln, I desire to say to you that although relations between Vice-Presidents and Presidents have not always been friendly as a rule, I pledge myself to be your friend and to render you the best advice and assistance in my humble power."

In 1864 Hamlin was not renominated with Lincoln. The reason was that the War Democrats were given greater recognition in making a "Union" ticket. Andrew Johnson of Tennessee filled the bill and was chosen by the nominating convention. On his return to private life Hamlin was made president of a Maine railroad, the Bangor and Dover line, now part of the Boston and Maine. But in 1868 he would be called back into politics and again elected to the United States Senate, serving until 1881 when he was appointed Minister to Spain. Hamlin was the last of the Lincoln intimates to survive, living in Bangor until 1891, a typical rugged "down-easter."

His inaugural journey was begun in Maine fashion. Whereas Lincoln's had commenced on a train in the rain, and Davis's in a rowboat on the river, the hardy Hamlin started out in a horse-drawn sleigh. Winter in Maine meant ice and snow and zero temperatures.

At four o'clock in the morning, Monday, February 18, Hamlin and his young wife set out from their home in Hampden to sleigh ride the six snow-mantled miles to Bangor. Happy townsmen made the leave-taking a gala occasion. Single sleighs and double sleighs and wagons on runners filled with bundled-up neighbors, escorted the first and only Vice-President-elect ever to come out of the Pine Tree State.

At Bangor he was greeted by the mayor and ex-mayors, and a great crowd of constituents. To the mayor's welcome, Hamlin responded briefly as the train was about to leave.

"I go to the discharge of official duties," he said from the back platform of the regular train from Boston, "which have been conferred upon me by a generous people; and relying upon Divine Providence, I trust that confidence shall never be betrayed.

"I know full well that dark clouds are lowering around the political horizon, and that madness rules the hour.

"But I am hopeful still that our people are not only loyal to the Government but they are fraternal to all its citizens; and . . . may we not reasonably hope that quiet will be restored and the whole country will advance in a career that will elevate man in a social, moral and intellectual condition. . . ."

The locomotive whistled and snorted. Cheers echoed on the sharp air. Sleigh bells jingled. Horses shied at the racket. The newly elected Vice-President of the United States was on his way to the federal capital, a journey to fame that would place him among the immortals through another and greater man who would always be his friend.

The 250 miles to Boston required all day, Hamlin making short speeches at train stopovers; Waterville and Portland, Maine; Portsmouth, New Hampshire; and Newburyport, Massachusetts. At other stations there were greetings and demonstrations when his presence on the train became known. The party included newly elected Maine congressman John N. Goodwin, John H. Rice, F. A. Pike, C. W. Walton, and such others as C. W. Goodard, president of the Maine Senate, and S. C. Fessenden, in whose office Hamlin had studied law, and who was the father of Senator William P. Fessenden, later Lincoln's Secretary of the Treasury.

In Boston crowds were waiting at the depots of the two Northern railroads, the Eastern Railroad and the Boston and Maine, not knowing by which route Hamlin would arrive. The train pulled in at the former at 8:00 P.M., half an hour late. By his request no formal reception or demonstration was attempted. He was ushered to a carriage that took him to the Revere House. It had been a long and arduous day. He retired at once.

To travel by rail from Boston to New York required passing over four separate railroads or by combinations of rail and steamboat. A through service was operated by the Boston and Worcester, "to New York without ferries or change of cars." It was called the New York and Boston Express Line, traveling the Boston and Worcester to Worcester, the Western Railroad to Springfield, then south over the New Haven, Hartford and Springfield, and into Manhattan on the New York and New Haven.

The through New York cars were departing at the same time as the Vice-President-elect, 8:30 A.M. Again there

[217]

was no special demonstration. Refreshed by a good night's rest and substantial breakfast, Hamlin entered the depot with his party and was cheered by those who were there. He acknowledged the greetings but made no speech. A local reporter said his appearance was much the same as usual and that "he wore his Newcastle hat fixed firmly on the back part of his head."

The Boston and Worcester provided a special car, patriotically decorated, comfortably appointed. Delegations acting as escorts were also on board. At Worcester, the first stop, an assembly of some fifteen hundred insisted on a speech. Introduced by a local dignitary who had been riding the train, Hamlin responded in these stirring words:

"Men of Massachusetts!" he cried out, "your generous tones speak truly for the heart of this great Commonwealth. You men who are gathered here are the best representatives of the blessings of intelligent, productive, free labor; and the sentiments of your hearts are worthy of the ancient fame of the old Bay State.

"I know you are sometimes charged with being too fanatical and I fear your complaint is chronic." (Laughter and cheers) "It came from old '76 and I have no apology to offer for you. I sympathize with it too deeply." (Cheers.)

The train pulled away, ending the speech in the middle of a paragraph. At Springfield, a five-minute scheduled stopover, Hamlin was again called to talk by an eager crowd. He detrained a few miles further on and spent the night with relatives at Windsor Locks, Connecticut.

Next afternoon he resumed the journey. By this time people along the route were aware of his presence. A throng greeted him at Hartford and a speech was demanded. The ladies presented Mrs. Hamlin with a handsome bouquet of flowers. At Meriden he had to speak from the baggage car, the only advantageous position. At New Haven he was introduced to the throng by the editor of the *New Haven Palladium*. At the close of his talk the crowd rushed to the car platform to shake his hand.

Hamlin, a friendly man with a big heart and a hearty handshake, grew so enthusiastic, and the people became so tumultuous that no one noticed the train had started moving. His hand in the grip of a well-wisher, he lost his balance and suddenly became one of the crowd. The train went on and left the Vice-President-elect, as one wit put it, widowed for a second time. The loss was discovered and the train halted. Hamlin put his muscle to work and was soon aboard the cars despite numerous shouted invitations to be New Haven's guest overnight.

At Naugatuck an accident below Bridgeport to the "up" train detained all movement on the single track. When Bridgeport was reached an immense crowd hurrahed for Lincoln, hurrahed for the Union, and hurrahed for Hamlin. But he would not respond. Possibly he was too upset by the New Haven episode. At Stamford, the next stop, he did respond, seeming to be his usual, cordial self, making a few pleasant remarks.

These were his last before arriving in New York at the New Haven depot on Twenty-sixth Street, forty-five minutes late. Greeting him was a concourse of friends that would have been much larger had he announced his itinerary. Several delegations had met the morning train from Boston. Even so, deputations were on hand from Kings and Queens counties as well as from Manhattan. They escorted him, cheering and shouting, to the carriages they had waiting. In charge of General James W. Nye of Brooklyn and Judge Lothrop of New York, the party was driven over Twenty-sixth Street to Fifth Avenue, down to Fourteenth, over to Broadway and down Broadway to the Astor House.

Hamlin did not leave New York with Lincoln. He stayed another day, holding a reception Thursday afternoon attended by some two hundred persons including such political notables as Thurlow Weed and former presidential nominee John C. Fremont. In the evening he and Mrs. Hamlin went to Niblo's Garden to hear the English opera, *Bohemian Girl,* starring Anna Bishop, billed as the greatest living soprano. Hamlin was discovered in the audience and given a rousing ovation. Madame Bishop sang in his honor "The Flag of Our Union Forever," assisted in the choruses by the entire troupe.

Early Friday morning, the twenty-second, the Hamlin party left for the federal capital. He did not tarry along the way but pushed right on to Washington. He arrived in the early evening and was met by Senator Seward and Congressman Washburne who were actually anticipating Lincoln's arrival, but did not tell Hamlin so.

The only departure Hamlin made from the regular schedule, in view of the rumors being circulated about Baltimore, was that before passing through that city he seated himself in another train. So reported Hamlin's grandson Charles, his biographer, using the notes left by his father, who had been the Vice-President's secretary and confidant. Charles wrote that some ruffians hanging around the railroad station boarded the cars and rushed through, presumably on the prowl for the President-elect.

Hamlin would be on hand in Washington to greet Lincoln, whose itinerary called for overnight stops at Philadelphia and Harrisburg. The scheduled arrival in Washington was Sunday. But there was destined to be a drastic change in Lincoln's program.

CHAPTER 21

THE handsome ship docked in the Cortlandt Street ferryslip was the newest and largest of the fleet. It was the ferryboat *John P. Jackson,* built the year before and named for the superintendent of the New Jersey Railroad and Transportation Company. The company also owned the railroad from Jersey City to New Brunswick as well as the great dockside terminal in Jersey City where five other rail lines ended their New York runs.

Aboard the decorated ferryboat Dodsworth's thirty-piece band was rendering selections from *Lucia di Lammermoor,* changing abruptly to patriotic airs as the President-elect and party were driven on board. Since Lincoln left the hotel at 8:00 A.M., an hour ahead of published departure time, few people had been present and there was no ceremony. Descending from the carriage, he was greeted by A. O. Zabriskie, chairman of the Jersey City citizens committee, who introduced him to the others. He shook hands with everyone on board.

The ferry got underway at once. As soon as it cleared the dock it was given a thirty-four-gun salute fired by the Cunard steamships *Africa* and *Jura* lying in their docks on the Jersey side. Both were ornamented in fine style;

pennants ran from water to masthead, from mast to mast, and from mast to water. The steamer *Granada*, passing at the moment, also fired a salute.

Foreign shipping in the harbor was especially decorated for the occasion—omnicolored bunting stretching through the rigging, flags flying in the stiff wind, the American ensign displayed at the position of honor, the stern. With the exception of a few Southern ships riding bleakly at their docks, unattended, the harbor presented such an animated spectacle that Lincoln was enraptured.

He had never seen it to such advantage before. Standing on the bridge of the powerful steamboat that could carry an entire regiment and its equipage, one that would be purchased by the government the next year for that very purpose, he watched the panoramic display of steamers, schooners, barks, brigs, tugs, barges and ferries. He expressed the hope of enjoying a fuller view at some future time.

To give him the best sight in the shortest time, the run was extended past the Battery to Bedloe Island, which did not yet carry France's gift to the American nation, the Statue of Liberty. Whistles shrieked, guns crashed and the band played as the presidential ferryboat steamed down the harbor and then turned west to the Jersey City terminal. As it neared the pier the Cunard liners ceased firing and the New Jersey salute was commenced by the Hudson County Artillery.

As the big ferry moored and the gangplank was let down, the party disembarked to lively national tunes, the Second New Jersey Regiment acting as guard of honor and presenting arms. Lincoln was welcomed by Jersey City's Mayor Cornelius Van Vorst, and by William L. Dayton, attorney general of New Jersey and chairman of the legislative reception committee. Arm in arm they walked into the huge depot, the band striking up the appropriate greeting, "Hail to the Chief."

The terminal was a huge structure, five hundred feet by two hundred feet. The gallery around its sides was packed with ladies waving handkerchiefs, the floor hidden by masculine faces. The men were yelling themselves hoarse. "Never before," asserted the *New York Herald,* "such a collection of Christians, at least twenty thousand." The *World* estimated that there were only twelve thousand, but still a mammoth gathering, it said, for New Jersey. Numbers and chauvinism aside, the assembly was immense and the greeting enthusiastic.

Up carpeted steps to the front end of a carpeted flatcar trimmed in tricolored bunting, Lincoln was conducted. Turning to him the mayor said, "I here extend the hospitalities of Jersey City to you, the President-elect of the United States." Lincoln bowed acknowledgment. The uproar was too great for him to speak.

Dayton then stepped forward. He waited until the outbursts had subsided and, addressing Lincoln, said in the absence of the governor and acting in his stead, "I give you a cordial welcome to the State of New Jersey.

"Sir," he continued, "we have assembled here to testify to our appreciation of your character, our unwavering loyalty to the laws and the Constitution, and our devotion to the interest of this great country and the perpetuity of the Union. . . ."

The applause reverberated through the high-ceilinged structure and increased as Lincoln stepped up to speak. He expressed his thanks for the warm greeting given "not to me as an individual, but as the representative of the Chief Magistracy of the nation . . .

"I am here before you, careworn, for little else than to greet you and say farewell. You have done me the very

[223]

high honor to present your reception of me through your own great man—a man with whom it is an honor to be associated anywhere—a man with whom no State could be poor. . . ."

He was referring to Attorney General Dayton who had been Republican Vice-Presidential candidate in 1856, the first time the Republican party had run in a national election. In the following (1860) Republican convention, New Jersey had supported Dayton as its favorite son for the Presidency. Lincoln would appoint him Minister to France, a sensitive and difficult position.

At the close of Lincoln's remarks the crowd pushed forward, determined to shake his hand. So great was their determination that the cordon of policemen surrounding the flatcar were overwhelmed. Brandishing their clubs they tried to push the mob back. It was no use. Lincoln and party were marooned in a roaring sea of people. He could not get down to reach his train. Asked to "hold them off" by saluting the ladies, he obliged.

"There appears to be a desire to see more of me," he said, moving to the front and holding up a hand for quiet. Stretching his head upward and turning to all sides, he remarked, "I can only say that from my position, especially when I look around the gallery (bowing), I feel that I have the best of the bargain, and I am for no compromises here."

The ladies thought highly of the sentiment. The men gave way amiably to this strategy of Colonel Ellsworth and to the impressive bulk of Colonel Lamon.

The depot clock pointed to 9:05 A.M. as the dressed-up locomotive *Governor Pennington* shrieked its warning and hauled the three bunting-bedecked cars out of the thundering terminal building. Preceded by the regular mail train which was clearing the track as a pilot, and followed at a safe distance by an excursion special of seven coaches, the Presidential Special drew to a halt in Newark at the railroad station on Division Street. The time was 9:30 A.M. Again guns were booming.

The Newark program was a last-minute affair. A committee of the common council had gone to New York and presented Lincoln with a copy of the resolutions inviting him to the city. He thanked them and referred them to manager Wood. Wood agreed to a half-hour stopover in Newark. Knowing from experience what generally happened, Wood stepped-up the departure a full hour.

Lincoln was to be received at the lower depot, parade the mile up Broad Street, and entrain at the upper depot. The populace was advised to avoid railroad stations and to view the parade along Broad Street. Lincoln was met in the ladies' parlor by a group of distinguished citizens, city officials, a party of ladies and the press. After replying to the mayor's welcome he was escorted to a barouche drawn by four splendid grays. Sitting with him were Mayor Moses Bigelow, the common council committee chairman and Attorney General Dayton. An imposing cavalcade of 150 horsemen headed the procession. The wide reaches of Broad Street were packed with 25,000 shouting spectators, despite a lively snowstorm. The event was a credit to the city, there was no disorder or confusion. At the upper depot on Chestnut Street, the Special waited. A dense crowd jammed the area but Lincoln had little difficulty boarding the train. He stood, as usual, on the rear platform bowing to the demonstrations as the cars rolled toward Trenton.

At Elizabeth a two-minute stop was made but no speech. At Rahway and succeeding points the train slowed that he might respond to "cheers, cannon and crowds." At New Brunswick there was a change of engines, the Camden and Amboy Railroad taking over the train.

At Princeton the student body was out in force, sending forth ear-splitting skyrocket cheers that fairly lifted the cars from the tracks. Lincoln acknowledged the exuberant demonstration as the train slowed. The college men piled into the excursion train that was following and regaled onlookers with organized cheering and college songs, "Gaudeamus Igitur," "Integer Vitae," "The Horn That Once Thro' Nassau's Halls," and "Upidee."

There were several snow squalls along the way, the sun coming through when Trenton was reached at 11:50 A.M. The depot had been thoroughly cleaned and was well-guarded by policemen. Lincoln was met by a welcoming group, addressed by the mayor, and escorted up State Street to the Capitol by a troop of horsemen followed by the Patterson Blues, the German Rifles, Shelton's New York band, civic officials and local celebrities. The procession was viewed by a rousing street audience of twenty thousand people, according to New York newspapers.

Arriving at the State House, he was ushered into the Senate chamber. Awaiting him were the Senate, state officers, a packed gallery of ladies, and two committees from Philadelphia. To the presiding officer's speech Lincoln listened carefully as he stood in the broad aisle in front of the Speaker. Removing his gloves and bowing to either side, he advanced a step forward. He began by expressing his gratitude for the warm reception:

"May I be pardoned if, upon this occasion, I mention that way back in my childhood, the earliest days of my being able to read, I got hold of a small book, such a one as few of the younger men here have ever seen, *Weems' Life of Washington.* I remember all the accounts then given of the battle-fields and struggles for the liber-

[226]

ties of this country, and none fixed themselves upon my imagination so deeply as the one here at Trenton, New Jersey.

"The crossing of the river, the contest with the Hessians, the great hardships endured at that time, all fixed themselves on my memory, more than any single Revolutionary event; and you all know, for you have all been boys, how these early impressions last longer than any others.

"I recollect thinking then, boy even though I was, that there must have been something more than common that these men struggled for. . . . I am exceedingly anxious that this Union, the Constitution, and the liberties of the people shall be perpetuated in accordance with the original idea for which that struggle was made. . . ."

The applause was tremendous. Shaking hands with the president of the Senate, with each member, and with the Philadelphia committees among whom he recognized several friends, he was conducted across the hall by the presiding senator to the assembly chamber. It was overflowing. The gallery, like the Senate, was jammed with ladies; the main floor packed with men admitted by ticket.

Lincoln stood in the broad aisle in front of the Speaker. As he turned to the audience to begin his response to the Speaker's welcome, the crowd pushed forward to get a better look. They cried, "Down in front!" "Take off your hat!" "Where's the President?" "Keep your seats please!" intermingled with the gaveling of the Speaker. Lincoln solved the confusion by mounting the rostrum.

"Mr. Speaker," he said, "the man does not live who is more devoted to peace than I am. None who would do more to preserve it.

"But it may be necessary to put the foot down firmly." Saying this he lifted his foot lightly, pressing it down with a quick but not violent movement. Pandemonium broke loose. When order was restored Lincoln finished his sentence, "and if I do my duty, and do right you will sustain me; will you not?"

Again the crowd broke loose. Shouts, cheers, whistles, foot stampings, desk poundings, produced a vast cacophony. Hats flew into the air. The gallery was a mass of waving handkerchiefs. Not since he had begun the journey had Lincoln reached beneath the calm surface of logic and reason to touch the wellsprings of emotion pent up in the American people.

In putting the foot down, even lightly, he released emotions wrought up by years of agitation. He touched off feelings made explosive by many things that had been inflaming the prejudices of his follow citizens; things that were angering them beyond reason, tensing their nerves to the bursting point.

Things such as these: Two books—one, a book of fiction written by Harriet Beecher Stowe called *Uncle Tom's Cabin* became a best-seller and was reprinted all over the world. The other book, written by North Carolinian Hinton R. Helper, who had to flee to New York when it was published in 1857, was full of facts and fury. It was a statistical indictment of slavery, entitled *The Impending Crisis*. The two big sellers made a devastating combination; the book of facts that set one's teeth on edge; the novel that tingled the spine with a harrowing tale of whiplashed Uncle Tom, and of the mulatto girl, Eliza, and her child, escaping from pursuing bloodhounds over the ice floes.

The two books were part of a larger picture; a picture that included a daily press eager to report agitations of the moment, no matter where. The magnetic telegraph, making possible transmission of news from distant points, was new and novel. News was traveling faster and farther than ever before, thanks to the clicking brass keys. News like that of the runaway slave from Virginia who was captured in Boston, one Anthony Burns. He had made the mistake of writing to his brother and the letter got into the owner's hands instead. When the slaveowner came to Boston to reclaim his "property" under the Fugitive Slave Law a mob threatened to take Burns away from him. A deputy United States Marshal was killed in the attempt, and the militia was called out. Burns was lodged in the courthouse jail for safety. To the vessel that was to transport them south, owner and slave were escorted by a military guard of eleven hundred soldiers, so fierce was the people's feeling. The outrage was a nation-wide sensation.

So was the caning of Massachusetts Senator Charles Sumner by hotheaded Preston Brooks, congressman from South Carolina. Sumner, in the heated debate on the Kansas-Nebraska bill, delivered a stinging attack on slavery, singling out Douglas and Senator A. P. Butler of South Carolina for personal remarks. He called his speech The Crime Against Kansas and said the bill raped a virgin territory, compelling it to embrace the harlot, slavery.

Congressman Brooks, relative of Butler, resented the attack against his state and the insinuations against his kinsman. He took the law into his own hands. Using a guttapercha cane such as gentlemen then affected, he quietly entered the Senate on the afternoon of May 22, 1856, and struck Sumner as he sat at his desk, raining blows on the dazed victim so hard the cane broke. Sumner suffered severe lacerations and possible brain concussion. He was laid up for two years. Thereafter both Northern and Southern congressmen went to their chambers fully armed. The public was inflamed

No single personal incident exerted such a powerful effect on the people's emotions as did Senator Sumner's beating in the Senate chamber. So far-reaching were its repercussions that students of the period have considered it a contributory cause of the war that followed. The stage also had been well prepared by the bloody events in Kansas.

"Bleeding Kansas" was made violent by the Kansas-Nebraska Act which put determination of the slavery question into the hands of the settlers. Slaveholders in adjacent Missouri moved to control the political destinies of the new Kansas Territory by sending in their men. Abolitionists, just as determined to keep Kansas "free," sent in groups of settlers carrying Bibles and bullets. Bloody collisions were inevitable.

Dispatches from the area were filled with hair-raising exploits of border ruffians, the Wakarusa "war," John Brown of Osawatomie, the sack of Lawrence, the Lecompton frauds, and other acts of villainy and violence. The plains of the Platte River witnessed the preliminary rounds of the coming war.

President Buchanan, who had triumphed over the first Republican ticket of Fremont and Dayton in 1856, had been hopeful of taking the slavery question out of the political arena where it had caused so many heartaches, making it a matter of jurisprudence. He promised in the Inaugural Address that his administration would bring a period of quietude to the problem of slavery in the new territories. "Most happy it will be for the country when the public shall be diverted from this question," he said, thus recognizing the artificiality of the agitation, "and besides, it is a judicial question which legitimately belongs to the Supreme Court before whom it is now pending."

Two days later the high tribunal obliged by emitting one of its most unrealistic opinions, the Dred Scott decision. The three-hour-long decision, written and read by Chief Justice Roger Brooke Taney, a slaveholder from Maryland, argued that "at the time of the Declaration of Independence . . . and for more than a century before, they (Negroes) had been regarded as so inferior that they had no rights which the white man was bound to respect." The decision held that a Negro slave was property and could not become a citizen of the United States. It also held that the Missouri Compromise was unconstitutional.

Gone before it could begin was Buchanan's promised period of quietude, no thanks to a confused judiciary. Lincoln made penetrating comments on the subject in campaign speeches and in debates with Douglas. He summed up with this wise counsel:

"Republicans believe as much as Democrats that the Supreme Court must be respected and obeyed. . . . But we think the Dred Scott decision is erroneous. We know that the court that made it often over-ruled its own decisions, and we shall do what we can to have it over-rule this."

Added to these highly-charged emotional incidents was a long series of economic controversies that had aggravated the antagonisms; the Homestead bill, the protective tariff, Pacific railway route and the program of internal improvements. Driving the wedge deeper was Democrat opposition to Field's proposed trans-Atlantic cable, the transcontinental mail service, the overland telegraph line, the deepening of rivers and harbors. A bill did get through Congress providing funds for certain harbor work, but Secretary of Treasury Howell Cobb of Georgia, under whose jurisdiction the disbursement came, refused to spend the money. The newspapers yelled, "Chicago to be Cheated Out of Her Harbor Appropriation by the Democracy."

Southern Democrats wanted to acquire Cuba, and sponsored a bill for that purpose. Senator Seward expostulated, "The Homestead bill is a question of land for the landless free men of the United States; the Cuba bill is a question of slaves for slaveholders."

The slave empire builders had also openly supported questionable methods, known as filibustering, of acquiring territory in Central America and Mexico. The acknowledged leader was William Walker, well known for his military machinations in tropical lands that seemed desirable for a slave-based aristocracy. Jefferson Davis in his speech at Atlanta during his inaugural trip spoke of the South's glorious future "stretching from the Atlantic to the Pacific, with the northern portions of Mexico forming part of the broad domain." Meaning plainly enough that the confederacy would reach out for lands and islands to be incorporated into the new cotton empire.

The "free" states opposed such adventures. They did not approve the continual political concessions being made to slaveholding states, such as permitting them to count non-voting slaves for congressional representation—five slaves were counted as three whites. Thus these states had a proportionately greater representation in Congress than the free states.

Of the many tensions, a climax came when John Brown raided Harpers Ferry. This government arsenal, established by Congress in 1796, was located at the confluence of the Potomac and Shenandoah Rivers in northern Virginia. Misanthrope Brown and eighteen of his followers seized it on the night of October 16, 1859. They were driven out two days later by Colonel Robert E. Lee and Lieutenant J. E. B. Stuart of the United States Army and ninety marines. Amid great excitement, Brown and the survivors of his folly were given a "fair" trial in a nearby county seat.

So widely has the event been chronicled in song and story over the years, it is only necessary to point out that, trivial as the incident appears today, at that time it exerted emotional power beyond all comprehension. The free states had a martyr and the slave states an omen when Brown was summarily hanged. The war was now virtually assured.

These were some of the factors that contributed to the uproar that followed Lincoln's mention in Trenton that he might have to set the foot down firmly. When quiet finally descended he presented the most telling point. New Jersey, it will be recalled, had not voted him full endorsement in the election. He needed its backing in the crisis looming ahead. This was the moment to elevate political competition into patriotic cooperation.

Bending forward, with a smile and manner that was both captivating and indescribable, he said to every straining ear, "And, gentlemen, if you think I am right, you will stand by me, will you not?"

"We will! We will!" cried the audience.

And Lincoln responded, "That is all I ask."

To those who might still oppose him politically he thereupon advanced the closing argument, "And if, as I have already suggested," he continued, "the majority of this Legislature do not agree with me in [political] sentiment, we will try and save the ship for this voyage; and the next time it may be hoped that even in your judgment a better pilot may be chosen in my place. . . ."

Crowding up to shake his hand, pushing to get closer to him, they made the passage from assembly chamber to waiting carriages virtually impossible to negotiate. The police were helpless. Lincoln had to make his own passage. Good-naturedly, reaching out his long arms, he moved those in the immediate front who were in the way, bending his tall form to the task, speaking cheerful words as he went, and eventually reached his vehicle.

The waiting procession resumed the trip to the Trenton House. Here was another impenetrable mass of people. Above the hotel entrance a small platform had been erected, and in response to repeated demands, Lincoln finally appeared on it. He said he supposed that when he spoke to the legislature "they intended I should speak to you through them as they are the representatives of all of you."

At 2:00 P.M. the dining room was opened for a "reception dinner given by State authorities." There were no speeches. There were no seats. There was no menu. It was a cold buffet luncheon. About three hundred persons participated. Lincoln and suite ate quickly, anxious to meet the train schedule in spite of continual interruptions by well-wishers.

Mrs. Lincoln and family, who had been guests of Attorney General and Mrs. Dayton at their home, returned directly to the waiting train. At 2:30 P.M. the Special moved toward Philadelphia.

The lanky Railsplitter had completely captured the Garden State.

CHAPTER 22

Philadelphians were waiting along the streets by the thousands, a hundred thousand at least, as Lincoln emerged from the Kensington depot of the Philadelphia and Trenton Railroad at 4:00 P.M. Escorted by a cavalcade of local and state dignitaries, two hundred citizens in carriages, and accompanied by police and militia, the procession moved down Frankford Road to Girard Avenue, winding its way over Sixth to Arch, to Sixteenth, to Walnut, to Ninth and up to the Continental Hotel at Chestnut Street.

Here the crush was so great that, despite precautions of the police, the broad halls and stairways of the hotel through which Lincoln had to pass were clogged with citizens. To reach the balcony where he would make his scheduled speech required more expert crowd manipulation. Even the room from which he entered the balcony was filled to suffocation.

After his response to the mayor's welcome, Lincoln re-entered the room and said to the escort:

"Gentlemen, I must now get some refreshment. After that I shall be glad to shake hands with all of you that I can. I will shake as long as I can shake and then will content myself with a look that will answer the same purpose. . . ."

Mrs. Lincoln and the boys had come directly from the depot. They awaited him in the adjoining apartment to which he now withdrew to have his much-needed supper.

Philadelphia's oversized newspaper, the *North American and United States Gazette,* proudly announced, "Our reporter had the opportunity of seeing them all from the little eight-year old to Master Robert, the sophomore from Harvard. . . . The boys are fine-looking fellows but lack the polish of city lads . . . and decidedly resemble their mother. As to Mr. Lincoln, we never before placed the proper estimate upon the picturesqueness of whiskers. Mr. Lincoln with whiskers is anything but the reverse of good-looking. His beard should never again be laid aside; with it he is a fine-looking personage."

After the hurried meal Lincoln made his way to the reception parlor where heads of city departments and members of the city councils were gathered. Along the corridor the citizens committee had ranged themselves, having no other place to go. He greeted them individually as he passed along.

Several representatives from Wilmington, Delaware, were presented as the committee delegated to invite him to their city. Lincoln took them to his apartment for a private interview. He expressed his fond remembrance of a previous visit to Wilmington when campaigning for the Whig presidential candidate who was subsequently elected, General Zachary Taylor. He said he regretted not being able to accept their kind invitation.

At eight o'clock the public reception was to begin, but it took half an hour for Lincoln to extricate himself from the many persons trying to see him. He took position at the head of the main stairway, the people coming up from the lobby and passing in front of him, an operation similar to Cleveland and Buffalo.

The scene was touching. Rough men, unaccustomed to the niceties of life, raised their hats as they came into his presence. Those who did not were the exception. Many made homespun remarks, "God bless you, Abe!" "Do the best you can for us, old fellow!" "You are our only hope, Mr. Lincoln!" Relieved of shaking hands, he bowed to all comers, smiled at those who spoke to him. The general comment was pleasant surprise that he was not nearly so ill-looking as represented.

A display of fireworks began at a little after ten o'clock. Lincoln retired from public view, worn out from sixteen hours of unremitting activity, the eleventh successive day of it. A brass band on the balcony entertained the twenty thousand spectators massed in the streets watching the brilliant pyrotechnics. The program ended at eleven o'clock with the firing of a triumphal arch erected over Ninth and Chestnut streets from southeast to northwest corner. The arch bore the name "Abraham Lincoln" in large letters, underneath, "The Whole Union."

Outside Lincoln's bedroom door several committees lingered till midnight, hoping he would come out to see them. He could not; he was closeted with close friends and advisers. They were bringing him disquieting news, the first hint of peril.

After a cold and gusty night the temperature moderated and the wind died, as "morn walked rosy o'er the hills. The lamps of heaven faded, the glorious Star of the Morning lingering latest in the sky. . . ." In this manner, the *Evening Bulletin* began its report of the events of Friday, February 22, 1861; including, as a practical contribution, the temperature at the *Bulletin* office, thirty six degrees at 9:00 A.M., forty-four degrees at noon.

The *Gazette* opined that a stranger would have wondered at the number of well-dressed people so early astir in the streets.

For many years past, continued the account, no Washington's Birthday in Philadelphia equaled in brilliancy this celebration. The whole day was made up of incidents, the high point being the elevation of the national ensign of thirty-four stars upon the flagstaff surmounting Independence Hall by the President-elect of the United States. "Into the history of Philadelphia," prophesied the writer, "this event will enter, and years hence when the now truant States have returned to the Union's fold, our grandchildren will read of it with gratitude."

The *Public Ledger* announced that at sunrise the booming of cannon in a national salute and the ringing of innumerable bells called forth the populace from their warm beds.

Just in front of the main entrance, and a few feet from Independence Hall, a large platform had been erected six feet high, the front was hung with the American flag, smaller ones floated from the framework. It was 7:00 A.M. when patriotic music was heard approaching along Chestnut Street. Crowds in surrounding streets increased to solid masses of people.

"A hum arose from the wide host; such as Byron describes the sounds of the army before whom Corinth fell, when their confused prayers arose at the muezzin call, and 'rustled like leaves from coast to coast.' . . ." the *Bulletin's* erudite reporter described the situation.

At the American Hotel across the square ladies crowded the windows and waved kerchiefs. The *Gazette* declared it "like a gorgeous floral piece, greatly enlarged."

Lincoln came out of his hotel on time, looking well rested. A handful of heroes of the Scott Legion, who had fought in Mexico, preceded by their band, formed his escort to Independence Hall. He was welcomed by the president of the city's select council. Standing in the room where the Declaration of Independence had been signed Lincoln replied to the welcome with an utterance that emphasized the underlying principle of American freedom. He said:

"I am filled with deep emotion at finding myself standing here in the place where were collected together the wisdom, the patriotism, the devotion to principle, from which spring the institutions under which we live.

"You have kindly suggested to me that in my hands is the task of restoring peace to our distracted country. I can say in return, that all the political sentiments I entertain have been drawn, so far as I have been able to draw them, from the sentiments which originated, and were given to the world from this hall in which we stand. I have never had a feeling politically that did not spring from the sentiments embodied in the Declaration of Independence.

"I have often pondered over the dangers which were incurred by the men who assembled here and adopted that Declaration of Independence—I have pondered over the toils that were endured by the officers and soldiers of the army who achieved that Independence.

"I have often inquired of myself, what great principle or idea it was that kept this Confederacy so long together. It was not the mere matter of the separation of the colonies from the motherland; but something in that Declaration giving liberty not alone to the people of this country, but hope to the world for all future time.

"It was that which gave promise that in due time the

weights should be lifted from the shoulders of all men, and that *all* should have an equal chance. This is the sentiment embodied in that Declaration of Independence.

"Now, my friends, can this country be saved upon that basis? If it can, I will consider myself one of the happiest men in the world if I can help to save it. If it can't be saved upon that principle, it will truly be awful. But, if this country cannot be saved without giving up that principle—I was about to say I would rather be assassinated on this spot than to surrender it. (Applause.)

"Now, in my view of the present aspect of affairs, there is no need of bloodshed and war. There is no necessity for it. I am not in favor of such a course, and I may say in advance, there will be no bloodshed unless it be forced upon the government. The government will not use force unless force is used against it."

"My friends, this is a wholly unprepared speech. I did not expect to be called upon to say a word when I came here—I supposed I was merely to do something toward raising a flag. I may, therefore, have said something indiscreet.

"But I have said nothing but what I am willing to live by, and, in the pleasure of Almighty God, die by," concluded the man from Illinois.

Members of the city councils and distinguished guests came forward to pay their respects. Lincoln expressed interest in the portraits of the early patriots adorning the walls, and made a short tour of Independence Hall. The procession moved to the platform outside, the appearance of Lincoln was greeted by waves of applause from the massed people, the sound rising and falling like the sound of the sea. His tall form, as he stepped upon

[240]

the platform, rose like Saul above the brethren. Introduced by a city official, he delivered a brief inspirational message.*

At the close, he stepped back and the Reverend Henry S. Clarke came to the railing. There being comparative quiet during the prayer, a photographer recorded the scene. The prayer finished, all but a few persons left the stand, allowing the President-elect more room for the flag-raising. He removed his overcoat, took hold of the halyard, and pulled, hand over hand.

As the tricolored bundle was raised aloft by the incoming Sixteenth President of the Republic, the band saluted with the "Star-Spangled Banner." The flag, folded into a roll, or what is known as "man-o'-war" style, stayed tight until it reached the peak of the flagstaff, then suddenly unfurled in a light breeze. The new banner of thirty-four stars was accorded special homage by the band. They played for the first time "The Stars and Stripes Are Still Unfurled," an anthem dedicated to Major Robert Anderson, then holding command at Fort Sumter. The Scott Legion, facing the stand as guard of honor, presented arms, and an artillery detachment of Washington grays, stationed in the square, fired the national salute. Press reports said it was impossible to describe the mad enthusiasm of the people.

The flag-raising ceremony over, Lincoln returned to the hotel, escorted by the Scott Legion, the band and a detail of police.

---

* The recent admission into the Union of Alaska and Hawaii as the forty-ninth and fiftieth states respectively, makes this sentence from Lincoln's remarks particularly significant: "I think we may promise ourselves that not only the new star (Kansas) placed upon that flag shall be permitted to remain there to our permanent prosperity for years to come, but additional ones shall from time to time be placed there, until we shall number, as was anticipated by the great historian, five hundred millions of happy and prosperous people."

At eight-thirty he left the hotel in the same open barouche with the plumed white horses and proceeded to the depot of the Pennsylvania Railroad in West Philadelphia where a special train of three cars awaited him. Cannon thundered, the band blared, the crowd cheered, and the Presidential Special took off for the capital city of the state.

In New Jersey with its Revolutionary battlefields, and in Philadelphia at the "cradle of liberty," Lincoln had been treading ground sacred to him; places noted for events he had pondered long and deeply. This day he had stood in Independence Hall. A Kentucky backwoodsman whose father had risen no higher than a log cabin on the prairie now appeared as the head of the great nation-state that had been fashioned in this very Hall. It seemed an unbelievable dream.

What method of government—what concept of political rule—could contribute to such an end? What underlying principle of this new nation-state in the New World made it so attractive? What, in essence, was the great centripetal idea that pulled men together and held them?

Lincoln had been groping for illumination. He said in Trenton that he had begun in boyhood to search for the answer. The quest had become imperative when his political allegiance had been taken from him. The Whig party, to which he had always adhered, had disintegrated under his very eyes. He had been the leading Whig politician in Illinois, and he had been elected to the state legislature four times, to Congress once, and once he had stood for United States Senator, each time as a Whig.

It wasn't going to be easy for him to change. Conservative in political action, in his thinking he was advanced. Between thinking and doing he always interposed the typical American denominator—would it work? He was a practical politician. To best friend Joshua F. Speed he confessed his uncertainty in 1855.

"You inquire where I now stand," he wrote Speed. "That is a disputed point. . . . I now do no more than oppose the extension of slavery. . . ."

Why Lincoln became a Whig no one knows. It has been a continuing mystery that despite widespread admiration for General Andrew Jackson among pioneers and backwoodsmen current in Lincoln's formative years, he had not become a Jacksonian Democrat. Neither he nor his friends ever shed positive light on the basic precept of his political career. Numerous explanations have been offered.

He often expressed admiration for the Whig leader and fellow Kentuckian, Henry Clay, whose efforts at harmonizing discordant political sentiments, and in holding to American ideals, appealed strongly to him. Clay had promoted the Missouri Compromise of 1850. Upon his death two years later Lincoln had delivered a touching eulogy of his hero.

The name Whig has an old and honorable background, almost forgotten in the jazz of the jet age. It was the party of the American Revolutionists. The Whigs opposed the king's men who were called Tories. Whig and Tory in America stemmed from long usage in England in a parallel relationship. The word itself has an obscure derivation and appears to have originated when Scotch Presbyterians raided cattle herds of the English Church of England border barons. Whig was applied to them as a term of derision. Over the years it grew to stand for the political party that represented the people as against the royalists, the Tories.

At the successful conclusion of the Revolution, the

only political party left in America was the Whig, the Tories having been killed, banished or converted. Then the thirteen colonies, banded together to gain their independence by a document of agreement known as the Articles of Confederation, moved toward a constitution to consolidate their unity and to establish themselves among the powers of the world.

Two points of view arose within the Whig party; those wanting a strong central government, and those opposed. The two viewpoints were represented in President Washington's cabinet by Alexander Hamilton and Thomas Jefferson.

It must be recalled that when the colonies freed themselves of the mother country, each colony retained for itself all powers not specifically delegated to the confederated authority. The Articles of Confederation were so framed that each colony was as independent as if there were no confederacy. Thus, state sovereignty was a very real thing. What is more, it was preferred by the people, who had a morbid fear of dictatorial central authority. No more kings for them!

Jefferson, author of the Declaration of Independence, was not opposed to a constitution, as were anti-federalists, but he wanted to be sure the instrument carefully defined and limited the delegated powers. He founded the Republican party; from the Latin, *res publica,* affairs of the public. Those favoring a strong central government called themselves Federalists. The Whig party, having performed its mission of freedom for the nation, faded out of the picture.

At this time France was struggling to become a republic. She had aided the United States in the struggle for independence and many Americans now wished to help her. Groups were set up in the United States on the order of the Jacobin clubs in Paris. Refusing to be called Republican, they took the name Democrat. They branded every opponent an enemy of the people. Denouncing the nation's first excise law and supporting the Whiskey Rebellion, they incurred the wrath of President Washington. They merged with Jefferson's Republicans and the party was called Democratic-Republican; later, the latter half was dropped.

A series of sedulous efforts had gotten under way to avoid a serious clash of the two opposing views toward a central government, and there began a number of compromises to harmonize the difficulties "by devising resolutions which might be construed at will in senses the most diametrically opposite." The results exceeded expectations. Under the Presidency of James Monroe the nation enjoyed an era of such good feeling that political parties were not needed. From 1817 to 1825, Monroe's two terms, the United States became a big, happy, unpolitical family.

Then came the Jackson period and plenty of turmoil. Political parties tended to follow political personalities. Jackson, conqueror of the British at New Orleans, was the undying hero of the Irish. By voting Jacksonian they could vote anti-British. Those opposed to Jackson's high-handed methods organized an anti-Jackson group.

James Watson Webb of New York (called "General" because of early military service; his father had been a famous general in the Revolution) read a letter before a political meeting suggesting the party opposing Jackson be called Whig. This was in 1832. When the letter was published in leading newspapers, including Webb's *New York Courier,* the idea caught on. Just as the early Whigs had opposed the King of England, these Whigs would oppose the kinglike rule of dictatorial President Andrew Jackson to prevent his further usurpation of power.

By 1834 the Whig party had advanced to control the New York common council, and it soon spread over the country. The Whigs looked to Henry Clay for national leadership.

Clay's untimely death, passage of the controversial Kansas-Nebraska bill and constant slavery agitation, all combined to make "good old Whig ground" no longer tenable. Extremists took over, splitting the old alignments. Radical splinter parties sprang up. Again the Whig party faded away. There resulted a fusion of political elements taking the name of Republican, coalescing on the principle of slavery restriction.

This, in briefest outline, was the political background of America when Lincoln wrote Josh Speed of his uncertainty. Being naturally conservative, he was careful in making new affiliations. He was not sure which new group would mirror his principles of moderation. He would not support radicalism under any guise.

The coalition that came to be called Republican demonstrated a moderate course and Lincoln joined its ranks. He was encouraged by the other Whigs who were joining. They added a wing of conservatism, together with the Jacksonian Democrats who were disgusted with the pro-slavery extremists of their party.

Thus stood Lincoln in the middle 1850's. Before his deep-set blue eyes, the entire record of American politics passed in review as he debated his political future. He put the rationale of political action to careful re-evaluation; as Euclid to propositions, so Lincoln to political principles. In doing so he isolated the centripetal *idea* of the American Republic. He discovered the one great

[246]

thing that pulled Americans together and held them together as a single people. Standing in the birthplace of the nation, he declared:

"The great principle that kept this Confederacy so long together was that which gave promise that in due time the weights should be lifted from the shoulders of all men, and all should have an equal chance."

This was the message Lincoln left behind in Philadelphia. The spirit of it was embodied in the phrase "in due time." This was to say that the equal chance was a goal to be striven for, not a fact. It was a condition to be reached; a practical counterpart of the spiritual injunction, "Be ye perfect even as your Father in heaven is perfect." The credo of American political rule was a shining light to guide the life of every man and every woman and every child, here and now. It represented a goal for today's living and for tomorrow's striving.

And Lincoln himself, plainest of the plain, elected to the highest office in the power of the plain people, was the living exponent of the American equal chance.

No one at the time had the slightest inkling of how great he would become. No one could foresee the heights to which he would travel. But what he said in Philadelphia that morning of George Washington's Birthday, what he had said in Trenton the day before, and what he said all along the line on his journey to be inaugurated, left no doubt that he was on his way. This was his journey to greatness.

CHAPTER 23

THE hundred-and-six-mile trip from Philadelphia to Harrisburg followed the familiar pattern. Leaving at nine o'clock, stops and hesitations were made in the next four and a half hours at Haverford, Paoli, Downingtown, Coatesville, Leaman Place, Lancaster, Elizabethtown, Mount Joy, Middleburg, and finally, Harrisburg. Lincoln bowed from the rear platform or made the usual remarks to the usual accompaniment of "crowds, cheers and cannon." He appeared no different than on any other occasion. Behind the outward calm, however, was a great underlying difference. A plot to assassinate him in Baltimore had been uncovered.

At Leaman Place the train stopped four minutes, and at the conclusion of Lincoln's speech he was greeted by loud calls for Mrs. Lincoln. So he went in and brought her out, telling the audience he concluded to give them "the long and short of it." A burst of cheers sent the train on its way.

"We are now approaching the City of Lancaster," wrote a local reporter riding the train, "and the boom of the first guns can be heard. . . . In crossing the Conestoga Bridge, Mr. Lincoln got out on the platform and took a view of the surrounding country, of which he expressed great admiration to the Lancaster committee."

From the train he was conducted across Chestnut Street to the balcony of the Cadwell House (now Brunswick Hotel), his escort being Peter B. Fordney, a local merchant who was two inches taller than Lincoln and who thereby became a local hero. "I being so tall," Fordney would relate, "Mr. Lincoln selected me out of the reception committee as soon as he alighted from the car. He took my arm and I took him over. In the hotel he said he recognized me to be the tallest of the crowd and was pleased to have an escort of that size in Lancaster."

When Lincoln was about to retire from the balcony after his brief, pleasant remarks he was presented with a handsome bouquet by a committee of ladies, which he accepted with a bow and an expression of thanks.

Harrisburg was out in full military and civilian force to greet his arrival near Second and Vine streets at one-thirty, the city being decorated in holiday style. President-elect and suite were taken at once to the Jones House on Market Square where Lincoln was met by Governor Andrew Curtin. From the portico of the hotel the governor introduced him with an appropriate speech, in response to which Lincoln said:

"Perhaps the best thing that I could do would be simply to indorse the patriotic and eloquent speech which your governor has just made in your hearing," and remarked that while he was proud to see the fine military array, "it shall be my endeavor to preserve the peace of this country so far as it can possibly be done consistently with the maintenance of the institutions of the country."

An hour later the governor conducted him to the hall of the House of Representatives. Here he addressed the legislature in joint session. In the course of his speech Lincoln pointed out that "Allusion has also been made by one of your honored speakers to some remarks recently

[249]

made by myself in Pittsburgh in regard to what is supposed to be the especial interest of this great commonwealth of Pennsylvania.

"I now wish only to say in regard to that matter," he emphasized, "that the few remarks which I uttered on that occasion were rather carefully worded. I took pains that they would be so. I have seen no occasion since to add to them or subtract from them."

Lincoln made it a point to know what he was talking about.

Returning to the hotel, the pressing matter of the alleged conspiracy to assassinate him was thoroughly discussed and a decision reached. Lincoln would later review the plot in detail.

He would tell a noted historian of the time, Benson J. Lossing, what the circumstances were. Accompanied by Isaac N. Arnold, member of Congress from Chicago and great friend of Lincoln's, Arnold probably arranged the interview when the historian came to Washington December 7, 1864. Here is Lincoln's version as set down by Lossing.

"I arrived in Philadelphia on the twenty-first," Lincoln related. "I agreed to stop over night and on the following morning hoist the flag over Independence Hall. In the evening there was a great crowd where I received my friends at the Continental Hotel. Mr. Judd, a warm personal friend from Chicago, sent for me to come to his room. I went and found there Mr. Pinkerton, a skillful police detective, also from Chicago, who had been employed for some days in Baltimore watching or searching for suspicious persons there. Pinkerton informed me that a plan had been laid for my assassination, the exact time when I was expected to go through Baltimore being publicly known. He was well informed as to the plan, but did not know that the conspirators would have pluck enough to execute it.

"He urged me to go right through with him to Washington. I didn't like that. I had made engagements to visit Harrisburg and go from there to Baltimore and I resolved to do so. I could not believe there was a plot to murder me. I made arrangements, however, with Mr. Judd for my return to Philadelphia the next night, if I should be convinced that there was danger in going through Baltimore. I told him that if I should meet at Harrisburg, as I had at other places, a delegation to go with me to the next place and then to Baltimore, I should feel safe and go on.

"When I was making my way back to my room through the crowd of people, I met Frederick Seward. We went together to my room, where he told me that he had been sent at the instance of his father and General Scott, to inform me that their detectives in Baltimore had discovered a plot there to assassinate me. They knew nothing of Pinkerton's movements. I now believed such a plot to be in existence.

"The next morning I raised the flag over Independence Hall and then went on to Harrisburg with Mr. [Colonel] Sumner, Major Hunter, Mr. Judd, Mr. Lamon and others. There I met the legislature and the people, dined and waited until the time appointed for me to leave. In the meantime, Mr. Judd had so secured the telegraph that no communication could pass to Baltimore and give the conspirators knowledge of a change in my plans.

"In New York some friend had given me a new beaver hat in a box and in it had placed a soft wool hat. I had never worn one of the latter in my life. I had this box in my room. Having informed a very few friends of the secret of my new movements and the cause, I put on an old overcoat that I had with me and, putting the soft hat in my pocket, I walked out of the house at a back door, bareheaded, without exciting any special curiosity. Then I put on the soft hat and joined my friends without being recognized by strangers, for I was not the same man.

"Sumner and Hunter wished to accompany me. I said no; you are known and your presence might betray me. I will only take Lamon (now Marshal of the District) whom nobody knew and Mr. Judd. Sumner and Hunter felt hurt.

"We went back to Philadelphia and found a message there from Pinkerton, who had returned to Baltimore, that the conspirators had held their final meeting that evening and it was doubtful whether they had the nerve to attempt the execution of their purpose. I went on, however, as the arrangement had been made for a special train. We were a long time in the station at Baltimore. I heard people talking around but no one particularly observed me. At an early hour on Saturday morning, at about the time I was expected to leave Harrisburg, I arrived in Washington."

This was a remarkable account. Considering that nearly four years had elapsed, the most desperate and bloody years the nation would ever experience, Lincoln's statement was remarkably accurate. He missed on three points. Judd did not accompany him; only Lamon went with him all the way. He said Pinkerton had returned to Baltimore; actually Pinkerton accompanied him from Philadelphia to Washington. The other point was about the train.

The two-car train that sped him from Harrisburg to Philadelphia was a special, but the one from Philadelphia to Washington was not, as his account had it. It was the regular overnight run to the federal city leaving

Philadelphia at 10:50 P.M., equipped with a sleeping car owned and operated by the railroad. Aside from these three points, Lincoln's statement provided an excellent account that included his own feelings toward the plot.

The uproar that followed his surreptitious arrival in the federal capital was tremendous. Disunionists flayed the Black Republican unmercifully. The press enjoyed a headline feast. Cartoonists had a field day. Even Lincoln's supporters were taken aback by his underground trip. The sensation shook the nation from coast to coast.

Baltimorean civic pride was cut to the quick. A committee was formed to demand explanation of the President-elect for his unseemly conduct. Such reaction was normal and natural. They did not know the facts which, when fully revealed, disclosed the existence of a conspiracy of hotheaded radicals whose actions could precipitate widespread bloodshed, and who had direct designs on Lincoln's life. Pinkerton told Lincoln, "They didn't have the pluck." Following their failure to kill him, however, their course became unrestrained and in a few weeks they roamed city and countryside, burning and pillaging.

It was in an attempt to run down recurring rumors that the so-called Baltimore Plot was uncovered through the efforts of Samuel M. Felton, president of the Philadelphia, Wilmington and Baltimore Railroad. He was being informed by loyal employees of secessionist plans to burn his bridges and destroy the Havre de Grace (Maryland) ferryboat that carried trains over the Susquehanna River. The rumors culminated in threats that "no Yankee abolitionist President would reach Washington alive."

Felton's first corroborative information came, according to his own account, from Miss Dorothea Dix of Massachusetts. Miss Dix was a social worker especially noted for her establishment of mental hospitals. She also organized a corps of nurses in Washington when the war broke out and became the first superintendent of United States Army nurses.

"I had known her for some years," said Felton. "Her occupation brought her into contact with prominent men of the South too. . . . For more than an hour she related to me what I had heard before in rumors. The sum of it was that there was an organized and extensive conspiracy to seize Washington . . . and then declare the Southern conspirators the *de facto* government of the United States. The whole was to be a *coup d'état*."

Felton at once sent a trusted employee to General Scott in Washington with the news. Scott replied that he already had the information from various sources and had asked President Buchanan for troops to garrison the seat of government. But no action had been taken, and Scott told Felton it might be necessary to inaugurate Lincoln in Philadelphia.

Felton kept getting reports of depredations being planned against his railroad by secessionist sympathizers organizing just below the Mason-Dixon Line in Maryland. Early in January he called in the Pinkerton Detective Agency of Chicago.*

---

* A word about the Pinkertons. Emigrating from Scotland in 1842, Allan Pinkerton settled in Dundee, Illinois, thirty-eight miles from Chicago. His father was a policeman, but Allan had learned the cooper's trade. He soon built a thriving business, at the same time performing voluntary detective work for the community. He was asked to become deputy sheriff. His natural skill manifested itself and he was invited to Chicago. Selling the cooperage business, he joined the Chicago police force as its first, and at the time, only plainclothes detective. In 1850 he went into detective work for himself as Pinkerton's North Western Police Agency. A wave of thefts had been plaguing the few widely-scattered railroads when operating in Illinois. They asked Pinkerton to set up a protective system. Underwritten by the rail lines entering Chicago, Pinkerton's National Detective Agency came into existence in 1855. Other roads became clients. Receiving Felton's urgent message in January, 1861, Allan Pinkerton went to Philadelphia.

Bringing some of his best operatives, Pinkerton set out to learn the situation firsthand. He paused at Wilmington, Delaware, and in Maryland at Perryville, Havre de Grace, Perrymansville and Magnolia. In Baltimore he rented a house on South Street that could be entered from four directions to serve as agency headquarters. He also rented a downtown office and set himself up as a stockbroker, using the name J. H. Hutchinson, of Charleston, South Carolina.

His first day's tour of the city disclosed that Felton's fears and employees' reports underestimated the actual danger. Disunionists ruled Baltimore. Pinkerton found the police under the thumb of Marshal George P. Kane, a determined secessionist who had brought his rank and file into the rebel cause. They could not be trusted for protection in case of trouble. Kane, who was to escape from prison where he was committed because of treasonable activities, would become a confederate officer. The mayor and other city officials were equally suspect.

Stationing his operatives at key points along the Philadelphia, Wilmington and Baltimore right-of-way, Pinkerton soon had startling reports from them. At Perrymansville, operative Timothy Webster joined a troop of cavalry organized ostensibly for protection against "Yankee aggression" but found they planned to destroy bridges and other railroad property so that "no damned Yankee could ever get through to sit in the Presidential chair."

Operative Kate Warne, smooth and disarming, wearing the cockade of secessionist sympathy, who had just come up from a Southern assignment on the Adams Express case, insinuated herself into the confidence of Baltimore's socially elite with her Alabama charm. She found sinister activity at top levels.

Of greatest importance was the work of skilled operative Harry Davies. Using the name Joseph Howard, he joined the conspiratorial band. He had gained an introduction through Marshal Kane to the leader, "Captain" Cypriano Ferrandini who was a follower of Orsini, the radical who had attempted the life of Napoleon III. Davies (or Howard) was one of the kneeling assembly in a darkened meeting room when the special oath of allegiance was taken, binding all to the utmost secrecy. Then lots were drawn for eight red ballots that designated those who would assassinate Lincoln on his way through the city.

Thus, eight zealots were picked and solemnly sworn. They believed they could destroy a government by murdering its elected head and become heroes by so doing. A steamer on Chesapeake Bay would be ready with a boat ashore to carry the assassins to a Southern port and (they were convinced) to everlasting glory.

This was enough for Pinkerton. He closed the house on South Street, instructing all operatives to continue their work as though nothing had happened and so not alarm the plotters into thinking they had been discovered.

Pinkerton knew Norman Judd, general counsel of the Chicago and Rock Island, one of the railroads that had joined in backing his agency. He also was aware of Judd's close association with Lincoln. As evidence piled up he wrote to Judd and finally arranged to meet him in New York. Unable to keep the appointment, he sent Mrs. Warne in his place. She added her own firsthand information to Pinkerton's reports. The charming Kate arranged with Judd for Pinkerton to meet Lincoln in the Quaker City.

It was in Philadelphia that Lincoln was first apprised of the plot to assassinate him in Baltimore. But he would not alter his program. He would raise the flag over Independence Hall and carry out his commitments to the Pennsylvania Legislature. After he had completed these engagements he was still reluctant to change the schedule. During a discussion of the situation that evening he asked Governor Andrew Curtin and a few others at the supper table, "What would the nation think if I were to sneak into Washington like a thief in the night?"

His advisers replied it was not for him to decide; that his safety had become a matter of public consideration. Lincoln gave in and agreed to follow Pinkerton's advice.

Essentially, Pinkerton's plan was simple. It would make sure the plotters continued to plot while their intended victim slipped by ahead of the published schedule. The arrangements demanded careful planning and precise timing, at both of which Pinkerton was adept.

A thorough account of the assassination plot, its double detection, Lincoln's secret night ride, and the biographers' aftermath, has never been told.

Pinkerton would tell his part twenty years later in a subscription book, now out of print, *A Spy of the Rebellion*. He would also issue advertising brochures that included affidavits supporting his activities in the counterplot. He had to distribute these, so he said, to rebut the claims of an arch rival in uncovering the conspiracy. The arch rival was the superintendent of New York's metropolitan police, John A. Kennedy.

Kennedy, an energetic and imaginative police officer, went far beyond his jurisdiction in sending detectives to Washington and Baltimore. Reports had reached him through New York affiliations of Southern Democrats and secessionists concerning treasonable activities against the government. He also received an invitation from a congressional committee to send detectives who could ferret out the rumored conspiracies.

Kennedy first sent detectives to Washington in December, 1860. He said that on Friday, January 4, 1861, he received a note from the Honorable Schuyler Colfax (member of Congress from South Bend, Indiana), requesting him to send a number of detectives into Washington for the same purpose.

"I then decided to go myself and take a man with me to look over the field," related Kennedy. "I don't know what induced me to select Captain Charles P. Stone of General Scott's staff in preference to Colonel Robert E. Lee, but I did so, and told him of my three detectives in the city and their findings."

Kennedy also put men in Richmond and Alexandria. In response to the alarming reports from Baltimore, he had an ace operative investigate fully. He sent David S. Bookstaver who posed as a music agent and who verified the plottings, reporting them to Washington according to Kennedy's instructions. As the hour of Lincoln's visit to Baltimore ticked closer, Bookstaver grew concerned. He hastened to Washington and laid his findings before Captain Stone who took them to General Scott. Scott in turn referred them to Senator Seward. Seward requested that Stone make a written report.

It was this report that young Frederick Seward had with him and which he showed to Lincoln, together with a letter from his father and a note written by General Scott to Seward. Stone's report began, "A New York detective officer who has been on duty for three weeks past, reports there is serious danger of violence to, and the assassination of, Mr. Lincoln, in his passage through the city should the time of passage be known. . . ." These documents authenticating young Seward's verbal report did much to convince Lincoln of the plot.

Back in New York Kennedy grew restive at the lack of any protective measures being taken. He decided to lend a hand in conveying Lincoln across the dangers of Maryland, and to meet him in Baltimore. Lincoln was then in Harrisburg, scheduled, according to the published program, to leave next morning. By a strange coincidence, Kennedy was in the front end of the same sleeping car in which Lincoln was making his secret ride from Philadelphia that night. They traveled together without either being aware of the other's presence.

What riled Pinkerton in later years was Kennedy's claiming credit for saving Lincoln's life and for distributing the credit among Scott, Stone, Seward and Bookstaver, not mentioning his agency at all. His ire was intensified by two of Kennedy's detectives so disturbing the conspirators at the critical moment by bumbling work that only the timely intervention of Pinkerton operatives saved their lives.

Bickering as to who did what over the years has tended to create an unrealistic impression of the whole affair. Many writings, including recent ones, have muddied the pool. There was credit enough for both Pinkerton and Kennedy.

Credit to railroad and telegraph personnel must also be given. It was the Philadelphia, Wilmington and Baltimore Railroad president, Samuel Felton, who brought in the Pinkertons—and paid for them. Operating executives of the Pennsylvania Railroad including Thomas A. Scott, then vice-president, carried out the Pinkerton plan and saw to it that Lincoln reached Philadelphia safely and secretly. E. S. Sanford, American Telegraph Company president, supervised the blacking out of Harrisburg, screening all telegrams through Philadelphia to prevent any upset in the program.

One may question all the trouble occasioned by Lincoln's trip through Baltimore. Why go through the city at all, knowing its secessionist activities?* The sea did offer an alternative, but it was a long voyage down the Atlantic Ocean, up Chesapeake Bay, and up the Potomac River to the seat of American government.

Only one railroad entered the District of Columbia, a single track angling the thirty-eight miles south from Baltimore. No bridge over the Potomac brought in a railroad from the South. The slender thread of two iron rails of the Baltimore and Ohio's branch line provided Washington's sole land transportation, save for poor roads and slow horses.

The plotters knew they could hold the federal capital at their mercy, surrounded as it was by hostile secessionists. They knew that trains from the North entered Baltimore at two separate depots, and that these depots were two miles away from that of the Baltimore and Ohio line going south. To cross this gap, passengers were forced to transfer by way of horse-drawn bus or carriage. At night the through sleeping cars were dragged by horses from one station to the other over dark streets. The situation was made to order for foul play.

Lincoln, as might be expected, offered the most effectual summary of the whole perplexing affair. He told Congressman Arnold in the course of the Arnold-Lossing interview: "I did not then, nor do I now, believe I should have been assassinated had I gone through Baltimore as first contemplated, but I thought it wise to run no risk where no risk was necessary."

---

* Eight weeks later it happened. The Sixth Massachusetts Regiment was changing depots on its way to Washington when it was attacked by an armed mob. Some estimate as many as one hundred were killed, the exact total has never been proved. Many were injured. On April 20, the assassination plotters really got going. They burned bridges in Maryland along the two railroads going north, destroyed railroad property, cut telegraph lines and shut up the Federal Government of the United States in the five-mile-square District of Columbia.

CHAPTER 24

Waiting at the Washington railroad station for Lincoln to arrive was Elihu B. Washburne, member of Congress from Galena, Illinois, trusted friend of the President-elect. Senator Seward also expected to be on hand but somehow had overslept. Alone, Washburne waited in the dimly lighted train shed as the long winter night slowly ebbed.

"I planted myself behind one of the pillars in the old Washington and Baltimore depot where I could see and not be observed," wrote Washburne of the eventful Saturday morning. "Presently the train came rumbling in on time. I saw every car emptied and there was no Mr. Lincoln. I was well-nigh in despair and about to leave when I saw slowly emerge from the last sleeping car, three persons. I could not mistake the long, lank form of Mr. Lincoln. The only persons that accompanied him were Pinkerton, the well-known detective, and Ward H. Lamon.

"I accosted the President-elect: 'How are you, Lincoln?'

"The others were startled, but Mr. Lincoln, who recognized me, relieved them at once by remarking in his peculiar voice, 'This is only Washburne!' Then we exchanged congratulations and walked to the front of the depot where I had a carriage waiting."

Entering Willard's Hotel on the Fourteenth Street side, Washburne noted it was before daylight. He asked the porter to show them to the little receiving room at the head of the stairs and then to go to the front office and have Mr. Lincoln assigned a room.

"We had not been in the hotel more than two minutes," continued Washburne, "before Senator Seward entered, much out of breath and somewhat chagrined to think he had not been up in season to be at the depot. The meeting of these two great men was full of emotion and thankfulness."

Washburne's account differed in certain details from the several variations that Pinkerton subsequently turned out. Pinkerton related that as the party was moving along the train shed a figure darted out of the darkness, grabbed hold of Lincoln's arm and called, "Abe, you can't play that on me, I know you!"

Following immediately behind Lincoln, Pinkerton said he jumped forward and punched the interloper, pushing him away. "Don't strike him, Allan! Don't strike him!" Pinkerton said Lincoln expostulated. "That is my friend Washburne—don't you know him?"

Pinkerton replied by warning everyone to keep his voice down. They hurried out of the station and succeeded in depositing the President-elect on the second floor of the hotel in room number thirteen, without having attracted attention.

Lincoln expressed himself as being rather tired from the evening's unconventional activities. The retinue dispersed to permit him to rest. He had been awake, said Pinkerton, during much of the tense night, telling stories in a low voice from an upper berth.

Leaving the hotel with Seward, Pinkerton spent an

hour in the New York senator's home reviewing the hectic events. He returned to the Willard, registered under his *nom de guerre* of E. J. Allen, and sent out a number of telegrams, wiring "all is well" to Judd in Harrisburg; also wiring the concerned railroad and telegraph people there and in Philadelphia. To his superintendent in Chicago he reported in code: "Plums has Nuts. Arr'd at Barley. All right." The "plums" meant Pinkerton; "nuts," the President-elect; and "barley," Washington.

Between chores Pinkerton said he ran into difficulties with Colonel Lamon. Lamon published his recollections some fifteen years later. While agreeing in the main with others, he did not mention incidents about himself that Pinkerton related; that he wanted to wire details of the secret night ride to a Chicago newspaper friend but that Pinkerton forbade him; that Pinkerton found him in a huddle with Hanscomb, the *New York Herald* man who had replaced Villard, spilling the whole story; and that Pinkerton demanded that Lamon leave his name out of it. Pinkerton noted in his record book that Lamon was drinking heavily, commenting he was a "brainless egotistical fool."

Through a chain of unusual circumstances Lamon later got to read about himself in Pinkerton's record book. He never again mentioned Pinkerton's name; and when the Kennedy competition came up in public prints, he maintained studied silence. The feud continued throughout their lifetimes, coloring their subsequent reports. It represented but one of the many crosscurrents flowing through the Lincoln story, making it difficult to sieve particles of truth out of the partisan sediment.

The unexpected and dramatic appearance of the President-elect in the national capital sent wild rumors flying about the city. Willard's Hotel was filled with a milling crowd all day long. Not until the *Washington Evening Star* hit the streets did the populace have definite news. The edition was sold out quickly.

Chronicling his movements, the *Star* said that at nine-thirty Lincoln breakfasted in his room and received no visitors. Shortly before eleven Senator Seward joined him and they drove to the executive mansion to call on President Buchanan. The cabinet was in session. Great was their surprise to be introduced to the incoming President whose safety had been the subject of so much speculation and wild talk. From the White House, Lincoln and Seward drove around to the war department to see General Scott. As he was not in, they returned to the hotel. Lincoln again retired and requested no visitors. Up to press time, one o'clock, he had received nobody. With that the *Evening Star* account ended, save for wondering verbally about the reason for Lincoln's hasty entrance into the capital city.

Piecing together various accounts of the rest of the day's activities, it appears that Lincoln's first afternoon callers were the Illinois members of Congress headed by Senator Douglas, who arrived toward three o'clock. From that moment on Lincoln had a busy time. General Scott marched in and they spent considerable time together. Other callers included Frank Blair and his son Montgomery; the latter Lincoln would appoint postmaster-general.

Shortly before five-thirty, with rain falling fast, Mrs. Lincoln entered the hotel. Accompanied by Senator Seward who greeted her at the depot, she arrived on the Presidential Special which had left Harrisburg at 9:00 A.M. and stopped over at Baltimore. The Messrs. Willard met her at the door of the hotel, then conducted the family to an apartment of five rooms on the second floor —suite six, facing Pennsylvania Avenue, overlooking the White House. Lincoln moved to the family apartment that night.

At six o'clock the secretary of the Peace Congress presented a request for Lincoln to name the time most convenient to him for members to call. He dined at Seward's home and returned to the hotel at precisely ten minutes to nine. On the hour, delegates of the Peace Congress filed into one of the reception rooms. Lincoln stood at one end, all alone, to greet them. The delegation was headed by former President John Tyler of Virginia, and ex-governor of Ohio, Salmon P. Chase. Chase introduced Mr. Tyler to the President-elect and the others in turn.

The reception was entirely informal. As each delegate was introduced, Lincoln greeted him with an appropriate word, and all gathered around the tall man in an ever-widening circle. His long figure and animated face towered above them, "the most striking personality in this group of Americans," noted a delegate, who also observed that Lincoln was making his future course clear to them.

A Virginia delegate replied to Lincoln's complimentary remark that, although he had retired from public life, he had answered his governor's call to unite in this effort to save the Union. "But," he demurred, "the clouds that hang over us are very dark. . . . I can do little—you can do much. Everything depends upon you."

"I cannot agree to that," replied Lincoln. "My course is as plain as a turnpike road. It is marked out by the Constitution. I am in no doubt which way to go. . . . Do you think it would work?"

"Permit me to answer that," interposed a delegate from western Virginia. "Yes, it will work. If the Consti-

[265]

tution is your light, Mr. Lincoln, I will follow it with you. . . ."

A New York delegate, greatly intent on compromise for business reasons, loudly protested that Lincoln should not go to war on account of slavery. Lincoln answered that "the Constitution must be respected, obeyed, enforced and defended, let the grass grow in city streets or where it may."

A large number of prominent citizens, senators, representatives and government officials who had gathered in the hotel's public rooms were now presented. Notified that ladies in the main parlor were desirous of paying their respects, Lincoln said for them to come along. Each was introduced by her accompanying gentleman. At 10:00 P.M. the Cabinet returned the courtesy of the President-elect's morning call.

Mrs. Lincoln, fatigued from the arduous trip, had not intended to receive company that evening, but learning of the rush of callers she requested the parlor adjoining her suite be opened and added her social grace to the first Lincoln reception in Washington.

The next morning was clear and sunshiny, a beautiful Sunday. About eleven o'clock Senator Seward came for Lincoln and together they walked to church. President-elect and Secretary-of-State-to-be strolled up Fourteenth Street, over F, passing Willard Hall in which the Peace Congress was holding its meetings, then around the Treasury on Fifteenth Street to Pennsylvania Avenue, and so to Lafayette Park. Through the park with its equestrian statue of General Jackson they walked arm in arm.

Before them, at the corner of Sixteenth and H streets, stood (and stands now) St. John's Church. Seward, a parishioner, guided Lincoln to his pew in front.

The services were conducted by the rector, Reverend Dr. Smith Pyne, who preached a text taken from one of Paul's letters to the Corinthians, "And they that use this world, as not abusing it: for the fashion of this world passeth away." I Cor. 7:31. Dr. Pyne made several allusions in the course of his sermon to the state of the country and to the change of administration about to take place. There was an appropriateness to the hymn he selected, based on Psalm 37:

> In all thy ways, trust thou the Lord,
> And he will needful help afford,
> To perfect every just design.
> He'll make, like light, serene and clear,
> Thy clouded innocence appear,
> And as a mid-day sun to shine.

So it came to pass that an obscure and undistinguished Kentuckian, newly arrived from Illinois, ended his immortal journey to the nation's capital and began his pilgrimage into the heart of every man. Into the heart of every man, that is, who believed with him that the highest goal of government was to provide its citizens with the opportunity of being free together.

The Civil War that would be waged between his fellow Americans for four terrible years would be one of the greatest events in the long history of civil government.

Much more than the fate of the American Union rested in Lincoln's hands; more even than the fate of Negro slavery. The fate of popular government all over the world was at stake. Men everywhere were watching in trepidation the rising conflict in America between a new government, established on the inequality of mankind, and an eighty-five-year-old Republic founded on the Utopian principle that all men are created equal.

Was there to be no more government in the world for the people by the people? Would this be the end?

"In *your* hands, my dissatisfied fellow-countrymen, and not in *mine*, is the momentous issue of civil war," he said on the east steps of the Capitol in the Inaugural Address he had been exposing piecemeal along the way. "The Government will not assail *you*. . . . *You* have no oath registered in heaven to destroy the Government, while *I* shall have the most solemn one to 'preserve, protect, and defend' it."

And then he closed the Address with what would become one of his most famous utterances and make every citizen proud of the rawboned backwoodsman who would save the American Commonwealth of States as it passed through the fiery furnace, proud of the renewed hope that he would give to all mankind in the integrity of a people's government. Said Abraham Lincoln the moment before he took the Presidential Oath of Office:

"I am loathe to close. We are not enemies, but friends. We must not be enemies. Though passion may have strained, it must not break our bonds of affection. The mystic chords of memory, stretching from every battlefield and patriot grave to every living heart and hearthstone all over this broad land, will yet swell the chorus of the Union, when again touched, as they surely will be, by the better angels of our nature."

I N D E X

Huntsville, Ala., 162
Hutchinson, J. H. (Allan Pinkerton), 254
Hutchinson family of singers, 73
"Hymn on Music" (song), 211

I

Illinois, 7-8, 11, 14, 18, 21, 38-39, 81, 97, 174, 177, 240, 264
Illinois Central Railroad, 12, 174-175, 176, 177, 196
Illinois-Mississippi (Caton) telegraph lines, 8
Illinois State Journal, 6, 30
Il Trovatore, 212
immigration during 1850's, 55-56
Inaugural Address, Buchanan's, 230
Inaugural Address, Jefferson Davis', 157, 166
Inaugural Address, Lincoln's 30-31, 39, 54, 78, 90, 139, 141, 157, 181, 268; Second, 132-133
inaugural trip (Davis'), 232
inaugural trip (Lincoln's), aims and motives, 132-142; arrival in Washington, 261-266; attempt to wreck train, 206; begins in Springfield, 4-5; complicated by number of railroads, 80-81; expenses of, 190-191; from New York to Philadelphia, 221-234; from Philadelphia to Harrisburg, 248-249; length of, 3; meeting delegations a purpose, 20; members of Lincoln's suite and military escort, 7-10; objective of harmony, 52-53; summary and significance, 267-268; timetables, 145, 171; see other topics under alphabetical headings
Independence Hall, Philadelphia, 238-240, 241, 250, 251, 256-257
Indiana, 11, 14, 18, 20, 21, 81, 97, 199
Indiana Legislature, 38, 199
Indianapolis, Ind., 3, 9, 18, 19, 24, 27-36, 37-45, 53, 63, 73, 97, 141
Indianapolis and Cincinnati Railroad, 41, 45, 46
Indians, 131-132
"Integer Vitae" (song), 226
inventions, American, 103
Iowa, 102
Irish immigrants, 127, 245
Irwin, Robert, 7
Iuka, Miss., 162

J

Jackson, President Andrew, 31, 90, 243, 245, 266
Jackson, Miss., 162
Jackson and Great Northern Railroad, 162
Jacksonian Democrats, 243, 246
Jacobin clubs, 245
Jameson, W., 10 (footnote)
Janesville, Wisc., 8

Jefferson, President Thomas, 51, 244
Jersey City, N. J., 127, 221, 222, 223-224
Jewett, Mrs. T. L., 77
John P. Jackson, (ferryboat), 221
Johnson, President Andrew, 215
Johnson, William, 43, 150
Jones, Thomas D., 140, 141
Jones House, 249
Judd, Norman B., 7, 174, 198, 250, 251, 252, 256, 263
Jura, (steamship), 221

K

Kane, Marshal George P., 255, 256
Kansas, 75, 102
Kansas-Nebraska Act, 101-103, 132, 230
Kansas-Nebraska bill, 213, 229, 230, 246
Kansas Territory, 230
Keene, Laura, Theater, 208
Kelley, William, 172
Kennedy, John A., Supt. of New York Police, 187, 199, 257-259, 263
Kentucky, 21, 38, 41, 51-52, 54, 97, 106, 242
Kings County, N. Y., 193, 219
Kingsland, ex-Mayor of New York, 202
Know-Nothings, 55, 103
Knox, the hatter, 203
Knox College, Galesburg, Ill., confers degree on Lincoln, 181
Knoxville, Tenn., 108
Knoxville Whig, 108, 157
Kohn, Abraham, 152
Krzyzabowski, 128

L

Lafayette, Ind., 18, 21-23, 43
Lafayette and Indianapolis Railroad, 23
Lafayette (Indiana) *Journal*, 204
Lamon, Col. Ward H., 7, 13, 19, 39-41, 60, 74, 121, 122, 136, 198, 224, 251, 252, 261, 263
Lancaster, Pa., 248-249
Lancaster (Pennsylvania) *Express*, 34
Lane, Senator Henry S., 19
Latham, George C., 7
Laura Keene's Theater, 209
Lawrence, Kansas Territory, 230
Lawrenceburg, Ind., 45, 46-47, 51
Leaman Place, Pa., 248
Leary, the hatter, 203
Leathers, Captain Tom, 160
Leatherstocking Tales, 96
Lebanon, Ind., 23-24, 84
Lecompton constitution of Kansas, 75
Lecompton frauds, 230
Lee, Robert E., 160, 233, 258
Leland's brass band, 111
Leonard, E. F., 10 (footnote)
Leonard, New York Police Inspector, 183
Leslie's Weekly, 111

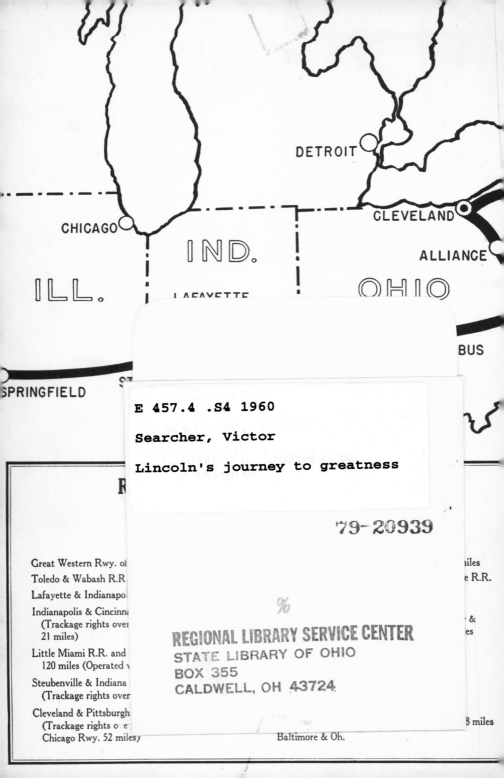

DETROIT

CLEVELAND

CHICAGO

IND.

ALLIANCE

ILL.

OHIO

LAFAYETTE

BUS

SPRINGFIELD

R

Great Western Rwy. of ...iles
Toledo & Wabash R.R. ...e R.R.
Lafayette & Indianapo...
Indianapolis & Cincinn...
(Trackage rights ove...
21 miles)
Little Miami R.R. and ...
120 miles (Operated ...
Steubenville & Indiana ...
(Trackage rights ove...
Cleveland & Pittsburgh ...
(Trackage rights o...e...
Chicago Rwy. 52 miles)

Baltimore & Oh.

...&
...es

...8 miles